Hold Fast Your Confession

Studies in Church Principles

Hold Fast
Your Confession

Studies in Church Principles

Edited by
Donald Macleod

The Knox Press (Edinburgh)

THE KNOX PRESS (EDINBURGH),
15 North Bank Street,
Edinburgh EH1 2LS,
Scotland

© KNOX PRESS (EDINBURGH), EDINBURGH, SCOTLAND

First edition 1978

Printed in Great Britain by
Robert MacLehose and Company Limited
Printers to the University of Glasgow

Preface

The articles in this symposium were all written by ministers of the Free Church of Scotland and give a contemporary vindication of the distinctive principles of that denomination. The points of view expressed, however, are shared by many Christians all over the world and it is hoped that the volume will be useful far beyond the confines of one particular tradition. Although a pretentiously academic approach was deliberately avoided, an attempt was made to achieve thorough and comprehensive treatment of the various problems.

The Editor's only contribution has been to collect the papers and apply a minimum of editorial revision. He is grateful to the various contributors for their co-operation.

One final word. This book is not an official document of the Free Church of Scotland. The discussion of each topic is judged to be in complete harmony with the ordination commitment of the author. But, within that, all enjoyed freedom to clarify and defend the principles as they saw them.

Glasgow,   DONALD MACLEOD
August, 1977

Contents

The Free Church:
An Outline of Its History
and Witness

GEORGE N. M. COLLINS, B.A., B.D.
Professor of Church History and Church Principles,
Free Church College, Edinburgh.

Just as many things are older than the names by which they are now identified, so the Free Church of Scotland is older than the new name which she chose at the Disruption of 1843. The decisive thing in determining the identity of a church is not, after all, the name by which she is known but the beliefs which constitute her testimony to the world around her; and by this standard the Free Church of Scotland claims unbroken continuity with the Church of the Scottish Reformation in 1560. Dr. Thomas Brown, in his Moderatorial address to the second General Assembly of the Free Church, in October of 1843, made precisely that claim. 'We meet not at this time,' he said, 'for the purpose of framing a new Constitution for the Church of Scotland. That Constitution, under the guidance of the Spirit of God, has been framed by the skill, and the wisdom of our forefathers—men of eminence, and men of God of former times—our Protestant Reformers; and it existed before it was brought into connection with the State at all. By that Constitution we abide steadfastly. Our Standards, our Books of Discipline, our Creed, our Confession of Faith, we retain in all their original integrity. To them we have adhered; to them we have appealed; by them we have sought to be tested in all our recent contendings . . . . We therefore, this being the case, maintain that we are the Church of Scotland.'

The decision to break with the Establishment in 1843, did not arise—as Dr. Brown so cogently argues, and so clearly shows—from any desire on the part of the protesters to change the long-existing relationship of Church and State in Scotland; on the contrary, the long struggle that led to the Disruption was, in fact, a determined effort to preserve that relationship in the terms of the agreement that had been made between both bodies at the time of the Scottish Reformation. If a new denomination *did* originate in Scotland on 18th May 1843, it was not the body meeting in Edinburgh's Tanfield Hall, but the residuary Assembly of the Church of Scotland which had sat on in St. Andrew's Church after the protesting party had withdrawn. Dr. Robert S. Candlish, second only to Chalmers himself in popular leadership at the time, expressed this view with perfect clarity; 'The date of the existence of the present Established Church of Scotland is 1843; the date of *our* existence is 1560.'

It is a reasonable requirement, however, that all such claims should be substantiated by unambiguous evidence, and the claim of the Free Church of Scotland to be in direct descent from the Reformed Church of Scotland of 1560 is one that will bear the fullest investigation. In a book like this which deals with its distinctive principles, let us look, to begin with, at *its attitude to the Holy Scriptures.*

Here, then, we find the fullest agreement between the Scottish Reformers and the Free Church of Scotland today. In formulating their creed in the *First Scots Confession,* the Reformers showed their anxiety that their work should be tested by Biblical standards where they wrote, in their *Foreword,* 'We conjure you, if any man will note in this our Confession, any article or sentence repugnant to God's Holy Word, that it would please him of his gentleness, and for Christian charity's sake, to admonish us of the same in writing; and we, upon our honour and fidelity, do promise him satisfaction from the Holy Scriptures, or due reformation of that which he shall prove to be amiss.'

Speaking nearly three centuries later, Thomas Chalmers drops into similar strain. 'We walk by no light,' he said, 'and submit to no authority in spiritual things but the light and authority of the enduring Book, the Bible—the common Statute Book for ministers and people.'

The ministers and other office-bearers of the Free Church of Scotland today submit themselves to the same authority where, in signing the Formula at their admission to office, they declare, '. . . I do sincerely own and believe the whole doctrine contained in the *Confession of Faith,* approven by former General Assemblies of this Church, to be the truths of God; and I do own the same as the confession of my faith; . . .' And the doctrine of Holy Scripture to which that pledge commits them may be examined in the very first chapter of the *Westminster Confession of Faith,* pin-pointed in particular, by the words in paragraph IV. 'The authority of the holy scripture, for which it ought to be believed and obeyed, dependeth not upon the testimony of any man or church, but wholly upon God, (Who is truth itself), the author thereof; and therefore it is to be received because it is the Word of God.'

Any tenets and dogmas which diverge from the clear teaching of

Holy Scripture are to be rejected and disavowed. The Bible is to be the last court of appeal. 'To the law and to the testimony; if they speak not according to this word, it is because there is no light in them,' (Isa. 8.20). It was a testimony that honoured God, and that, by His blessing, quickened the soul of Scotland in the 16th century and effected Reformation. It gave nerve to the martyrs of the Covenant to glorify God at the stake and the gibbet in their defence of Scotland's spiritual and civil independence in the 17th century. It strengthened the hearts of the Disruption Fathers to sacrifice their all in the same cause in the following century. And when, later in the same century, under the influence of rationalistic liberalism, the majority in the Free Church surrendered the principle of the sovereignty and inerrancy of Holy Scripture and, in the interests of Church Union, worked for such Constitutional change as would bring them into line with the Voluntary position of the United Presbyterian Church, the same testimony decided the action of the Constitutionalist party in the Free Church who were determined that the Reformed witness of the Scottish Church should be maintained, and who continued the Free Church of Scotland after the 1900 Church Union.

Again in the realm of *Church and State* relations, the position of the Free Church of Scotland today is that of the historic Presbyterian Church of Scotland. In the early post-Reformation years, it is true, we do not see the Presbyterian system in its full development and in its normal operation, due, in the main, to the fewness of the Church's ministers. Knox's 'superintendents' cannot by any stretch of the imagination be regarded as prelatic bishops. Their appointment was a temporary arrangement, and it passed with the emergency. The intensely democratic spirit of the Reformed Church, which became articulate in its formularies from the beginning, expressed itself eventually in the full Presbyterian system. which grew up under the competent leadership of Andrew Melville. King James's subtle attempts to foist upon the people a diocesan episcopacy which they regarded as alien to the spirit and teaching of the New Testament Church met with determined resistance, and Kirk and Crown were in frequent conflict throughout what remained of the Stewart dynasty until, under new auspices, the persecuted Church won its final victory under the Revolution Settlement of 1690.

The remonstrance addressed to James by Melville, when the king, in overbearing mood, charged the Church with sedition because it had dared to meet in General Assembly without his permission, is memorable, and worth repeating as an expression of the view of Church and State relations which the King was attacking. 'There are two kings and two kingdoms in Scotland,' said Melville. 'There is King James, the head of this commonwealth, and there is King Jesus, the King of the Church, Whose subject James the Sixth is, and of Whose Kingdom he is not a king, nor a head, but a member. We will yield to you your place, and give you all due obedience; but again, I say, you are not the head of the Church.'

Church and State, in this view, are twin departments under the crown of Jesus Christ, each under obligation to help the other, and neither usurping any of the prerogatives of the other. To such a doctrine as the Divine Right of Kings the Holy Scriptures gave no support; rather the reverse. In the Second Reformation the Covenanters resisted it to the death. Their slogan, 'For Christ's Crown and Covenant', roused the people, and in the reckoning that followed, the usurping Stewarts lost the throne. 'The genuine Covenanters,' writes Dr. King Hewison, 'from first to last never resiled from those definite principles on which the Reformed Church in Scotland was founded. Those principles, in fine, were the absolute authority of the Word of God over all men; the exclusive jurisdiction of the Church in spiritual concerns; the exclusive power of the ruler in civil affairs only, according to the Word, and in Scotland, according to its ancient Constitution.'

The authority of the King, argued Samuel Rutherford in his *Lex Rex*, is a trust originating indeed with God, but reaching the King by the suffrages of the people. It is a trust, not a gift; and, if it be abused, it can be properly recalled by the people, for *they* are the fount of power. The King's will is not the law; *Lex est Rex*.

The leaders of the Free Church in 1843 took precisely that ground. Again to quote Chalmers, 'We hold that every part and every function of a commonwealth should be leavened with Christianity, and that every functionary, from the highest to the lowest, should in their respective spheres, do all that in them lies to countenance and uphold it. That is to say, though we quit the Establishment, we go out on the Establishment Principle; we quit a vitiated Establishment, but would rejoice in returning to a pure one.'

In the full terms of the Establishment Principle a national recognition of religion is clearly implied, either with or without endowment. This Principle continues to be a vital part of our Free Church testimony. It was not in disagreement with it that the Evangelical

Party who formed the Free Church in 1843 left the Establishment, but, ironically enough, in defence of it. For they held that the body retaining the name of the Church of Scotland had departed from the historic position of that Church by conceding to the civil power, in the Patronage controversy which precipitated the Disruption, a jurisdiction which belongs alone to the spiritual power, and that was guaranteed to the Church by the Revolution Settlement in 1690. The Free Church of Scotland, to quote Lord Haldane, 'left their *Claim, Declaration and Protest* to stand for all time as a clear exposition both of their reasons for leaving the Church of Scotland, when they did leave it, and as a profession of their faith as the true Church of Scotland though separate from the Establishment, which, in their view, was itself heretical from its submission to the temporal power in what they regarded as purely spiritual.'

The re-imposition of Patronage upon the Church—which was at the root of the pre-Disruption conflict—had been a clear breach of faith with the Church, on the part of the State. The recognition of her spiritual independence, and the maintenance of her Presbyterian government, guaranteed at the Revolution Settlement, and re-affirmed in the Act of Union of the English and Scottish Parliaments in 1707, seemed a sufficient and permanent settlement of Church and State relations in Scotland; yet in 1712 the breach of faith was made. Jacobite intrigue was still rife, and even Queen Anne herself was not opposed to it, for she had always hated her brother-in-law, King William, and the prospect of the passing of the throne to a German succession after her death made the restoration of the Stewarts an event to be looked upon with favour. The Jacobite party, still committed to their restoration policy, regarded the prevailing Church and State situation as one that could be exploited to their advantage. To bring Kirk and Crown into conflict in Scotland would react in favour to their cause. Accordingly, they coalesced with the High Church party and the Tories to bring about the passing of the 1712 Act which re-imposed Patronage on the Scottish Church. 'The toleration of Epicopalians, and the restoration of Patronage,' declares Principal Story, 'were advocated for the sole purpose of regaining their lost ascendancy to the Episcopalians and Jacobites of Scotland.' The Act appealed to Queen Anne because it was her aim 'to make Churchmen more dependent on the aristocracy,' and thus the way was prepared to make the Church once again a mere department of the State.

The powers conferred upon the patrons were increasingly used to the disadvantage of the congregations until, eventually, the call of the people became a mere formality. And when the Courts of the Church endeavoured to exercise their guaranteed rights it was to find themselves in direct collision with the civil courts. Auchterarder, Strathbogie and Lethendy are place-names that stand out prominently in the story of this conflict. The Church resisted every encroachment upon its province by the civil courts, and was unsparingly denounced for its boldness in challenging the authority of these judicatories. But it had its doughty defenders even within legal circles. Commenting on the Strathbogie case in particular, Lord Cockburn remarked, 'Those who rail at the audacity of the Assembly, had as well reflect on the comparative audacity of the Civil Court, by which, in effect, not seven ministers, but the whole Church was suspended.'

Undeterred by the secessions which had already taken place as a result of patronage, the Moderate party in the Church continued to countenance the Erastian policy of the Courts until it became fully evident that the benefits of Establishment would have to be relinquished if the spiritual independence of the Church was to be retained. For this contingency Dr. Chalmers and his associates had planned the Sustentation Fund, whereby the ministry of the Free Church, if separation became necessary, would be supported by the liberality of the people, without any benefit from the Church's patrimony. Few in the Government, or in the Moderate following, took this plan seriously, or regarded it as having any prospect of success, unless, perhaps, in the hot-headed enthusiasm of the first few years of the dissenting Church's separate existence. The springs of Christian liberality would soon dry up and the dissenters would be forced under sheer economic pressure to return to the fold.

There was one factor, vitally affecting the situation, however, which the Erastians in Church and State had left out of their calculations, namely, that the period prior to the Disruption had been singularly marked by spiritual revival up and down the country, in consequence of which a people awake to their spiritual duty and appreciative of their spiritual heritage were resolved that, cost what it might, the crown-rights of Jesus Christ in His own Church, guaranteed by contract of Church and State at the Reformation, contended for even to the sacrifice of liberty and life by the Covenanters in their epic struggle, recognised by the Revolution Settlement after the Killing Times had ended, re-affirmed by the Union of Parliaments in 1707, should still be upheld. But separation from the State was to be the last resort, and every effort was made to prevent such a calamity. The aggrieved Church addressed its final appeal to the Government, setting out its case in masterly fashion in its *Claim, Declaration and Protest*, a 'solemn instrument,' as Dr. Robert Buchanan described it, in which 'the Church took all men to witness that there was now but one or other of two alternatives open to her—either to get her *Claim* acknowledged and allowed by the Legislature, or to abandon her civil establishment.'

Their appeal was refused, and the refusal was regarded by some in high places of government as a method of calling the bluff (as they saw it) of the appellants. But the protesters had counted the cost, and now proceeded to act upon the plan which they had devised as their alternative to an Erastian Establishment. The die was cast, and the Church of Scotland, Free, became a reality within a few weeks. In bitter disillusionment, Sir James Graham, who, as Home Secretary, had uncompromisingly opposed the Church's *Claim*, wrote, within a few years of the Disruption, 'I have never ceased to regret that occurrence; and when I look at its consequences I take great blame to myself and have a painful misgiving that more might have been done by me to avert so great a calamity.'

But it was not until 1874 that the State took any practical step to correct its mistake of 1843; and when it did, its action was inspired by politics rather than by principle. For by this time a strong dis-establishment movement was agitating the country, and the Act of 1874 abolishing Patronage was an astute attempt to foil it. It was Patronage that had caused the secessions of 1733 and 1761, and that lay behind the Disruption of 1843. If Patronage were now removed, a dis-Establishment crusade could be made to look foolish, and the way for an honourable return to what Chalmers had called a 'pure Establishment' would be open. But an Establishment from which Patronage had been eliminated would not of itself have satisfied Chalmers. Speaking in Disruption year, he had plainly said so. 'The abolition of Patronage,' he declared, 'will not satisfy us; we must have an independent power of discipline; we must have an independent jurisdiction in things ecclesiastical.' And this requirement was certainly not met by the Patronage Act of 1874. Professor William Milligan, of Aberdeen University, warned his Church of Scotland brethren at the time of the passing of this measure that 'no Union could be looked for between the Church of Scotland and the Free Church on the ground of the Patronage Act of 1874, because the Free Church held a principle which the Establishment had rejected, viz., the independence of the Church in spiritual matters.'

By the time this Act reached the Statute Book there was a spirit of change at work in the Church which was to prove more divisive than Patronage itself. This concerned the Church's relation to its own Confessional standards. The negotiations for Union between the Free Church and the United Presbyterian Church had broken down in 1873 when it became evident that the Establishment Principle was not the only, or even the major, matter of disagreement between them. When charges of heresy were made against Professors Brown and Balmer these had been glossed over in such a way as to reveal that the doctrine of the United Presbyterian Church was no longer that of the Secession Fathers. There was evidence of a drift away from the clear-cut definitions of the Reformed theology, and the substitution for them of vague ambiguities that would facilitate the entry of the Critical movement which had arisen in the German theological schools. This drift eventually issued in the United Presbyterian *Declaratory Act* of 1879. The rashness of Professor William Robertson Smith of the Free Church College, Aberdeen, which brought him to trial for heresy in the Free Church General Assembly in 1881, revealed that theological liberalism had gained a footing in the Free Church also, and in 1891 a *Declaratory Act*, very similar to the United Presbyterian Act of 1879, was passed by the Free Church General Assembly and sent down to Presbyteries under the Barrier Act.

Suffice it to say, by way of criticism of these measures, that their most objectionable feature was the allowance that they made for 'diversity of opinion' on such points in the *Westminster Confession* as do not enter into 'the substance of the Reformed faith,' without any guidance being given as to which doctrines fall into this category, or into the alternative one. The Church arrogated to herself the right to determine from time to time 'what points fall within the description'. Thus the recognised standards of doctrinal orthodoxy were virtually set aside, and the Church was left without fundamentals, without essentials, without 'things most surely believed,' and, consequently, without powers of discipline. Opponents of the Declaratory legislation urged that the course of common honesty for the critics of the *Confession* would be to show where they judged it to be at variance with the Holy Scriptures in its teaching, and to specify clearly which of the Confessional statements they wished to change. But the challenge was not accepted, for the obvious reason that investigation would reveal that what they were really calling in question was not so much the teaching of the *Confession* as that of the Scriptures themselves.

It was on this foundation of sand that the Church Union of 1900 between the United Presbyterians and the majority of the Free Church was built. The Church of Scotland subsequently drove a hard bargain with the United Free Church, promising not to oppose the passing of the Act of Parliament for the settling of questions between the Free Church and the United Free Church, provided that a clause were added that would give the Church of Scotland the right to qualify subscription to her Standards, just as the United Presbyterian Church and the undivided Free Church had arrogated to themselves. The right was conceded, and the way was opened for the Union between the Church of Scotland and the United Free Church which was effected in 1929.

The section of the Free Church which declined to enter the 1900 Union was now left with the responsibility of continuing the name and distinctive witness of the Church of the Disruption Fathers of 1843, and in greatly diminished numerical strength and resources she faced her task. The invitation extended to her to participate in the later and larger Union of 1929 was regretfully declined, not, however, from sectarian motives, but for reasons set forth in a circular issued in that year. In concluding this brief survey of Free Church history, the terms of the circular are worth quoting as setting forth the position of the Free Church still.

'It would be the occasion of much joy to us, as Free Churchmen,' runs the pamphlet, 'to see the re-union of the sundered Presbyterians of Scotland on the ground held by our Reforming and Covenanting Fathers. It is a matter of sincere regret that we cannot regard the Union that is soon to be consummated as one that at all, worthily, answers such a description.

'In the uniting Act which gives the basis of the intended Union there are mentioned, under the heading of General Constitution, as "leading documents setting forth the constitution of the united Church":

1. United Free Church Act anent Spiritual Independence (1906).
2. Articles Declaratory of the Constitution of the Church of Scotland in Matters Spiritual (1926).

'The Spiritual Independence that is claimed in both these documents is not that which our Disruption Fathers claimed, but a revolutionary counterfeit which is divorced from a definite Constitution.

'Under the heading of Doctrine there are named, along with the *Westminster Confession of Faith* (1647):

1. *United Presbyterian Declaratory Act* (1879).
2. *Free Church Declaratory Act* (1892), with *Act* (1894) relative thereto.
3. *Church of Scotland Act on the Formula* (1910).

'Thus the doctrine that is recognized as Standard in the projected Church is seriously at variance with the exhibition of the Reformed Faith, that has been historically, from the 17th to the 20th century, the Standard of the Church of Scotland.'

The last paragraph of the above-quoted statement sets forth succinctly the basic reason why the Free Church of Scotland still maintains a separate denominational existence. Like David the son of Jesse we have our brethren who chide us, but to these we reply, in David's words, '*What have I now done? Is there not a cause?*'

The Westminster Confession of Faith

CLEMENT GRAHAM, M.A., B.D.
*Professor of Apologetics and Practical Theology,
Free Church College, Edinburgh.*

I The Ordinand's Pledge—Three Worthy Emphases

'Do you sincerely own and believe the whole doctrine contained in the Confession of Faith, approven by former General Assemblies of this Church, to be founded upon the word of God; and do you acknowledge the same as the confession of your faith . . . ?'

Anyone who has attended a minister's ordination or induction service in the Free Church of Scotland has heard this question put to the ordinand and responded to with an unqualified affirmative. For generations, Presbyterian ministers the world over affirmed their devotion to the Confession in similar terms, for the famous document was acknowledged and, though in some cases with modifications in varying degrees, is still acknowledged as a constitutional element in most Presbyterian Churches tracing continuity with the Reformation in Great Britain. The fact that the Confession still has significance for so many, more than three hundred years after its compilation is a signal of its excellence. The fact of the three hundred years may be sufficient to suggest to some that the time must be ripe to make changes. But the real motivation for up-dating does not come from reflection on the changes in language and idiom over the centuries, but from an entirely altered concept of what a Christian's and a Church's confession ought to be and the purposes it ought to serve. To this point we shall, no doubt, return. For the moment we just observe that the compilers of the Westminster Confession deemed it to be the mark of a Christian that he would 'think God's thoughts after Him,' and so witness to the truth which God has revealed. They reckoned it to be worthy of a Church to give a somewhat formal and systematic expression to the doctrine of Holy Scripture. That was what they tried to achieve in the Confession of Faith. They would have wished their production to find general acceptance as a declaration of the faith of the Church only as long as it was seen to be an adequate formulation of the doctrine of Scripture, for they pleaded no exception in their own case from the principle they engrossed in the Confession, that 'The supreme judge, by which all controversies of religion are to be determined, and all decrees of Councils, opinions of ancient writers, doctrines

HOLD FAST YOUR CONFESSION

of men and private spirits, are to be examined, and in whose sentence we are to rest, can be no other but the Holy Spirit speaking in Scripture,' (Conf. I, 10). Sadly it has to be acknowledged that the quarrel of many who today agitate for the complete re-writing of the Church's creed—or the abolition of creeds—is not primarily with the Confession of Faith, but with the Scriptures the Confession expounds.

To return to the question quoted at the beginning of this article —it presents three very worthy emphases of which it is good to take particular notice.

(1) There is recognition that for today as well as for the great confession—making epochs of the Church, the Word of God, which is Holy Scripture, is the only rule of faith and life. Preceding the question quoted is one which is quite basic—'Do you believe the Scriptures of the Old and New Testaments to be the Word of God and the only rule of faith and manners?' Unless the position adopted here is accepted, a confession has no objective value. It is merely descriptive of belief and experience; it can be a monument of history but it cannot be a beacon, for its light has gone out. What the Scriptures teach is 'worthy of all acceptation' for all time. What is not taught in Scripture may never be made a requirement of Christian life. This principle found most attractive and colourful expression by the compilers of the Scots' Confession—which preceded the Westminster by almost a century—whom we hear, 'Protesting that if any man will note in this our Confession any article or sentence repugning to God's holy Word, that it would please him of his gentleness, and for Christian charity's sake, to admonish us of the same in writing; and we of our honour and fidelity do promise unto him satisfaction from the mouth of God (that is, from His Holy Scriptures) or else reformation of that which he shall prove to be amiss.'

When the Confession of Faith is described as a subordinate standard of a Church (as of the Free Church of Scotland) this is what is clearly intended. It is subordinate to Scripture—it is subject to scrutiny and examination in the light of Scripture. It is a fair representation of the teaching of Scripture and this is the measure of its authority.

(2) The second emphasis follows naturally and is to the effect that Scripture is perspicuous. God makes His meaning clear in His word. If Scripture be compared with Scripture the essential doctrine becomes clear to the man who is taught by the same Spirit as

gave utterance to the Word in the first place. So it is possible to summarise the main points of Biblical teaching. The making of such a summary will in itself be an aid to clarifying the understanding, and it is entirely worthy of the man of God and of the Christian community (the Church) to seek and to express its clear understanding of the Word of God in a confession. God's truth has found propositional expression in Scripture: it can find propositional summary in a Christian confession.

(3) The third emphasis of the question which invites a man to pledge himself in terms of the Confession of Faith is one which is not always specifically appreciated. It is that a Confession of Faith is an intimately personal thing, giving expression to truths which have gripped the heart and illumined the mind. As such it is at the polar extreme from stiff, formal, clinical abstraction. An interesting feature of some of the Reformed Confessions is that the first draft was prepared by individuals for their private use. The second Helvetic Confession, for example, was a development of a statement prepared by Bullinger for personal edification. Not everyone has an equal gift of utterance. Few are strangers to the experience of hearing others articulate more precisely and beautifully than ever they could hope to, truths that are most precious to them. The fact that some-one else has given the verbal expression does not make the truth so formulated any less magnificent: it does not diminish the passion of personal devotion by a breath. When I acclaim my Risen Redeemer as 'My Lord, and my God' my confession is not drained of sincerity because some-one else uttered these very words almost two thousand years ago! Why then should it be deemed a burdensome thing to subscribe a confession just because this specific articulation of faith was made three hundred years ago? Paul Woolley assessed the situation accurately, declaring —'Most modern people hold the view that a creed is something to be forced, or imposed on other people. That is utterly perverse . . . . Nothing could be further from the proper function for a creed. It ought to be a very joyful affirmation of the truth which has benefited the affirmant, and which he wants to pass on to others in a clear and simple form.' (*Scripture and Confession*, ed. John H. Skilton. Article 'What is a Creed for?'—By Paul Woolley, p. 98). The ordinand who acknowledges the Confession of Faith as the Confession of his own faith is not reluctantly bowing to pressures he cannot resist—but gladly confessing truth about which he cannot be silent. To miss this point is to fail to recognise the vital inter-action between the

Word of God, the man of God and the faith by which the man of God lives.

II   The Biblical Authorization of Confessions

The inter-action between the Word of God and the faith and declaration of the man of God is basic to all discussions about a Confession of Faith. There are people who argue that the Reformation insistence on Scripture alone, (sola Scriptura) is prejudiced by an emphasis on creeds which inevitably attract to themselves a respect and reverence, which, in time, is little to be distinguished from the Roman obedience to tradition in the form of 'consensus of the fathers' and 'conciliar decisions.' Necessary as it is to recognize the perspicuity of Scripture, it is equally necessary to have a lively sense of the sufficiency of Scripture and this principle, it is argued, is distorted when creeds are given prominence. This can hardly be regarded as a serious objection when it is recalled that no more than a subordinate position is claimed for a Confession. Appositely Dr. A. A. Hodge observes—'While the Scriptures are from God, the understanding of them belongs to the part of men. Men must interpret to the best of their ability each particular part of Scripture separately, and then combine all that the Scriptures teach upon every subject into a consistent whole, and then adjust their teachings upon different subjects in mutual consistency as parts of a harmonious system. Every student of the Bible must do this; and all make it obvious that they do it, by the terms they use in their prayers and religious discourse, whether they admit or deny the propriety of human creeds and confessions. If they refuse the assistance afforded by the statements of doctrine slowly elaborated and defined by the Church, they must make out their own creed by their own unaided wisdom. The real question is not, as often pretended between the Word of God, and the creed of man, but between the tried and proved faith of the collective body of God's people, and the private judgement and the unassisted wisdom of the repudiator of creeds' (*A Commentary on the Confession of Faith*, pp. 1-2).

The Biblical answer to the question of the propriety of confessions of faith may be learned, in part, from reflection on the activity of faith. The Scriptures show faith as a compulsive talker. 'I believed, therefore have I spoken' said the psalmist: and Paul exhibiting this as a feature of his own and his contemporary witnesses' faith, echoes—'we also believe and therefore speak.' Nor is this an attitude familiar only to men directly inspired to speak the very words of God. It is the spontaneous reaction of all those who receive the truth. They recognize it as both intimately personal and also as public property. The truth will out, and if assistance can be got in its articulation from the formulas of the Church, so much the better. The passion of conviction is not diminished when faith achieves satisfactory utterance.

Plainly, the Biblical approval of Confessions is more direct and specific. There is no need to research every occurrence of the action or summary of the content, of confessions referred to in Scripture. Paul lays his young disciple Timothy under a solemn charge of obedience by recollection of Jesus Christ and His good confession 'before Pontius Pilate,' and the writer of the Epistle to the Hebrews has a parallel line of argument in fixing the attention of people who needed to re-affirm their faith on 'the apostle and High Priest of our profession.' More than once when He was with them the Lord Jesus Christ invited the disciples to make open and specific profession of their faith in Him. (John 6.67 ff. Luke 9.18 ff.). Paul tells of the relation between inner conviction and vocal expression, belief in the heart and confession with the mouth (Romans 10.9 ff.) and John lays emphasis on some facts about the Lord Jesus Christ which are inseparable from a Christian confession, (John 6.69; 15.26 f.).

No doubt, the passages of Scripture to which we have referred, and others of similar import, lay considerable stress upon the importance of relationship and activity. There must be a vital relationship between the disciple and his Lord expressed in the activity of confession. But it is an inadmissible artificiality which tries to seal off this from the specific content of the confession. 'The act of confession cannot be thought of apart from either the faith exercised or the faith summarized and expressed in words,' (*Scripture and Confession*, Ed. John H. Skelton. First Article by Norman Shepherd, p. 14). Norman Shepherd rightly observes that the New Testament writers declined the use of the Greek word *homologesis* which focuses attention on the act of confession. 'Instead, another noun *homologia* (e.g., Heb. 4.14) is used, which implies the act of confession but draws particular attention to that which is confessed,' (*Ibid.*, p. 13).

There can be no belief in the Lord Jesus Christ without some knowledge of facts about Him. There can be no significant confession of Jesus which does not include facts about Him. To this the apostle John, in particular, gives explicit testimony: and Paul observes that Hymeneus and Philetus overthrew the faith of some by declaring the resurrection to be past already. Quite obviously as early as the times when the New Testament was being compiled the Christian community recognized that 'the faith' not only referred to relationship and activity, but also to doctrinal truth. This truth focused on the Lord Jesus Christ, the Incarnate Word of God, but it was not Christomonistic. Jesus Christ was known as the one sent by the Father and by whose promise the Spirit came at Pentecost. The concern of Christians was not with how little they needed to know and believe to sustain a Christian confession, but to understand the truth in its manifoldness.

'To summarize,' says Shepherd, 'we are not compelled to choose sides in the false dilemna: living faith—system of doctrine; faith in Jesus—faith about Jesus; faith to be confessed—confession to be believed. The apostle John does not call upon us to sacrifice the things that are written for the sake of the faith; rather they are written that we might believe, and believing, have eternal life (John 20.31). The things written are the things that have been revealed; they belong to us and to our posterity (Duet. 29.29).

'The fact that the truth has been revealed to us in words to be received in faith and to be proclaimed in the world makes possible the composition of confessional documents as summaries of the things most surely believed among us, (Luke 1.1). The confessional documents are confessions of faith.' (*Ibid.*, p. 18).

III   The Emergence of Confessions
There are evidences in the New Testament that short statements of Christian belief were gaining currency in the Church during the life-time of the apostles. A common explanation is that converts to Christianity were required, when offering themselves for baptism to make such a statement. An example is the declaration by the Ethiopian Eunuch (Acts 8.37), 'I believe that Jesus Christ is the Son of God.' In such circumstances a man might declare his conviction that 'Jesus Christ is come in the flesh' and the Church acknowledging the sincerity of the declaration and recalling that no man could make such a confession 'but by the Spirit of God' would recognise him as a brother.

The two basic confessions just instanced serve to highlight the twin impulses to confession-making. These are the joy of discovery and passion for the truth.

Archimedes is said to have experienced the joy of discovery in his bath and shouted 'Eureka.' With more reason and still greater and enduring joy people have re-echoed the disciple Andrew's words—'We have found the Messiah.' Doubtless these spontaneous utterances retain the virtue of brevity and concentration upon essential facts. The creed which has came to be known as 'The Apostles' Creed' and which most historians trace back to about the second century as a baptismal creed in use at Rome, can lay claim to these virtues. The compilers of the Westminster Confession regarded this formulary as of sufficient use and prestige to warrant its being printed at the end of the Shorter Catechism with an explanatory note in the following terms—'Albeit the substance of that abridgement, commonly called the Apostles' Creed, be fully set forth in each of the Catechisms, so as there is no necessity of inserting the creed itself; yet it is here annexed, not as though it were composed by the apostles, or ought to be esteemed canonical Scripture, as the Ten Commandments and the Lord's Prayer, but because it is a brief sum of the Christian faith, agreeable to the Word of God, and anciently received in the Churches of Christ.'

But whilst a short simple composition like the Apostles Creed may express the Christian joy of discovery, it cannot adequately express the Christian passion for truth. Perhaps this is, in part, because the preciousness of many aspects and elements of truth is only realized, when misguided people try to rob the Church of some of its treasures. When parts of divine revelation are denied and/or distorted the faithful are roused to secure the doctrine against error. This is how, as a matter of history, the great creedal statements came to be composed. No great insight is required to realise how powerless against many heresies a statement like the Apostles' Creed is. John Macpherson of Findhorn exposed its weaknesses thus—'On examination we find in it no doctrine of Holy Scripture, of divine decrees, or of divine Providence; no statement of the doctrines of grace. It is simply a résumé of leading historical truths. The incarnation and sufferings of Christ are related, but there is no reference whatever to the purpose for which He lived and died. The existence of the Church is acknowledged, but there is no doctrine of the sacraments. Belief in the forgiveness of sins is expressed, but it is not said that this is in any way connected with the redemption wrought by Christ. The resurrection and everlasting life are confessed, but how the resurrection of the just is to be attained unto we are not told . . . . Certainly there is no heresy in it, but of the heresies that have actually appeared through-out the history of the Church, there are few which those adopting the apostles Creed as their symbol might not maintain' (*The Westminster Confession of Faith*, p. 6).

The passion for truth requires greater elaboration in the exposition of the essential elements of the faith. Truth is seen in its full splendour when set in contrast with what is not the truth. To accuse the Church of living by negation in some of its confessional statements is to miss the point. When, for example, in the Definition of Chalcedon the union of the two natures in Christ is described as 'without confusion, without conversion, without division and without separation,' these are not 'four bald negative terms . . . Rather these limiting terms make a positive contribution to the brightness and sharpness of the outline of the image of Christ presented to us . . . and a glorious image it is' (Ed. John Skilton, op. cit., p. 100).

The debates of the early Church were concerned mainly with the Biblical doctrine of the Trinity and of the Person of Christ. At times, argument and counter-argument seemed to accomplish little but the disunity of the Church. Yet the resultant Confessional Statements—of Nicea (in 325) of Ephesus (431) and of Chalcedon (in 451), received a marvellously wide-spread acceptance and these creeds are still held in great respect by Churches in the Reformed family. Associated with the controversies about the Person of Christ is the name of the great Athanasius of Alexandria. So great was his passion for truth that he was prepared to stand against the whole world and the picture of Athathasius 'contra mundum' ranks with that of Luther before his accusers—'Here stand I, I can do no other,' as among the most inspiring examples of devotion to the truth, which the world has known.

When the collector of precious pearls discovers the one which is peerless he experiences an inexpressible transport of delight in the thrill of which he sells up his whole collection to gain the one 'of great price.' So our Lord tells us in a well known parable. The Reformation brought just such an explosion of joy into the Church of the 16th century. Too often the reader of history listens so much to the 'clash of tongues' voluble in controversy that he fails to hear 'the melody of joy and health.' But the song swelled in rapture to gladden the whole of Europe and make even sacrifice and martyr-dom yield sweet notes of joy.

For truth had been re-discovered; the Bible had been put into the hands of the common man in the language of his every-day life. People eagerly exhibited to one another the different facets of glory. Lines of communication were opened from Germany to Scandinavia and from Switzerland to Scotland, for the truth re-discovered was to be shared. It was not just the perk of the scholar but the shared bounty of the man who followed the plough. It was not just a series of academic propositions to be agreed, but the living word of God to be held in trust by the living people of God. Even at this distance in time there is something surpassingly thrilling in discerning the commerce of different leaders and Churches: in marking the mutual respect with which the Churches of different countries received each others' formularies of faith: in observing not resolutions to dominate but concern to be helpful in service one to another.

Out of all this joyful prospecting and digging in the mines of truth came the classical statements of the Christian faith which have endured to the present day. The Augsburg Confession, in its first draft mainly the work of Luther and Melancthon, has been the recognized statement of faith of the Lutheran Churches. Bullinger, the successor of Zwingli, contributed the essential ground-work both of the second Helvetic Confession and the Heidelberg Catechism. The influence of Calvin is more or less direct in the Gallican Confession (*via* the Paris Confession) and the Belgic which, however, was mostly the work of an individual, Guido de Bres. John Knox was the chief architect of the Scots Confession as Cranmer and Ridley were of the English Thirty-Nine articles.

More obviously the products of large conferences were the Canons of the Synod of Dort, and the Confession of Faith and the Catechisms of the Westminster Assembly. The famous Synod of Dort met from Novemebr 1618 to May 1619 to settle the controversy which had arisen over the teachings of Arminius. 'The Canons of this Synod were received by all the Reformed Churches as a true, accurate, and eminently authoritative exhibition of the Calvinistic System of Theology. They constitute, in connection with the Heidelberg Catechism, the doctrinal Confession of the Reformed Church of Holland and of the (Dutch) Reformed Church of America' (A. A. Hodge, op. cit., pp. 10–11). Of the circumstances leading up to and the work of the Westminster Assembly a brief account will be given in the next section.

IV   The Making of the Westminster Confession (1643–1647)

The cause and work of Reformation had fared quite differently in the Kingdoms of Scotland and England. Scotland had experienced a radical and complete renewal in Church life extending from doctrine to government and practice: in England the doctrines of grace had indeed prevailed as witnessed by the Thirty-Nine Articles, but government and discipline had remained episcopal with powers hitherto credited to the Pope, now vested in the monarch. This was much to the liking of the Stewart kings who had been resentful of the restraints placed upon the Royal prerogative by the Scottish Church. Both James VI and I, and Charles I had resolved to secure an absolute control of the Church in the two kingdoms and Charles found Archbishop Laud an energetic ally. Charles found however, that his pretensions to absolutism in Church and State were stoutly resisted by the English Parliament —and Scotland was in a ferment of dissatisfaction with the policies of Laud. The English Parliament, recognising that the King drew much of his support from the prelatic party, and having in many of its members principial objection to episcopacy, banned bishops and proposed in 'The Grand Remonstrance' (November, 1641) the holding of a General Synod with representatives from the Churches of England and Scotland and some from abroad to consider 'of all things necessary for the peace and good government of the Church;' this Synod to report to Parliament. For a time this proposal was thwarted by the King's resolute refusal to give his assent to the necessary Act and eventually Parliament passed an Ordinance to have the effect of law without dependence on royal assent. This fixed the 1st July, 1643 as the date for the meeting of 'an assembly of learned and godly divines and others, to be consulted with the Parliament, for the settling of the government and liturgy of the Church of England, and for vindicating and clearing of the doctrine of the said Church from false aspersions and interpretations.' This Assembly met as appointed on first July, though some who had been called by Parliament failed to appear out of respect to a Royal proclamation forbidding the Assembly. The first meeting was in the Chapel of Henry VII, but with the advent of colder weather the assembly moved (2nd October) to the quarters with which their name is inalienably associated, the Jerusalem Chamber. There they were to meet regularly from time to time for the next six years. Their last recorded minutes indeed are dated 25th March 1652.

Though in the intention of Parliament primary consideration was to be given to the government and liturgy of the Church of England, and matters of doctrine were regarded as less urgent, involving only the repudiation of mis-constructions, in actual fact the first task specifically allotted by Parliament was the revision of the Thirty-Nine Articles. Possibly, this was somewhat of a temporising measure, for relations between King and Parliament had deteriorated still further and Parliament was in need of help from the Scots.

The Scots were in no mood for merely civil treaties. The signing of the National Covenant in 1638 had marked the high tide of national religious feeling. So when the English Commissioners came to them proposing a civil league they insisted on a religious covenant—'The Solemn League and Covenant.' Much has been written about the alleged impractical idealism of the Scots in insisting on this Covenant as the price of their aid against the King. Not sufficiently appreciated is the risk they took in the cause of truth. B. B. Warfield justly commented—'The Scots had nothing to gain from the alliance which was offered them, unless they gained security for their Church from future English interference; while on the other hand by entering into it they risked everything which they had at so great cost recovered for themselves. Their own liberties were already regained; the cause of Parliament in England, on the contrary, hung in the gravest doubt. It really was an act of high chivalry, to call it by no more sacred name, for them to cast in their lot at this crisis with the Parliament' (B. B. Warfield, *The Westminster Assembly and Its Work*, p. 23).

In August 1643 the Commissioners of the English Parliament duly swore the terms of the Solemn League and Covenant. This document was in fact accepted by Church and Civil authority in Scotland, by Parliament and the Assembly of Divines in England and then circulated in both nations for popular signature as the National Covenant had been in Scotland five years earlier. By the terms of the engagement, Warfield recalls, 'The contracting parties bound themselves to "the *preservation* of the reformed religion in the Church of Scotland, in doctrine, worship, discipline and government, against our common enemies," on the one hand; on the other to "the *reformation* of religion in the kingdoms of England and Ireland, in doctrine, worship, discipline and government, according to the word of God and the example of the best reformed Churches"; to end that thereby, "the Churches of God in the three kingdoms" might be brought " to the nearest conjunction and uniformity in religion, confession of faith, form of Church government, directory for worship and catechising" ' (B. B. Warfield, op. cit., p. 24).

One immediate result of the acceptance of the Solemn League and Covenant by both countries was that a number of Scottish theologians went to England as Treaty Commissioners. A Committee of the English Parliament was formed to confer with them and this 'Grand Committee' undertook the work of the Assembly of Divines regarding uniformity of religion. The Scots Commissioners were also invited to sit in the Assembly of Divines though without vote. The Scottish deputation comprised Robert Baillie, George Gillespie, Alexander Henderson, and Samual Rutherford, ministers; with Lord Maitland and Johnston of Warriston, elders.

There being so much political manoeuvring associated with the institution of the assembly, the competence of the membership might be called in question. As men of ability, integrity, and piety, they had nothing to fear from the closest scrutiny of men. 'The Divines there congregate' wrote Richard Baxter, 'were men of eminent learning and godliness, and ministerial abilities and fidelity; and being not worthy to be one of them myself, I may the more freely speak that truth which I know, even in the face of malice and envy, that, as far as I am able to judge by the information of all history of that kind, and by any other evidence left us, the Christian world, since the days of the apostles had never a Synod of more excellent Divines than this Synod and Synod of Dort were' (quoted in E. MacRury, *The Symbol of Division*, p. 14). Each member of assembly took the following vow—'I do seriously promise and vow in the presence of Almighty God, that in this assembly, whereof I am a member, I will maintain nothing in point of doctrine but what I believe to be most agreeable to the Word of God, nor in point of discipline but what I shall conceive to conduce most to the glory of God, and the good and peace of His Church.' When one reflects that the membership comprised Presbyterians and Independents and Erastians and considers the excellence of the doctrinal statements produced, one realises both how seriously the vow to follow Scripture was honoured, and how graciously the Holy Spirit led those good men to their conclusions.

When the Solemn League and Covenant had been duly subscribed and the Commissioners from Scotland had joined the Assembly of Divines, that body got down seriously to the business agreed upon in the Covenant. The first part of the work to be completed was a Directory of Ordination and 'Propositions concerning Church Government.' These propositions did not commend themselves to the English Parliament and were never formally approved by it as by the General Assembly in Scotland. Parliamentary approval was eventually forthcoming for a 'Practical Directory of Church Government,' mainly the work of Alexander Henderson, which confined itself to prescription of the framework of Presbyterian government, rather than argument about the principles.

The Assembly's next task was one in which general agreement was more easily secured. This was the preparation of a Directory for Public Worship and this work was done and the approval of civil and ecclesiastical bodies in the two countries signified by February of 1645. The Directory is not a book of common order in the sense of prescribing a mandatory ritual of worship. It gives advice, proposes how the various elements of worship may be honoured and suggests paradigms of public prayer. In large measure it was the work of the Scottish Commissioners and drew upon the Book of Common Order known as Knox's Liturgy. The order of service observed in the Free Church of Scotland today is not greatly different from that suggested in the Directory. B. B. Warfield's general appraisal of it is worth reproducing at length.' At this distance of time we may look upon it dispassionately; and so viewed, it can scarcely fail to commend itself as an admirable set of agenda, in spirit and matter alike well fitted to direct the public services of a great Church. It is notable for its freedom from petty prescriptions and "superfluities" and for the emphasis it places upon what is specifically commended in Scriptures. Its general tone is lofty and spiritual; its conception of acceptable worship is sober and restrained and at the same time profound and rich . . . and it is singular among agenda for the dominant place it gives in the public worship of the Church to the offices of reading and preaching the Word . . . the paragraph on the Preaching of the Word, is, in effect, indeed a complete homiletical treatise, remarkable at once for its sober practical sense and its profound spiritual wisdom, and suffused with a tone of sincere piety, and of zeal at once for the truth and for the souls which are to be bought with the truth' (B. B. Warfield, op. cit., pp. 51–52).

The third part of the remit to the Assembly concerned the compilation of articles of Doctrine and though this was not regarded as the most urgent, having regard to the Reformed tenor of the

Confessions already acknowledged in both countries, it was a task very congenial to the members of the Assembly. The result of this was the Confession of Faith, which in its thirty three chapters covers all the essential points of a Biblical theology. It was presented to Parliament complete with proof texts in April 1647, approved by the General Assembly of the Church of Scotland the same year and by the Scottish Estates in February 1649. The English Parliament demurred at some of the Presbyterian principles and gave approval to a modified version in March 1660—but by then, so far as England was concerned, the mood for acceptance was passed. The Restoration of the monarchy in 1660 ensured that the document would only have historical interest in the Church of England.

But though in the land which gave it birth the Confession of Faith never achieved the place of honour it merited, its influence became paramount in Scotland and in the Presbyterian Churches descended from the Church of Scotland. Some of the younger Churches made modifications in the section on the relations between Church and State and others toned down the references to the Pope as Anti-Christ. The unique position achieved in Scotland was retained as long as the Scottish Churches retained their confidence in the Scriptures as the Word of God, but when rationalist philosophies prevailed, and higher critical theories of Scripture were given hospitality, the Confession began to be a burden and a judge and divider. No longer did it voice the joy of discovery, for men were listening to false prophets. No longer did it articulate the passion for truth, for people had become unsure as to what is truth. Little wonder that movements that aimed to modify an ordinand's relation to the Confession were hailed as movements of liberation. The wonder is not that the Declaratory Acts by which the Church of Scotland (following the pattern of the United Presbyterian and the United Free) has made acknowledgement of the Confession quite tenuous, have had such a welcome. The wonder is that there has been such a reluctance to make a final break with the Confession To many it would seem the more open and honest course to dispense with a Confession which no longer expresses the faith of the Church, rather than to retain the Confession with a pledge which dies the death of a thousand modifications. Our better part, however, is to encourage more candid study of the Confession and comparison of its doctrinal statements with Scripture, in the hope and with the prayer that this will yield in the National Church a

new discovery of truth with the joy that brings, and a new passion
for truth with the concern for precision of articulation which that
engenders. We are not bound to the very letter of the Confession
as though it were itself Scripture, but to the doctrine it articulates;
and a new formulation of the same doctrines which could demonstrate an equal loyalty to Scripture could equally and gladly be
acknowledged as the confession of our faith.

V The Content of the Confession

Volumes of expositions have been written on the contents of the
Confession of Faith and it would be over-ambitious to attempt to
summarize the whole doctrine here. A list of the thirty-three chapter titles will have to suffice to indicate the extent of the territory
covered. These titles read: Of the Holy Scriptures; Of God and of
the Holy Trinity; Of God's Eternal Decree; Of Creation; Of
Providence; Of the Fall of Man, of Sin and of the Punishment
thereof; Of God's Covenant with Man; Of Christ the Mediator;
Of Free Will; Of Effectual Calling; Of Justification; Of Adoption;
Of Sanctification; Of Saving Faith; Of Repentance unto Life; Of
Good Works; Of the Perseverance of the Saints; Of Assurance of
Grace and Salvation; Of the Law of God; Of Christian Liberty,
and Liberty of Conscience; Of Religious Worship and the Sabbath-
day; Of Lawful Oaths and Vows; Of the Civil Magistrate; Of
Marriage and Divorce; Of the Church; Of Communion of Saints;
Of the Sacraments; Of Baptism; Of the Lord's Supper; Of Church
Censures; Of Synods and Councils; Of the State of Man after Death,
and of the Resurrection of the Dead; Of the Last Judgement.

So wide a spectrum of Christian doctrine does this cover that it
is not surprising that many have objected that it is in fact too
comprehensive and that something considerably more selective and
brief would win more widespread acceptance. This raises the issue
of the purpose a Confession is designed to achieve. Without doubt,
short concentrated statements are suggested today, whose whole
purpose is to secure genearal approbation. Ecumenical interest
seems to dictate concentration of creedal statement. This is a
radical change from the passion to express truth as comprehensively
and precisely as possible. Dr. Gresham Machen exposed this contradiction quite pointedly. Referring to modern 'supposed doctrinal
statements' he observed: 'These . . . are constructed for a purpose
which is just the opposite of the purpose that governed the formation of the great historic creeds. The historic creeds were exclus-

ive of error; they were intended to exclude error; they were intended to set forth the Biblical teaching in sharp contrast to what was opposed to the Biblical teaching, in order that the purity of the Church might be preserved. These modern statements on the contrary are inclusive of error. They are designed to make room in the Church for just as many people and for just as many types of thought as possible' (Ed. J. H. Skilton, op. cit., pp. 151–152). The end-result in the formation of a creed, it would seem, depends on how honest and frank the creed-makers wish to be.

That unnecessary length would be a blemish in a Church Confession most will be ready to admit, for the Confession is not an exposition of the whole body of theology, which would require a multiplicity of volumes. Content is what matters and the interests of what is fundamental will determine length. John MacPherson properly remarked—'A Confession should be, not vague, but definite. We must guard against the notion that the interests of freedom are to be advanced by rendering the formulary short and vague in expression. It is quite a fallacy to suppose that greater liberty is enjoyed under a brief statement of beliefs than under a detailed enumeration of doctrines. When care is taken in admitting doctrinal statements only on leading and fundamental points, definiteness and fullness in a symbolical book will prove a high recommendation' (John MacPherson, op. cit., pp. 4–5).

In the determination of what the fundamental points are, it is not sufficient to isolate a few texts or passages of Scripture. The embryonic confessional statements in the New Testament, to which reference was made earlier do indeed highlight truths necessary to be believed for salvation. But the Church cannot pretend that its history has never been: it cannot ignore the lessons, the struggles and the hard-won elucidations of truth which that history has yielded. Nor can the Church pretend not to be aware of matters, without uniformity on which, no orderly progress and life would be possible even though these do not come within the category of things necessary to be believed for salvation. These factors, no doubt, persuaded the compilers of the Confession of Faith to incorporate into the formulary somewhat more than would be required as a confession from an individual claiming to be a Christian. That is why the Church does not make acceptance of the Confession of Faith a requirement for admission to its membership —but a requirement of those who are to undertake the propagating of the faith for the edification of the Church.

That it has attempted to say too much, is not however the most grievous complaint brought against the Confession. Many protest that some of the things the Confession says are totally unacceptable. We have already observed that the formulation of the Church-State relationship proved unacceptable to most of the American Presbyterian Churches and the reference to the Pope as anti-Christ made other people unhappy. But more radical than these have been the objections taken to the place assigned to the Divine sovereignty and the eternal decrees, as also to the supposed exclusion of children dying in infancy from the benefits of salvation. Some of those objecting have caricatured the Confession's doctrine of God, failing to observe its emphasis on grace as well as sovereignty. Nor have they sufficiently appreciated the discriminating language of the Confession in regard to the election to life and the 'passing by' of those who for their sin are ordained to dishonour and wrath. In regard to the statement about 'elect infants,' it has not always been appreciated that the concern of the Confession was to leave open a question which Scripture itself does not answer in regard to the possible application of the benefits of salvation to those whose minds cannot be illumined in the ordinary way to the apprehension of truth.

Restraint, is indeed one of the shining virtues of the Confession. Rightly, it begins with the recognition of Scripture as the sufficient and authoritative revelation of God, and in assigning first place to Scripture it stakes a claim to contemporary relevance which cannot be lightly dismissed. Having acknowledged Scripture, the Confession keeps within the limits of its teaching and refuses to be drawn into speculations and abstract thinking beyond these limits. Writing on 'The Theology of the Westminster Confession,' Professor John Murray observed—'In respect to fidelity to Scripture, precision of thought and formulation, fulness of statement, balanced proportion of emphasis, studied economy of words, and effective exposure of error, no creedal confession attains to the same level of excellence characterising that of Westminster,' (Ed. Skilton, Op. cit., p. 145).

VI Contemporary Relevance

However impressed one may be by the virtues of the work accomplished by the Assembly of Divines in 1647, one cannot parry the question—Is the Confession they compiled relevant to the situation of the Church today? The issue is not merely one of language

HOLD FAST YOUR CONFESSION

for it would not be an impossible task to re-write the Confession in the idiom of this decade, given the contemporary relevance of its content.

This question cannot be answered without reference to basic first-principles and to the uses for which a Confession is intended.

In regard to first principles it has to be re-iterated that the Confession proceeds upon the acceptance of Scripture as the Word of God. Not just as containing God's word: not just as the record of God's word: not just as the witness to God's word: Scripture is the revelation of God. God spoke and revealed His will and this speech and revelation we have in Scripture. This is what invests Scripture with final authority and requires that all Church doctrine be determined by it. If there are Churches which deny this first principle: if there are Churches which give priority to human reason: if there are Churches which look on Scripture as the history of a religious evolution: it has to be recognized that the Westminster Confession has minimal relevance to them. It has the relevance only of a witness of what was once believed and of a summons to return to pristine faith. The same verdict must be given in regard to those who require that a Confession be a record of contemporary Christian experience. The Westminster Divines were not lacking in Christian experience, but they deemed it their business to expound Scripture. Experience is to be judged by Scripture.

The foregoing considerations may compel recognition that the province of relevance for the Confession of Faith—other than as a witness to what ought to be—is depressingly narrow. But within this area the sense of relevance may be all the more intense, and the Confession recognized as a standard around which almost all of Reformed conviction may rally.

This leads us to consider the uses of Church Confessions and to ask whether the Westminster formulation answers to the classical uses. These can be simply stated as to identify, to unify, to edify and to multiply.

(a) *To identify.* By means of a Confession a Church makes an honest avowal of its attitude to Scripture and its conviction as to what the Scriptures principally teach. This it does both positively and negatively, setting the truth acclaimed over against the errors repudiated. There should be no muffing of important issues. A Christian Church should have Christian convictions and be unashamed of them. Christian convictions the Westminster Confession does proclaim and as such can usefully identify those who hold to 'the faith once for all delivered to the saints.'

(b) *To unify.* True unity is in the truth and there can be no more than a pretence of unity when the positive assertions of the faith have to be muted or silenced. Truth is not in such flux that it can never be honestly expressed: and for men of the 20th century to listen to the truth of divine revelation conveyed in words of the 17th century is not to absolutize what is passing and relative, but to perceive the relevance for their own time and circumstances of truth which has activated generation after generation. Ecumenical interest is often said to be prejudiced by creedal statement. This can only be argued when the ideal of unity is greatly impoverished. Among the Churches of the Reformation there was a strong sense of unity because, though formularies might vary, the doctrines of grace professed were the same. The Westminster Confession can still give to its professors coherence in the truth.

(c) *To edify.* Presenting, as they do, succinct statements of Biblical doctrine the creeds of the Church have been used from the beginning to build up the members of the Church in their most holy faith. The Christian has a charge to grow in grace and in the knowledge of the Lord Jesus Christ, and the researching of Scripture which the Confession summons him to make is a helpful method of procuring that growth. Ignorance of Confessional truth on the part of Church members, when discovered by the pastor, is a signal to him of the emphases he needs to make in the public ministry of the Word. As discipline is a part of Christian edification, a Biblical Confession is of use in this also. So used, the Confession is not an instrument of persecution but a method of expressing pastoral care. To this situation in a Biblical perspective the Westminster Confession is still relevant.

(d) *To multiply.* By this we mean that a Biblical Confession stimulates the outreach of the Church. Truth possessed is not to be hidden. The Lord lays His people under a charge to let their light shine. This a confession does both by assertion and negation. If we have been right in attributing confession-making in part to the joy of discovery, this is a joy which the Christian wishes to become infectious. The man who has studied the Word of God and compared the Confession of Faith with it makes a happy declaration when he acknowledges it as his own, but his happiness is increased by sharing.

The conclusion that 'the doctrine of the Confession is the doctrine which the Church needs to confess and hold aloft today as much as in the seventeenth century' (Ed. Skilton, op. cit., p. 146) does not mean that we regard the Confession as perfect and beyond improvement. Nor does it mean that we claim that no doctrinal advance is possible from the high point of enlightenment granted by the Holy Spirit to the Church in 1647. 'Doctrinal advance is certainly conceivable,' Dr. Gresham Machen conceded. 'It is perfectly conceivable that the Church should examine the particular errors of the present day and should set forth over against them, even more clearly than is done in existing creeds, the truth that is contained in God's Word. But I am bound to say that I think such doctrinal advance to be just now extremely unlikely . . . . I think it is clear that ours is not a creed-making age.' (Ed. Skilton p. 156). To agree with this statement is not to indulge a spirit of *'laissez-faire'* or indifference. It is simply to face facts. But neither are we to give way to spiritual indolence. We still have a mandate 'to search the Scriptures' and to 'try the spirits.' Let us continue to do so with a readiness to receive whatever can show that it is of God. In this we shall have help and no hindrance from the formulary of Westminster.

Bibliography

A. A. Hodge, *A Commentary on the Confession of Faith*, T. Nelson & Sons. Re-issued 1958, Banner of Truth Trust.

John. H. Skilton (Ed.), *Scripture and Confession*, Presbyterian & Reformed Pub. Co., 1973.

John MacPherson, *The Westminster Confession of Faith* ('Hand Books for Bible Classes'), T. & T. Clark.

E. MacRury, *The Symbol of Division*, Pickering & Inglis.

B. B. Warfield, *The Westminster Assembly and Its Work*, Oxford University Press, 1931.

Church and State

NEIL A. MACLEOD, M.A., B.D.
Minister of Duke Street Free Church, Glasgow.

Although the Free Church of Scotland assumed its present designation at the time of the Disruption of the Church of Scotland in the year 1843, it claims continuity with the true church of Christ back to Reformation times, to Apostolic times, and indeed to its very institution in Old Testament times. And when we thus trace the roots of our church back into Old Testament times, we find it hard to forbear quoting at some length, because of their exquisite felicitousness and their crucial relevance to our later argument, the words of James Walker of Carnwath, in this connection. He writes: 'The old writers did not think so much as we are apt to do, of Christianity beginning with the actual historical appearance of our incarnate Lord among men. They much more usually regarded the Christian church as the Old Testament Church in a new manifestation,—as ancient Israel, its shackles exchanged for a crown, the types and shadows gone in the rising of the Sun of righteousness, the merely local and temporal thrown away, with, as it were, such new dress, in the form of sacred ordinances, as befits altered circumstances—breaking out from its confinement among the hills of Judah, to clasp in its embrace all the nations in the order and way of that special providence which still as of old belongs to the covenant people and the holy kingdom; that is to say, the Christian Church is really the old theocracy on a grander scale, and with a more glorious Shechinah of the Holy King in its truths, and ordinances, and spiritual influences—in which, indeed, as in a kind of open Holy of Holies, He abides; and, in short, none but Himself, the theocratic Saviour, must rule or legislate within it' (James Walker, *Scottish Theology and Theologians*, pp. 129-130).

Inasmuch, however, as the church–state problem was the one which precipitated the Disruption, that era has a special interest for us in the present connection. Our church's position vis-à-vis the proper relationship between church and state is crystallized in the relevant sections of the Westminster Confession of Faith, and we shall have occasion to discuss the terms of these at a later stage, but no question of church principles can be handled with any kind of

45

relevance or adequacy without indicating its historical genesis and development. We must, therefore, first of all, touch upon some of the more significant epochs in the history of the problem of the church and the state, and not only as it has been the concern of the Free Church of Scotland, for we have need to remind ourselves that our Confessional statement of the issue represents the anguished contendings of the true church of Christ in many nations and through many centuries, the tireless labours of countless scholars and theologians, and the nameless agonies, and even the blood, of fearless martyrs, who flinched before no foe that they might assert and defend what came to be described, in Covenanting times in Scotland, as the Crown Rights of the Redeemer. It is essential, in a word, to establish some sort of historical perspective as we proceed to a consideration of the problem.

We use the term *problem* purposely, as it was it was only with the emergence of the Christian religion on the scene of world affairs that the question of the relationship between religion and the state became a problem at all. As P. Carnegie Simpson reminds us: 'In earlier religions the deity was tribal or national, and no conflict or even contrast existed between the god that was the object of worship and the god that was a political patron or ally. So when outlying nations fell before the conquering might of the Roman Empire—to go no further back into history—their religions, with the notable exception of Judaism, fell with them. Belief in their power and even in their reality could not survive the political overthrow which, as national protectors, they should have been able to avert.' (The Church and the State, pp. 14–15). Even Judaism, surviving as it did, enjoyed the statutory protection of the Roman Empire, being, as it was termed, a *religio licita*, and until Christianity became identified as a religion distinct from Judaism it flourished under the same official shelter. The thinking which lay behind the policy of the Roman Empire to afford to some faiths the status of a *religio licita*, with all the privileges that accompanied it, was that people could believe and practise what they liked *provided* that, first, they acknowledged and took part in the imperial cultus. The refusal of the Christians to become involved in Caesar worship, which was decreed as the only acceptable gesture of allegiance to the imperial authority, opened the conflict which created the problem, which, from that time to this, has been known as the problem of the church and the state. From the moment that the Christian religion came under the general outlawry of the imperial decree, '*Non vobis esse licet*' (You have not the right to exist) the first period of barbaric persecution against the Christians began.

It is not our present assignment to trace the course of these persecutions, but we should remind ourselves that, for by far the greater part, they occurred because of the threat that Christianity appeared to offer to the integrity and security of the Roman empire. The votaries of other religions could be tolerated and their particular devotions and practices actually welcomed, but the Christians, unlike even the Jews, were religious propagandists and the *majestas* of Rome was not prepared to accommodate religious fanatics and moral faddists whose views and practices, if allowed to proceed unchecked, bade fair to rend assunder the very fabric of imperial society and civilisation. The story of these persecutions is recounted in numerous volumes of church history dealing with that period. Suffice it to say here that they went on with unbelievable ferocity and with every conceivable refinement of torture, there occurring only brief periods of respite, for about three centuries. It is significant, by way of understanding the main motivation that lay behind the persecutions, to note that Marcus Aurelius, who is generally recognized as probably the most cultured and humane of the emperors, was not by any means the least noted in pursuing this policy of ruthless suppression. The last persecutions of this period, and doubtless the worst, took place under Decius and Diocletian; and it has been remarked that the atrocities perpetrated reached such a surfeit of savagery that defeated itself, for human nature could stand no more of it. One chronicler has stated that, 'these emperors renewed the persecution until the swords became blunt and the executioners weary.' The future was not to be secured through sickening barbarities. Some other way had to be found.

It is at this point that the name of the emperor Constantine appears upon the scene, and for an understanding of the controversies which have convulsed the church down the ages, and not least our own church, in its relations with certain other churches, particularly during the past century and a half, it is of critical importance to establish precisely what it was that Constantine did in relation to the Christian church. Constantine has had imputed to him the odious distinction of having done more than probably any other person to introduce degeneracy, ambition, avarice, and corruption into the Christian church, and this, because he brought to an end the long period of savage persecution, and passed legislative measures to provide for the toleration of the Christian church as an organized society in the empire. These allegations have been made, and continue to be made by those who hold to a Voluntary view of the church's relation with the state, which, to put it quite bluntly, means no relation at all. (We shall have occasion to explain later what the term Voluntary, in this connection, means, as also the other terms which have been employed to distinguish the various positions which have been taken by the several branches of the Christian church). It has been said, again and again, by many people through many centuries that Contsantine made Christianity the *established* religion of the Roman Empire. *He did no such thing.* It has also been alleged that because of Constantine's action vis-à-vis the Christian church he was responsible for the introduction of worldliness, heresy and almost every mentionable and indeed, unmentionable evil into the church, leading to the emergence and ultimate ascendency of the papacy during the Dark Ages. This is the case as stated by the churches which take a view of church–state relations different from that taken by ourselves as a denomination, and particularly those of a Voluntary persuasion, and that includes the greater part of what, in the spirit of charity, has to be described as the evangelical community of the world. But what are the historical facts?

The first effective act of toleration was introduced, not by Constantine at all but by Galerius, one member of a college of four imperial rulers which Diocletian had set up in order to assist him in the government of the empire. Indeed it is alleged that it was Galerius who prompted Diocletian to his dreadful orgy of blood against the Christians, and it was on his deathbed that he issued the edict which heralded a welcome era of toleration for the Christian church. Notwithstanding the action of Galerius it was, without doubt, the Edict of Milan in 313, brought into statute by Constantine, that was the decisive turning-point in the early history of the church's relations with the state. Its main provisions were that Christians 'and all others' should have full religious liberty, that all previous edicts to the contrary should be abrogated, and that whatever property had been taken away from the Christian church should be restored, the state to make good the cost to those who had thus become liable to loss. There is certainly nothing in this edict to indicate the *establishment* of the Christian religion. The truth is that Constantine established no religion but rather made provision for a kind of religious eclecticism. The most that can be said with regard to his attitude towards Christianity, as reflected in this edict, is that he accorded it a certain preferential treatment. The notion that Constantine established and endowed the Christian religion as a result of his personal conversion to the Faith is a tendentiously conceived historical myth. Those who argue against the national recognition of religion, never tire of raising the spectre of Constantine, and pointing with horror and self-justification to the corruptions introduced into the church by Constantine's 'establishment' of Christianity. Almost their entire case is built on this. In other words, their case has as its main historical basis a grave error or a deliberate fabrication. It reminds one of the fact that the gigantic edifice of the mediaeval papacy was based on the twofold historical fiction of the forged 'decretals of Isidore of Saville,' and the fictional 'Donation of Constantine'! As a matter of historical fact it was the emperor Theodosius, in the year 380 who took the decisive and official step of making Christianity the official religion of the empire. The edict by which this was effected was issued with the threat of divine and imperial punitive sanctions and it was imposed, not in terms of what 'establishment' represents in theory, but rather as a matter of practical expediency. It has to be said that Constantine did, in the later years of his reign, show imperial favour towards Christianity which expressed itself in preferential laws, in personal liberality and in general public observances and enactments. In his new capital on the shores of the Bosphorus pagan religion and practices were proscribed, and it was decreed that the only recognized religion should be the Christian. 'The net impression of Constantine's policy of favour towards the Christian faith was that in feeling and in fact, if not actually in law the Church of Christ was becoming—and in the new capital had become,—the church of the Roman state' (F. Carnegie Simpson, *The Church and the State*, p. 33).

It cannot be denied that the changed attitude of the imperial authorities towards the church had certain unhappy effects, but these arose not as a result of imperial favour, but from the inherent weakness and sinfulness of human nature. 'Worldliness is no monopoly of state churches.' Theologically, the church, which under the pressure of persecution had been preoccupied with the notion of the *parousia*, the second coming of the Lord, turned its attention more to the goal of making conquest of the world in His name. And with the hindsight of many centuries can we say that this change in outlook and emphasis was one to be altogether

D

deprecated? Morally, certain unhappy developments took place. It became more to a man's advantage to be a Christian and, as a result, hordes of unfit persons rushed into the church to receive baptism. Ecclesiastically, the influence of the emperor in church affairs increased and he began to concern himself not simply with matters of government such as the calling of synods and councils, but also with doctrine. This, in a way, was inevitable in days when the church was rent apart into two violently opposing factions, as a result of the Arian controversy, and he had to determine which Christianity was to enjoy the privilege of his favour. The outcome of this was that he came to be regarded as *summus episcopus*. Any theory of Erastianism, however, simply did not arise. The course of events during this period was dictated, not by theory, but by practical exigency.

We must attempt now, to answer the constantly repeated allegation that the alliance between church and state initiated by Galerius and Constantine was the source from which all the error, spiritual degeneracy, and appalling corruption of the Middle Ages stemmed. It has been argued, and still is argued, that the emergence, ascendency and tyranny of the papacy was the direct result of their policy. Is there any substance or validity in the argument? The argument, if argument it can be called, is to be found in the writings of Voluntaries—that is, those who abjure any sort of alliance between church and state, and, as an example, we may quote one of the leading apologists of that view from last century, Dr. Wardlaw, as quoted by James Gibson in his volume, *The Church in relation to the State*, (p. 16): 'the hindrance to the development of this anomalous power (the man of sin), this strange and wicked mystery, was 'taken out of the way' when the emperor and empire of Rome ceased to be pagan, and became (in the language of courtesy) Christian. It was then that every barrier to the progress of corruption was thrown down and by its gradual or rather rapid and accelerating increase the Antichristian Pope succeeded to the Christian Emperor; and thus from an event which has too often been boasted of as one of the most splendid triumphs of Christianity, and most signal manifestations of divine favour to the church, were introduced the terrors of papal tyranny, and all the ignorance and superstition, the degradation and misery, and thralldom of the dark ages.'

The assumption underlying this extraordinary statement is that error, ignorance and superstition were unknown, or almost so, prior to the toleration and establishment of Christianity and, therefore, 'Voluntaries with one voice speak of the state of Christianity, in the first three centuries, as such that it affords positive proof of such a total, sudden, pernicious, and universal depravation, on the accession of Constantine, as to furnish a complete argument against a national church' (op. cit., p. 16). But a fair and even cursory examination of the circumstances which prevailed from New Testament times down to the age of Constantine will show that numberless and complex corruptions prevailed long before he became emperor, that almost every corruption in doctrine and practise that afterwards disfigured the church not only existed but was widespread and had gained a firm hold on the life and thought of the church, that the church's wealth was acquired by voluntary contributions, that even imperial gifts were of this kind, that whatever evils then existed sprang from the Voluntary principle and not from the connection of church and state, and that Constantine on becoming a 'Christian' could hardly have done less in favour of the church than he did, and that, much as he has been blamed, he was tolerant even of the pagans. We have already pointed out that in reality he never endowed the church. One or two points may be mentioned by way of illustration. Even during the earthly ministry of our Lord we have record of rivalry and ambition among the apostles; in apostolic times there was abounding error and corruption as we may readily learn from the New Testament documents themselves —'For the mystery of iniquity doth already work' (2 Thess. 2.7, and cf. 2 Pet. 2.15, 16, 21; Rev. 2.6, 15, the Epistle of Jude, 1 Tim. 6.4, 5.; and the letters to the seven churches). During the second and third centuries corruptions and heresies of all sorts appeared, and this without the alleged corrupting influence of any state favour or alliance. It is from this period that heresies took their origins as, for example, the doctrine of purgatory, prayer for the dead, transubstantiation, and various errors regarding baptism and the Lord's supper. It was also during this time that monarchical episcopacy took its beginnings, and there are not wanting evidences of the rapacity and unbounded ambitions of persons in places of ecclesiastical influence. It is therefore a shameless falsification of the facts of history to maintain that the errors and evils which corrupted the church during the Dark Ages are attributable to the alliance formed between the church and the state, dating from the time of Constantine.

The church was first despised by the state; then, persecuted;

then tolerated; then favoured; then established. In the course of the succeeding centuries it became the inheritor of the imperial prestige and, with a mightier power than old Rome had ever known, went on to rule the world.

In bringing this section to a close we turn again to the words of James Gibson: 'who that knows anything of the dreadful sufferings of those early followers of the Redeemer—who "had trial of cruel mockings and scourgings; yea, moreover, of bonds and imprisonment; who were sawn asunder, were tempted, were slain with the sword,"—does not sympathize with the following pleasing strain of feeling, in which (Eusebius) indulged, on the accession of Constantine, and the overthrow of their pagan persecutors, as recorded in these words—"A bright and glorious day, no cloud overshadowing it (μηδενὸς νέφους αὐτὴν ἐπισκιάζοντος) did enlighten, with rays of heavenly light, the churches of Christ over all the earth; and among all Christians there was an inexpressible joy, and a kind of celestial gladness!" We can scarcely believe, that if some of our modern sentimentalists, who mourn so pathetically over the evils of Constantine's conversion, and inveigh, with such declamatory bitterness, against the succeeding, or, as they say, the consequent corruptions, had "come out of so great tribulation," they would have failed to accept with gladness the peace which God had provided; that *they* would have chosen strangling and death rather than life' (op. cit., pp. 77–78).

We must now overleap the centuries and come down to Reformation times, and we shall do no more in this connection than state that all the reformers, with varying degrees of emphasis insisted on an alliance between the church and the state. Indeed, as every theological schoolboy knows, the Reformation could never have triumphed without such an alliance. We pass over this momentous period with this brief comment because the general consensus of the opinions of the reformers finds expression in the Westminster Confession of Faith to which we now turn our attention. But before doing so it may be well to state, as we indicated earlier, that we would state what the various positions are which, historically, have been held with regard to the question. There is, first of all, the view that the state should be subject to the church in everything both civil and spiritual, which is the papal position, or, as it is known in its extremest form, Ultramontanism. The reverse of this, namely, that the church should be subject in all respects to the civil authority, is the second we take up for mention, and is usually referred to as Erastianism, although it is sometimes described by continental writers as Byzantinism. A third view is that which has come to be known as Voluntaryism, which abhors and abjures any kind of contractual relation or alliance between the two spheres, civil and ecclesiastical. There is, fourthly, the position to which we as a church subscribe, and is based upon what is known, historically, as the Establishment principle. According to this view the two jurisdictions of church and state are clearly distinguished, and their functions clearly defined. The leaders of the Church of Scotland in 1590, with Andrew Melville at their head, in a memorable document, addressed King James in the following terms: 'There are two jurisdictions exercised in this realm: the one spiritual, the other civil; the one respects the conscience, the other external things; the one directly procuring the obedience of God's word and commandments, the other obedience unto civil laws; the one persuading by the spiritual word, the other compelling by the temporal sword; the one spiritually procuring the edification of the Kirk, which is the body of Jesus Christ; the other, by entertaining justice, procuring the commoditie, peace, and quietness of the Commonweal, the which, having ground in the light of nature, proceeds from God, as He is Creator, and so termed by the Apostle Humana Creatura.' (Quoted by James Walker, op. cit., pp. 143–144.) But the respective boundaries and functions of the two jurisdictions are not only carefully defined, their mutual relations and obligations are clearly set out. Hear Rutherford, in his magnificent treatise, *Lex, Rex,* 'God is the author of civil laws and government, and his intention is therein the external peace, and quiet life, and godliness of his church and people, and that all judges, according to their places, be nurse–fathers to the church (Is. 49.23)' (Lex Rex, p. 105). This view accords with that of many of the Reformed Confessions, namely that the first duty of the civil magistrate is to recognize, to countenance, to protect, to promote and to maintain with the nation's resources, the true religion. Not all these Confessions maintained that this was his *first* duty, but with one accord they insisted that it was a principal part of his magisterial responsibility. The church, on its part, had its responsibilities towards the state. It was its duty to pray for the civil rulers, to offer them guidance in spiritual and moral matters, to admonish them when their conduct of civil affairs was in conflict with the teaching of the word of God, and generally to lend its support to the advancement of the spiritual interests of the people. In the interests of historical accuracy it has to be said that, in his later thought, Rutherford moved away from the position above stated, that the promotion of religion was the civil magistrate's *first* responsibility.

But before proceeding to discuss the matter in any greater detail let us see how it is dealt with in the Westminster Confession, and consider some of the objections which have been made against it. In chapter 20, section 4, we read, 'And because the powers which God hath ordained, and the liberty which Christ hath purchased, are not intended by God to destroy, but mutually to uphold and preserve one another; they who, upon pretence of Christian liberty, shall oppose any lawful power, or the lawful exercise of it, whether it be civil or ecclesiastical, resist the ordinance of God.' In chapter 23 the question relating to the position of the civil magistrate is stated as follows, and although it is fairly lengthy we give it in full as it is of crucial importance for our present purpose. The chapter is entitled, 'Of the Civil Magistrate,' and these are its terms:

'God, the supreme Lord and King of all the world, hath ordained civil magistrates to be under him over the people, for his own glory, and the publick good; and to this end, hath armed them with the power of the sword, for the defence and encouragement of them that are good, and for the punishment of evil-doers.

II. It is lawful for Christians to accept and execute the office of a magistrate, when called thereunto: in the management whereof, as they ought especially to maintain piety, justice and peace, according to the wholesome laws of each commonwealth; so, for that end, they may lawfully, now under the New Testament, wage war upon just and necessary occasions.

III. The civil magistrate may not assume to himself the administration of the word and sacraments, or the power of the keys of the kingdom of heaven; yet he hath authority, and it is his duty, to take order, that unity and peace be preserved in the church, that the truth of God be kept pure and entire, that all blasphemies and heresies be suppressed, all corruptions and abuses in worship and discipline prevented or reformed, and all the ordinances of God duly settled, administered and observed. For the better effecting whereof, he hath power to call synods, to be present at them, and to provide that whatsoever is transacted in them be according to the mind of God.

IV. It is the duty of the people to pray for magistrates, to honour their persons, to pay them tribute and other dues, to obey their

lawful commands, and to be subject to their authority for conscience sake. Infidelity, or difference in religion doth not make
void the magistrate's just and legal authority, nor free the people
from their due obedience to him: from which ecclesiastical persons are not exempted; much less hath the Pope any power of
jurisdiction over them in their dominions, or over any of their
people; and least of all to deprive them of their dominions or
lives, if he shall judge them to be hereticks, or upon any other
pretence whatsoever.'

The terms of this Confessional statement are so comprehensive,
unambiguous, and so precise that little, really, needs to be added
by way of exposition. It may, nevertheless, be helpful to make a
number of comments upon it. In his book, *The Claims of the Church
of Scotland*, G. D. Henderson tells a story, which, though humour-
ous, contains within it a statement which summarizes the teaching
of the Confession. The story is evidently told by Ian MacLaren,
'which he holds to be at least *ben trovato*.' He tells about a serious
mother asking her child as it supped its porridge, 'What is the true
relation between Church and State?' The innocent promptly re-
plied: 'co-ordinate jurisdiction with mutual subordination' (G. D.
Henderson, *The Claims of the Church of Scotland*, p. 154). Humor-
ous in its own way though the story is, the alleged reply of the
infant is a fair summary of the position known as the Establishment
principle (at least in some of its aspects), and it also represents a
fairly crisp summary of the teaching of the Westminster Confession,
as quoted above. But some further observations must be made.
Although the civil and the ecclesiastical spheres are quite distinct
they have, as has been remarked already, mutual relations and
obligations. As Cunningham says, 'though the promotion of religion is not an end of civil government, it is yet an end which civil
governors, in the execution of their official functions, may be called
upon to aim at . . . . though not *finis operis*, it may yet be the *finis
operantis*' (*Discussions on Church Principles*, p. 199). When Cunningham and others speak or write of civil rulers working for the 'promotion of religion' they do not intend to signify by that or similar
phrases that the civil ruler has any right of authoritative interference in the strictly spiritual affairs of the church. They mean,
simply, that it is the responsibility of the civil magistrate, or ruler,
in his administration of civil affairs to have that as his ultimate and
controlling objective. In other words the civil ruler has no power

in sacris. He has, of course, where civil matters impinge upon purely spiritual ones, power *circa sacra*, but we shall come to that in due course. We merely comment, in the meantime, in the words of James Gibson, that, 'if the State does not interfere *circa sacra* there is no possible check to the usurpations of churchmen' (op. cit., p. 73). We may remark, in passing, that this statement is made by Gibson in the course of arguing that the rise of the Popish domination was due to Voluntary principles and not, as has so frequently been alleged, to the supposed Establishment principle, allegedly introduced by the Emperor Constantine. The church has, as has been indicated above, its own responsibilities to the state in terms of prayer for its officers, guidance of them, and admonition where that is called for. In civil matters the church is subordinate to the state, and in spiritual matters the state is subordinate to the church. The authority which constitutes and limits the power in each province, civil and ecclesiastical, is the will of Christ expressed in his own word. The whole matter may be summed up in the time-honoured Latin tags; the state has no power *in sacris* but has power *circa sacra*; the church has no jurisdiction *in civilibus* but only *circa civilia*. As the church has to do with injuries done to persons or property, not as they are civil offences, injurious to civil society, but only as they are ecclesiastical scandals; so the state has to do with distinctly religious offences, not as they are religious, but only as they may be breaches of civil order. If, for example, a church member is guilty of a civil offence, such as the theft of property, he may be proceeded against, not on the basis that he has committed a civil offence, but that he has behaved in a way that is a violation of his profession as a Christian and of the terms of his acceptance as a member in the church. Or, on the other hand, as Bannerman points out: 'In exercising . . . their undoubted powers of jurisdiction, civil courts may be called upon to judge of spiritual acts and sentences insofar as these are conditions on which pecuniary interests depend, and to determine whether, in this light, they do or do not carry with them civil effects. They may be called upon to say whether the proceedings of Church courts are good, not as spiritual sentences, but good as legal conditions of temporal rights.' And again, 'As the courts of the State are the guardian's of a man's character as well as of any other of his civil rights, they must have the power, no less than in the former case (i.e. pecuniary) of granting redress when character is maliciously injured . . . .' (*The Church of Christ*, Vol. II, Appendix D, pp. 395 and 396.)

We must now, however, give some attention to the objections which have been raised, and that with condsiderable indignation and vehement disapprobation, to the way in which the Westminster Confession deals with the question of the Civil Magistrate. Parts of chapters 20 and 23 have already been cited. Along with these may be taken section 2 of chapter 31; 'As magistrates may lawfully call a synod of ministers and other fit persons to consult and advise with about matters of religion, so if magistrates be open enemies to the Church, the ministers of Christ, of themselves, by virtue of their office, or they, with other fit persons upon delegation from their churches, may meet together in such assemblies.' As a matter of interest, before going on to consider the statements of the Westminster Confession of Faith, it may be worth remarking that the first time in the history of the Christian church that any statement was made, in an authoritative church Confession, of 'Church Power,' especially in relation to the civil power, was in the Augsburg Confession of 1530, which was mainly the work of Melancthon. Again, before proceeding to deal with the Westminster Confession specifically, it may be well to remind ourselves of the contendings, the achievements, and the ultimately established position, of the Scottish church long before the Assembly of Divines ever met at Westminster. In writing of the Scottish Act of Parliament of 1567, P. Carnegie Simpson says: 'It is a most remarkable settlement. In the statutes of the Scottish Parliament of that year, the reader suddenly comes upon a section which uses language strangely unfamiliar in legislation, speaking of another King than the Scottish monarch. What this means is that this Settlement besides formally ratifying the abolition of Romish authority, and securing the Protestant succession and other matters of this semi-political kind, embodies *en bloc* the Church's Confession and constitution including the statement of the Church's spiritual freedom and final jurisdiction in all ecclesiastical issues' (op. cit., pp. 145–146).

But now to the Westminster Confession itself and its detractors. Two main charges have been brought against it vis-à-vis the right biblical relationship between the church and the state. These are that the Confessional statement allows for, if it does not encourage, Erastian principles, and that it makes provision for 'persecuting principles.' It is also alleged that it violates the rights of the individual conscience. Before making comment upon these allegations let us assert, with the greatest possible emphasis, that there is not in the Westminster Confession the merest hint of Erastianism, nor of persecuting principles, and so far from stating a position which would do violence to the conscience of any person, it states a case which, we believe, has never been equalled in any document of its kind, to safeguard the due rights of the individual conscience. With regard to the alleged violation of the realm of conscience we may give the words of Hallam in his *Constitutional History* with reference to the Puritans: 'Though no friend,' said James Bannerman, (op. cit., Vol. II, Appendix D. p. 382), 'to the Puritans, and pretending no sympathy with their religious tenets . . . he (i.e. Hallam) has felt constrained to acknowledge that their struggles and sacrifices in behalf of spiritual independence kept alive the flame of political freedom, at a time when the cause was almost lost in England, and that the Puritan controversy has left its permanent mark on our national polity, in the principles of right and liberty which it impressed. And the same may be said,' adds Bannerman, 'with equal if not greater truth of the fierce struggles through which religious freedom was won in Scotland.' As F. F. Bruce says, in his foreword to J. D. Douglas's volume on the Covenanters, *Light in the North*: 'the story of the Scottish Covenanters . . . brings out in sharp outline a crucial issue which the Christian Church has had to face from its earliest days, and which is as acute today as ever it was. This issue is not the question whether episcopacy or presbytery is the more apostolic church order . . . The issue is that of the relation between the church and the State.' (*Light in the North*, by J. D. Douglas, p. 7). Or take the words of Dr. Thomas McCrie, in his book, *Vindication of the Covenanters*: 'what we assert is (and we make the assertion without the slightest fear of refutation) that, in opposing Prelacy, Erastianism, and the Indulgence, the Covenanters were standing up for the civil rights and political liberty of their country. Prelacy in Scotland was always combined and leagued with arbitrary power. The prelates, to use an expression of one of themselves (Archbishop Gladstanes), were *the king's creatures*; they derived their power entirely from him; they were supported by him in opposition to the inclinations of the nation; and they uniformly showed themselves disposed and ready to gratify his will, and to sacrifice to it the liberties and best interests of the people. What is Erastianism? Is it not the principle which ascribes the whole power of modelling and regulating the government of the church to civil rulers? (Thomas McCrie, *Vindication of the Covenanters*, p. 206).

58

The charge of violation of conscience brought against the position, as stated in the Confession, on church–state relations is unwearyingly made by those who are Voluntaries. This alleged violation is a chimera, excogitated by tendentiously diseased minds. We quote from Balfour's treatment of the subject: 'Conscience has always been the citadel in which Voluntaryism has sought to entrench itself. It has been resorted to by all kinds of men, from the days of Adam till now. The prophets of Baal could plead conscience as well as the holy apostles and martyrs of Jesus Christ. It was at the professed dictate of conscience that the High Priest pronounced sentence of death against the Lord of conscience. There have been as many dark deeds of villainy perpetrated under the guise of conscience, as there have been noble sacrifices to the cause of truth laid upon its altar.' (op. cit., Rev. William Balfour, p. 56.) Balfour further remarks, and very much to the point, that the conscience of the civil magistrate 'is no more subject to the commandments of the people in matters of faith and worship than are theirs to his. And it is no more competent to him to lay his conscience aside when he assumes the office of a magistrate, than for any of his subjects when they become parents or ecclesiastical rulers' (op. cit., p. 68). The remark of Dr. Thomas McCrie, in his celebrated *Statement*, expressed the matter with his usual clarity and cogency. 'The magistrates cannot but take to do with matters of conscience . . . if he is to rule over *men*.' 'Men are not to *herd* together like a number of cattle, making provision merely for their external protection, accommodation, and order, forgetting the God that is above.' (Dr. McCrie's *Statement*, p. 114.) What statement could more succinctly and effectively assert and safeguard the rights of conscience than the words of the Confession, quoted above, 'God alone is Lord of the conscience?' And we know that the Lord of the conscience has spoken clearly and authoritatively in his word.

What answer do we give to those who charge the Westminster Confession with asserting Erastian principles? Before giving our answer, we are bound to make two points (and these apply as much to the charge of conscience-violation and persecuting principles as to this): the statements of the Confession, or of any similar document, must be taken in their entire context, and also in terms of the particular signification attaching to them at the time that they were used. Now no honest mind, taking the terms of the Confession as they stand, can allege against it anything in the way of making provision for the violation of the rights of conscience; similarly, no honest mind, taking the terms of the Confession as they stand, and understanding them in the sense they bore when first used, can bring against it any charge of Erastianism. The phrases which have been used to this mistaken, or nefarious, end occur in section 3 of chapter 23, reproduced above. No better answer could be given than that given by Principal Cunningham: 'The introductory words, that "he (i.e. the civil magistrate) hath authority, and it is his duty," do not necessarily or even naturally mean more than that it is competent to, and incumbent upon him, and then the next phrase, "to take order," on which the meaning of the whole statement essentially depends, can easily be proved, according to the *usus loquendi* of that and the preceeding period, to mean,—*to attend to, to aim at, to see about, to provide for, to labour to effect.* It is indeed just a translation of *procurare,* or *providere,* or *dare operam,* the expressions used in the same connection to convey the same idea in the Confessions of the Reformed churches . . . . The words then, do not necessarily or naturally mean more than that the civil magistrate is entitled and bound to aim at, and to seek to effect, the different objects here specified, which are all comprehended under the general heads of the welfare of religion, and the purity and prosperity of the church of Christ. This is just the principle of national establishments, which we believe to be not only true, but important. The Voluntaries, in opposing this principle, used to allege that it necessarily implied the right of the civil magistrate to exercise authority or jurisdiction in religious matters, and over the concerns of the church. This was denied and disproved by the defenders of Establishments, who showed that there was a clear and palpable distinction between the object of the magistrate's *care,* and the sphere or subject of his *jurisdiction*; and that while he was entitled and bound to aim at the promotion of the interests of religion and the welfare of the church, he had no jurisdiction, or right of authoritative interference, in religious or ecclesiastical matters:—that the sphere of his jurisdiction was only the persons and the property of men,—and that his jurisdiction in these civil things he was to exercise for promoting the religious and ecclesiastical objects which it was his duty to aim at and promote' (op. cit., pp. 223–224). This explanatory statement we believe to be adequate for any reasonable mind, and indeed to be unanswerable.

The phrases in the Confession which seem to have provided a handle to those who want to indict it with the grave charge of promulgating persecuting principles occur in the 20th chapter, where those who are found to be guilty of propagating erroneous opinions, or conducting themselves in a way that is destructive to the peace and order which Christ has established in the church should be proceeded against 'by the power of the civil magistrate.' The Free Church of Scotland has taken such accusations seriously and carefully examined those parts of the Confession which have occasioned them, and has consistently, and officially, expressed itself of the mind that, on the basis of fair and contextual interpretation, they are unfounded. The history of the church in Scotland through three centuries and more is sufficient vindication of the integrity and validity of this judgement.

The position of our church is, as the child, supping his porridge, declared, 'co-ordinate jurisdiction and mutual subordination,' but the crucial question for us all is, WHAT SAITH THE SCRIPTURE? To this all-important question we must now address ourselves. Our appeal is to the entire word of God, both Old and New Testaments. There are many who, under the influence of Dispensationalism, or radical, hostile, Modernist criticism, or some other school of thought (or for that matter, of non-thought!) who discount any appeal to the scriptures of the Old Testament for the establishment or confirmation of any truth or doctrine by which our thought or lives in these days are to be determined or regulated. We do not pause to argue the validity of such an appeal, but simply proceed to examine what the word of God, as a whole, has to say. We merely permit ourselves a reminder of the words which we have already cited from James Walker of Carnwath: 'The old writers did not think so much as we are apt to do, of Christianity beginning with the actual historical appearance of our incarnate Lord among men. They much more usually regarded the Christian church as the Old Testament church in a new manifestation.'

When we turn to the Old Testament scriptures in order to discover whether there is anything there to guide us in determining the question whether it is obligatory, or even proper, for the civil ruler to use his position and authority, as a ruler, to advance the general interests of national religion, certain principles of a general nature emerge.

The broad general principle to which we wish, first of all, to refer is this, that it is the duty of any person, in whatever place of authority and influence he may be placed, to use that influence and authority to promote the interests of religion. In Genesis 18.19, Abraham is commended by God, as one who would exert his

HOLD FAST YOUR CONFESSION

influence as the head of a family, to promote the interests of religion, and in Genesis 35.1–3 Jacob is described with approbation as having acted in the same spirit with respect to 'his household, and to all that were with him.' In Exodus 20.10 the whole form of the Sabbath commandment plainly intimates that it is our duty not only to hallow the Sabbath ourselves but also to ensure that it is hallowed by all who are within the circle of our influence, and for whom we are responsible. The phrase, 'and all that are within thy gates,' is specially significant in this regard. It does not mean simply, 'all who are within your towns,' or, 'all who gather in your market-place or at your bazaar,' but, 'all who are under your civil jurisdiction.' The gate, or gates, was the place where the elders and judges, or king, sat officially (Deut. 21.19; 22.15; Ruth. 4.1, 11; 2 Sam. 18.24; Isaiah 29.21). It was thus synonymous with the court or place of judgement (Amos 5.12, 15). It was in fact the civic centre of the community. What is being enjoined is not only that the individual is obliged to keep the Sabbath holy but that the civil magistrate, in his capacity as a magistrate, is to take all proper measures to ensure that the Sabbath is hallowed within the sphere of his jurisdiction. Reference may here be made to the way in which the kings of Judah are admonished with regard to the Sabbath and the general promotion of the interests of righteousness and godliness. (cf., for example, Jeremiah 17.19–27, and 2.1–9). It was not as private individuals that they were so addressed but in their public capacity as kings. A classic example of the way in which the kings of Judah, under divine obligation, made the prosperity of the nation's religion their special care is the reformation carried out by Josiah when the book of the law was discovered in the temple. And although there were instances where kings sacrilegiously intruded upon purely religious functions there was no question, in relation to the kind of care and action we are discussing, of any unwarrantable interference with the work and responsibilities of prophets and priests. The very fact that these kings acted under divine command, and that those who did intrude without warrant upon purely religious affairs met with such stern judgement, should make quite clear to us what the divinely ordained order was, and we believe still is, in respect of the right relationship between the civil and ecclesiastical spheres.

What is of equal, if not greater, significance, for the purpose of our present argument, is what is recorded of non-Jewish monarchs who used their civil power and material resources for the benefit of

Israel's religion. And the relevance of this cannot be challenged because, to say the least, there is not the remotest hint of censure of their actions. There is, for example, the decree issued by Darius, king of Persia, requiring that all possible assistance and provision should be made for 'the elders of the Jews for the building of this house of God,' Ezra 6.8–10. By what conceivable reasoning could it be shown that God is now less concerned that the civil magistrate should make the interests of truth and godliness his concern? And how are we to put sense into the notion that the rulers of nations where the Christian religion exists be expected to do less in this respect than the kings of Persia? In numerous places in the Old Testament there are references to kings, rulers and nations using, with divine approval, and indeed under divine obligation, their power and wealth for the advancement of the cause of God (cf. Isaiah 60.9–12; Zech. 14.17–19). We read of Nehemiah using his magisterial authority to prevent the profanation of the Sabbath day (Nehemiah 13.17–18), and similarly he used it in order to ensure that just and adequate provision was made for the Levites (Nehemiah 13.9–14).

It is a significant fact that there is not one instance in the Bible of rulers who concerned themselves exclusively with the secular interests of the people; and, further, those who attained eminence as the greatest and best of Israel's rulers always took a profound interest, *as rulers*, in the spiritual affairs of the nation. There are Moses, Joshua, David, Solomon, Asa, Hezekiah and Josiah. It is also, surely, of deep significance that, frequently, rulers were raised up specifically to co-operate with the religious leaders. Was it purely fortuitous that there appeared on the scene of Israel's history such combined leading figures, civil and ecclesiastical, as Aaron and Moses, Joshua and Eleazar, David and Abiathar, Solomon and Zadok, Hezekiah and Azariah, Zerubbabel and Joshua? We think not. We believe, rather, that this took place because it is the purpose of God that all the material resources of the universe, all the authority which he has ordained in human society, and 'all the cattle upon a thousand hills,' should be requisitioned to the furtherance of the interests of his spiritual kingdom upon the earth. We may remark, too, that when there were no Jewish rulers to act, the help of Persian rulers was enlisted.

It should go without saying that the case being presented does not purport to establish that all that was done by rulers among the Jews may be done by magistrates in a state where Christianity has, in some measure, been embraced. Careful distinctions have to be made. Jewish rulers performed certain action as rulers, and certain other actions in some other capacity. The functions of Moses as a ruler and as a prophet have to be distinguished, as do those of David as a king and as a prophet. Such distinctions may raise in the minds of some the thought that because of the peculiarities inhering in the Jewish constitution, and because absolute identity of status and function cannot be predicated of rulers among the Jews, on the one hand, and the position of a magistrate in the kind of society we have indicated above, on the other, nothing can be argued from the structures of the Old Testament situation to that of the New. Reasoning of this kind, casts us down into the Stygian darkness of the position that holds that the greater part of the Old Testament has to be set aside, so far as any practical application of the examples it contains are concerned. The same process of reasoning, would bring us to the situation where examples from New Testament times would, because of the very different circumstances in which we live, have to be discarded as anachronistic, irrelevant and misleading.

The case being argued is not that every detail which characterized the Old Testament order of things should, without alteration or modification, be applied in the New Testament era. This would be folly, and would contradict the very things which are taught us in the Old Testament itself, not to mention the New. All that is being contended for is that what we find there may be applied by way of analogy; that is, there is a broad correspondence between the order which existed in Israel and that of a Christian state, or of a state in which Christianity has gained acceptance. If we take the position that nothing at all can be inferred from the functions and activities of Jewish rulers because of the distinctiveness, the peculiarity, of their status, then we must, in consistency, take the view that the functions and activities of priests and prophets in Israel were so absolutely peculiar that nothing can be applied from them to men in comparable offices in New Testament times. But would this way of thinking and reasoning correspond with what we read in the New Testament Scriptures? When the apostle Paul was authoritatively stating the proper arrangement for the support of the Christian ministry he appealed to the practice in Israel with respect to the priests. In 1 Corinthians 9.13-14 he says: 'Do ye not know that they which minister about holy things live of the things of the temple? and they which wait at the altar are partakers with the altar? Even so hath the Lord ordained that they which preach the gospel should live of the Gospel.' Similarly, the judgements which were inflicted upon Israel were of a distinctive kind, and were visited upon them for distinctive reasons, yet Paul is able, without embarrassment, to appeal to these judgements by way of administering warning to the Corinthians. 'Moreover, brethren, I would not that ye should be ignorant, how that all our fathers were under the cloud, and all passed through the sea; And were all baptized unto Moses in the cloud and in the sea; And did all eat the same spiritual meat; And did all drink the same spiritual drink: for they drank of that spiritual Rock that followed them: and that Rock was Christ. But with many of them God was not well pleased: for they were overthrown in the wilderness. Now these things were our examples, to the intent we should not lust after evil things, as they also lusted. Neither be ye idolators, as were some of them; as it is written, The people sat down to eat and drink, and rose up to play. Neither let us commit fornication, as some of them committed, and fell in one day three and twenty thousand. Neither let us tempt Christ, as some of them also tempted, and were destroyed of serpents. Neither murmur ye, as some of them also murmured, and were destroyed of the destroyer. Now all these things happened unto them for ensamples: and they are written for our admonition, upon whom the ends of the world are come' (1 Cor. 10.1–11). And to take another instance of a similar kind, was there not something quite distinctive about the prayer of Elijah on Mount Carmel, and yet James had no difficulty about applying it to the duties and experience of believers in New Testament times? In the light of all this the question we have to ask is: If the writers of holy scripture found no problem and felt no embarrassment, so far as these matters were concerned, on what basis is the position and function of the civil ruler made an absolute exception? Several wretched expedients have been resorted to in order to evade the force of this argument, such as that the kings of Old Testament times were types only in a spiritual sense, but if this be so then by pure logic (a department in which Voluntaries and neo-Voluntaries do not ordinarily excel) nothing at all may be applied to the New Testament times. The absurdity of this is surely apparent.

It is further confirmation of the view that the work of Jewish rulers, in furthering the cause of religion, expressed a principle that was to be universally applied, that Scripture approves the action of non-Jewish rulers when they acted in the same way towards Israel (cf. Dan. 3.29; 4.6–26). And in Ezra and Nehemiah there are edicts of several Persian monarchs not only permitting but positively favouring and publicly recognising the rebuilding of the temple. It certainly cannot be made out that they were 'types' or that they acted in virtue of the peculiarity of the Jewish constitution.

Equally significant with the principles and pattern which obtained in the church of Old Testament times are the promises given with respect to what should be its experience in New Testament times. It has already been remarked that the church is one in all ages. There is a direct line of continuity from its first form as domestic and patriarchal through until New Testament times when it embraces all nations. The church in its essence is spiritual but it has an external form, and thus may be injured and persecuted, or, alternatively, protected and supported. God gave promises to the church in Old Testament times that it would enjoy the recognition, support, and protection of kings and nations. Although the authority of the civil magistrate is ultimately from God as God, it has been given to Christ, as Mediator, to hold and exercise the authority by which 'kings reign and princes decree justice,' and this has been given to him in order that the power and resources of the nations may be applied to the advancement of his redemptive kingdom. It is the duty, therefore, of these kingdoms and their rulers to make the furtherance of Christ's church an important, if not the primary, end of their existence. 'The shields of the earth belong unto God' who 'is gone up with a shout,' and who 'reigneth over the heathen,' and He, therefore, has right to their service, Psalm 49.9. In Psalm 2 we have the record of God's proclamation of Christ as the king whom He has 'set upon his holy hill of Zion.' The kings and rulers of the earth are solemnly admonished to serve Him in the character in which he is presented to them. 'Be wise now, therefore O ye kings; be instructed, ye judges of the earth. Serve the Lord with fear, and rejoice with trembling. Kiss the Son lest he be angry, and ye perish from the way' (vv. 10–12). It was in their public capacity as rulers that they had opposed Christ, (vv. 2–3) and it is, therefore, in their public character as rulers that they are now to serve him. Dr. McCrie, in his *Statement*, quotes the following words from a sermon preached by John Owen before Parliament; 'Judges and rulers, as such, must "kiss the Son" .... Some think, if you were well settled, you ought not, *as rulers of the nation*, to put forth your *power* for the interest of Christ. The good Lord keep your hearts from that apprehension!' (p. 135).

In Psalm 72 there is another striking prophecy relating to the glory and extent of Christ's kingdom and, among other things, the subjection and service of the nations and their rulers are particularly mentioned: 'The kings of Tarshish and the isles shall bring presents; the kings of Sheba and Seba shall offer gifts. Yea, all kings shall fall down before him; all nations shall serve him,' vv. 10–11. A further promise to the same effect occurs in Isaiah 49.23: 'And kings shall be thy nursing-fathers, and their queens thy nursing-mothers; they shall bow down to thee with their faces toward the earth, and lick up the dust of thy feet, and thou shalt know that I am the Lord; for they shall not be ashamed that wait for me.' Along with this may be taken the words of Isaiah, 60.10, 12, 16: 'And the sons of strangers shall build up thy walls, and their kings shall minister unto thee, for in my wrath I smote thee, but in my favour have I had mercy on thee . . . . For the nation and kingdom that will not serve thee, shall perish; yea, those nations shall be utterly wasted . . . . Thou shalt also suck the milk of the Gentiles . . . .' Numerous such promises could be mentioned but sufficient have been cited to show that it was the purpose of God that the church in New Testament times should enjoy the protection and support of the nations of the world.

It has often been alleged that there is nothing in the New Testament to support the position which has just been argued on the basis of evidence drawn from the Old Testament scriptures. Even if this were so, it would be quite irrelevant as an objection, because we take the Old Testament, equally with the New, as our rule of faith; and if a case can be made out from the Old Testament for a position which is not specifically abrogated in the New then it is perfectly valid, and we are under inescapable obligation to receive it. And so far from any abrogation, in the New Testament, of the order which obtained under the Old, in this respect, there is added emphasis and confirmation. We refer to one or two passages, by way of example. In 1 Timothy 2.1 Paul says, 'I exhort therefore, that, first of all, supplications, prayers, intercessions, and giving of thanks, be made for all men; for kings, and for all that are in authority; that we may lead a quiet and peaceable life in all godliness and honesty.' Now what Christians are required to pray for, on behalf of rulers, it is the duty of the latter to promote. That is to say, it is the duty of rulers to advance the interests not only of honesty but also of godliness. What else is this but a clear intimation that it is the duty of kings and magistrates in their public capacity to countenance, to support and protect the true religion? With regard to the words of our Lord, enjoined upon his followers, to 'render unto Caesar the things that are Caesar's, and unto God the things that are God's,' we quote the words of Principal Cunningham: 'This implies that there are some things which belong to the province of Caesar, or the civil magistrate, which are subject to his jurisdiction . . . . and (he) is ordinarily to be obeyed; reserving, of course, the great principle which is of universal application, namely, that 'we must obey God rather than man.' It implies also that there are some things which are God's, in such a sense as not to belong to Caesar at all—not to belong to the province, or be subject to the authority, of the civil magistrate' (op. cit., p. 208).

Various objections have, from time to time, been made against the position of church–state relations as it has been here expounded. It has been said, for example, that to give the civil ruler this power can result, and has resulted, in a tyrannical abuse of the power. Of course there have been abuses both on the part of the church and of the state. There were the attempted abuses on the part of the state which led to the Disruption of the Church of Scotland when it sought to invade the proper province of the church. There have also been periods when the church, in some of its branches, has exercised tyranny over the state. This kind of situation obtained through the Middle Ages when, in the words of Dante, 'the sword is joined with the crook.' In the year 1300 Boniface VIII appeared at a great papal function not only wearing the tiara, but also girded with a sword and proclaimed before the multitudes, 'I am Caesar, I am Emperor.' He declared, too, in his famous Bull, 'Unam Sanctum,' that both the spiritual and the temporal swords are in the hands of the church. Things had come to such a pitch, indeed, that Wordsworth could write of them without exaggeration:

> 'Unless to Peter's chair the viewless wind
> Must come and ask permission when to blow,
> What further empire would it have?'

But are we to argue that because powers and privileges may be abused and violated there is no place for their proper use?

It has also been objected that to accord to the civil authority the power above defined involves an encroachment upon the prerogative of Christ. This has indeed been attempted in history, but it is not a necessary consequence of the principle. When parliament enacts laws for the preservation of the sanctity of the Sabbath day it does not pretend to add, and it cannot be regarded as giving added, authority to the divine command. By way of analogy, we read in Isaiah 44.26 that God claimed it as his prerogative that he would build the temple. It was not inconsistent with this that the royal mandate which was issued by Cyrus was used as a means for the accomplishment of this purpose (cf. Ezra 4.3 and 6.14). In the same connection it is objected that a spiritual kingdom cannot be promoted by a secular power. But we must not confuse what is merely secular with what is properly civil. The civil power is a divine ordinance and He requires that all that He has created and ordained should be consecrated to His worship and to the advancement of his kingdom. It is a pseudo-spirituality that regards the church as liable to be corrupted by the material wealth of nations. The church can of course be corrupted by anything; it can be, and has been, corrupted by learning, for example. But is everything which, because of the corrupt nature of man (including Christian men), may be misused, to be rejected? If God requires a thing of a man or of a nation then it becomes a duty, and we may not reject it because we fear it may corrupt.

Certain passages of Scripture are urged against the argument for the national recognition and support of religion. For example, Zechariah 4.6, 'Not by might, nor by power, but by my Spirit saith the Lord of Hosts.' But what was God, in fact, saying to his people through these words? He was intimating to a depressed and dispirited people that the work would be effected by the power of his Spirit, and that they need not, therefore, be dismayed. But was Zerubbabel, the civil governor, instructed, on this account to take no part? Or was it a contradiction when God turned the heart of the king of Assyria to strengthen their hands? (Ezra 6.22). These passages are from the Old Testament, and as Balfour says, 'The Old Testament is a portion of the Word of God in which Voluntaryism has always found difficulty in breathing' (op. cit., p. 91). So let us take up one passage from the New Testament which is seldom off the lips of those who oppose the national recognition of religion. The passage is the statement of our Lord addressed to Pontius Pilate, 'My kingdom is not of this world.' Let us hear Balfour's comment: 'The saying of Christ affords not the slightest conceivable countenance to Voluntaryism; but, on the contrary, in so far as it can be referred to, in connection with the controversy, it may be shown to favour the Establishment principle. When he uttered these memorable words, the Great Head of the Church stood before Pontius Pilate, who was about to countenance the withdrawal of the support and protection of the law from him and his cause; but before doing this he addresses himself to Jesus, saying, 'Thine own nation, and the chief priests have delivered thee unto me; what hast thou done?' It was in answer to this that Jesus said, 'My kingdom is not of this world.' And that man must be a rare expositor of Scripture, or he must have a curious power, if we may so say, of voluntaryising all he looks at, who can discover the Voluntary principle in this memorable saying. As if Christ had not specially before him, when uttering these words, the dream of the Jews regarding the kingdom of Messiah as a wordlly kingdom which was to subject to its power the nations of the earth! As if it were not his special design to allay the fear which had been awakened in the mind of Pilate concerning his being the king of the Jews, by declaring that his kingdom is a spiritual kingdom, diverse from all secular kingdoms, so that these kingdoms had nothing to fear, but everything that was good to expect from it! As if he had not present to his view, when uttering these words, the friendly relation which so long subsisted between His Church and the Jewish nation, as that which will and ought to exist between His Church and every nation to which the Gospel comes that *does not sinfully reject him*, as the Jews were then doing! As if the fact of its being a spiritual kingdom, and not of this world, were not the very thing that rendered it capable of entering into an alliance with the State!' (op. cit., pp. 157–158).

It is often said by Evangelicals that this whole question of seeking the national recognition and support of the Christian faith is pointless and irrelevant because we live in what is called a pluralistic society. Those who speak in this way do not seem to realise the implications of their view. It represents in fact a concession to the religious relativism which lies at the basis of the whole concept of comparative religion, which is both the father and mother of doctrinal and theological nihilism. Whatever the 'pluralism' of the religious scene in our own land or of any other, and however complex the problem may be of securing the practical implementation of its principles, the Christian church may not bate one jot or tittle of the absolutism of its claims to exclusive national recognition and support. The Free Church of Scotland took its beginnings, as such, over the church–state issue—the spiritual independence of the church and its claim to recognition and support by the state—

and it regards that issue as being just as relevant and crucial now as it was then.

Bibliography

William Balfour, *The Establishment Principle Defended*, Johnstone, Hunter & Co., Edinburgh 1873.

James Bannerman, *The Church of Christ*, Vols. I and II, T. & T. Clark, Edinburgh 1868.

James Begg, *Free Church Principles*, Johnstone, Hunter & Co., Edinburgh 1874.

John Brown (of Wamphray), *An Apologetical Relation, etc.*, Robert Ogle and Oliver & Boyd, Edinburgh 1845. Reprinted from the original edition of 1660 in *The Presbyterian's Armoury*, Vol. III.

G. N. M. Collins, *The Heritage of our Fathers*, The Knox Press, Edinburgh 1974.

William Cunningham, *Discussions on Church Principles*, T. & T. Clark, Edinburgh 1863.

William Cunningham, *Sermons from 1828 to 1860*, T. & T. Clark, Edinburgh 1872.

J. D. Douglas, *Light in the North*, The Paternoster Press, Exeter 1964.

James Gibson, *The Church in Relation to the State*, Johnstone, Hunter & Co., Edinburgh 1872.

George Gillespie, *Aaron's Rod Blossoming*, Robert Ogle and Oliver & Boyd, Edinburgh 1846. Reprinted in *The Presbyterian's Armoury*, Vol. II.

G. D. Henderson, *The Claims of the Church of Scotland*, Hodder & Stoughton, London 1951.

Charles Hodge, *The Church and its Polity*, Thomas Nelson & Sons, London 1879.

J. Marcellus Kik, *Church and State*, Thomas Nelson & Sons, New York 1963.

Lectures on Church Establishments (Various contributors), Fraser & Co., Edinburgh 1835.

John MacLeod, *Scottish Theology*, The Knox Press, Edinburgh, Second Edition 1946.

John MacPherson, *The Doctrine of the Church in Scottish Theology*, MacNiven & Wallace, Edinburgh 1903.

Sir Henry Wellwood Moncrieff, *The Free Church Principle*, Mac-Niven & Wallace, Edinburgh 1883.

Thomas McCrie, *Statement*, C. F. Lyon, Edinburgh 1871.

Thomas McCrie, *Vindication of the Covenanters*, Fourth Edition, William Whyte & Co., Edinburgh 1845.

C. G. McCrie, *The Confessions of the Church of Scotland*, MacNiven & Wallace, Edinburgh 1907.

Samuel Rutherford, *Lex Rex*, Reprinted by Robert Ogle and Oliver & Boyd, Edinburgh 1846, in *The Presbyterian's Armoury*.

Alexander Shields, *A Hind Let Loose*, 2 vols., Reprinted by R. Drummond & Co., Edinburgh 1744.

P. Carnegie Simpson, *The Church and the State*, James Clarke & Co., London 1929.

Stewart and Cameron, *The Free Church of Scotland, 1843–1910*, William Hodge & Co., Edinburgh and Glasgow 1910.

J. Walker, *Scottish Theology and Theologians*, T. & T. Clark, Edinburgh 1888.

Presbyterianism

Murdo A. Macleod, m.a.
Director, Christian Witness to Israel.

The doctrine of the church and particularly that aspect of it which deals with its government has in recent decades been relegated to the place of non-essentials. In ecumenical circles an attempt has been made to fuse the distinctives of each denomination, whether congregational, episcopal or presbyterian, resulting in a modified episcopacy as in the Church of North India. In evangelical circles the question has been almost totally ignored, resulting in the growth of independency as a counsel of despair. This is true even within the organized denominations whether episcopal or presbyterian, where congregations remain while operating almost totally independent of the denomination. In neither fold has there been a serious attempt to grapple with the scriptures and determine the order that Christ instituted for his church. Within the short compass of one chapter it is not possible to do this and no pretence is being so made. What is intended is merely to show that the outline of presbyterianism conforms to the scriptural data.

There are essentially three forms of church government. The independents, congregationalists and separatists (such as the Plymouth brethren), maintain that each congregation is self-contained and self-governing and cannot accept any decision outside of its own narrow limits as binding upon it. Episcopalians on the other hand, and also the church of Rome, hold a connectional view of the church, maintaining that there is a unity in the body of Christ and seek to express this in a monarchical bishopric structure. They fail, however, in that each bishopric is a self-contained monarchy and the unity is sought by the creation of a visible human head, whether it be pope or queen.

Presbyterianism, however, seeks to express the fundamental unity of the people of God in a harmonious interdependence of the smallest unit with the largest in a progressive series of courts.

In 1643 one of the Scottish commissioners to the Westminster Assembly in London wrote home, 'as yet a Presbyterie to this people is conceived to be a strange monster, the passing of the years does not seem to have brought great enlightenment.' George Eliot amusingly portrays this, 'In point of fact,' says one of her characters, 'these Evangelicals are not Churchmen at all: they're no better than Presbyterians . . . . a sect founded in the reign of Charles I, by a man called John Presbyter who hatched all the brood of Dissenting vermin!' A great number of misconceptions regarding the question still remain. Unfortunately these are as prevalent even amongst presbyterians themselves.

It is necessary that each generation applies itself to this question. Robert L. Dabney wrote during the controversy in the Presbyterian Church of America concerning the function of the eldership: 'It strikes many Presbyterians with surprise, that the General Assembly and our leading periodicals in this year 1860, one hundred and fifty years after the beginning of our church in America, should be largely occupied in discussing the question, 'What is Presbyterianism?' The good brethren who thus deplore these renewed discussions of the first principles misconceived the nature of the human mind and of free institutions. While man remains the creature he is, such discussions are to be expected and desired. Each generation must do its own thinking, and learn for itself its own lessons in first truths and general principles. If we insist that this generation of Presbyterians shall hold our fathers' principles on trust, and by mere prescription, the result will be that they will not hold them sincerely at all.' (*Discussions Evangelical and Theological*, Vol. II, p. 119).

Too often what belongs to the *bene esse* of the system has been regarded and defended as belonging to the *esse*, and often other factors which have historically accompanied the practice of presbyterianism have been confused with the system itself.

J. N. O. Ogilvie wrote: 'Presbyterianism as an ecclesiastical distinction has to do solely with questions of church polity and although the Presbyterian churches of modern times vary considerably in the details of their organisation and in the power assigned to various office-bearers there are three marks common to all which they cannot forfeit without at the same time forfeiting their Presbyterianism.' He enumerates these as:

(a) The Recognition of the Priesthood of the Christian People, by the Institution of the Eldership.
(b) The parity of the Presbyters.
(c) The Unity of the Church, represented by a Conciliar System of Government.

(The Presbyterian Churches of Christendom, pp. 1, 2).

This is a brief but comprehensive statement of the essence of presbyterianism.

While calvinistic doctrine and puritan simplicity of worship have largely accompanied the practice of presbyterianism, neither is essential to it. Liturgical worship for example existed in the churches of Switzerland and Scotland in the formative period of pesbyterianism in both countries. In Scotland during the period after the Reformation the presbytery as a court did not appear for nearly a quarter of a century; at first there was nothing between the weekly meeting of the kirk-session and the half-yearly meetings of synod, and the original bodies to send commissioners to the General Assembly were the weekly 'exercises.' (Details of this may be found in the writings of Erskine of Dun's description of the church in the *Spalding Club Miscellany*, Vol. IV.)

It is important, therefore, to distinguish between the essential and the incidental factors in the polity. There are two methods by which we can approach this question. We can either adopt the inductive method, by which we consider all the relevant texts relating to the government of the church and show from our studies that the general principles of government which are arrived at are those of the presbyterian polity; or on the other hand we may first of all state these principles and go on to show how the scriptures support them. I intend to follow the latter, in order to high-light what these distinctive principles are, and also because it is fundamental to our understanding of the distinctive nature of presbyterian polity that we consider the doctrine of the unity of the visible church. To approach this inductively would involve us in a much longer study than is now possible.

It may also be well to remind ourselves that in our interpretation of the scriptures the hermeneutical principles of *analogia scripturae* and *analogia fidei* (the analogy of scripture and the analogy of the faith) apply here as they do in the interpretation of any passage which is used to establish any other doctrine.

We will endeavour to deal with the question in the following way:
I   The organization of the local congregation.
II   The unity of the visible church.
III   The expression of this unity.

I   The Organization of the Local Congregation

What are the offices that God intended for his church? In the lists recorded in Eph. 4, 1 Cor. 12, and Rom. 12, we do not have lists of offices but of gifts that God has given to his church. Even if it is allowed that there is an element of office implied in the use of the words in one or other of these lists, the fact that the office is immediately given or appointed by God (and not an appointment by or through the church) would seem to limit these terms in their context to the establishment of the church. It is of considerable importance that the only offices to which appointments are made by the church are those of 'deacon' and 'presbyter' or 'bishop' (concerning the identity of the last two, see below).

In historical order, the office of deacon was the first to be established. This is understandable. The primary function of the apostles was to teach; but doctrine must result in works, so in order that the function of the apostles might not suffer, and yet the practical fruit of the gospel might be gathered, the founding of the order of deacons was a logical necessity. It is argued by some that the appointment of the Seven (Acts 6) was not the founding of such an order, but simply the setting aside of these men for a specific task. This indeed may be so, but even allowing for this the division of function as being necessary or desirable for the good of the church is clearly taught. Whatever may be the relationship of the Seven to the diaconate it is undoubted that such an order existed in the church by the time of the letter to the Philippians and certainly by the time of the pastoral epistles where we have listed the qualifications sought in those who would hold the office of deacon (1 Tim. 3.8–13). There is little evidence for the existence of women deacons, apart from the controversial verses in 1 Tim. 3.11 and Rom. 16.1. Very little is told us concerning the function of the diaconate but from the qualifications required the handling of monetary matters appears to have been their province. They were to be serious and discreet and their being free of greed and addiction to wine is stressed more than in the case of bishops. If the appointment of the Seven is taken in conjunction with this passage a fuller picture of the deacons' duties emerges.

The second ecclesiastical appointment is that of the presbyter or bishop and here the distinctives of presbyterianism begin to emerge in the plurality, parity and governmental authority of these officers. It is almost unanimously agreed by scholars of all persuasions that these two terms are interchangeable for the one office. Sometimes in the New Testament there are references to *presbuteroi*, 'elders' or 'presbyters' and sometimes to *episkopoi*, 'bishops'. The evidence for their identity appears conclusive (cf. Leon Morris, *Ministers of*

God, pp. 72–76). The classical argument for their identity is given by Bishop J. B. Lightfoot. It is worth quoting this more extensively: 'Of the identity of the "bishop" and the "presbyter" in the language of the apostolic age, the following evidence seems conclusive. (1) In the opening of this epistle St. Paul salutes the "bishops" and "deacons." Now it is incredible that he should recognize only the first and third order and pass over the second, though the second was absolutely essential to the existence of a church and formed the staple of its ministry. It seems therefore to follow of necessity that the "bishops" are identical with the "presbyters".... (2) In the Acts (20.17) St. Paul is represented as summoning to Miletus the "elders" or "presbyters" of the church of Ephesus yet in addressing them immediately after he appeals to them as "bishops" or "overseers" of the church (Acts 20.28) (3) Similarly St. Peter appealing to the "presbyters" of the churches addressed by him, in the same breath urges them to "fulfil the office of bishops with disinterested zeal"' (1 Peter 5.1–2). Bishop Lightfoot gives two further arguments and then (5) the same identification appears still more plainly from the apostle's direction to Titus (1.5–7), 'that thou shouldest set in order the things that are wanting and ordain *elders* in every city, as I appointed thee; if anyone be *blameless*, the husband of one wife having believing children who are not charged with riotousness or unruly; for a *bishop* must be *blameless*, etc.' (Epistle to the Philippians, pp. 93–97).

It is also interesting to note that the identity of the two titles in the New Testament i.e. presbyter and bishop, is recognized by the Peshito Syriac Version which commonly translates *episcopos* by *kashisho* i.e. presbyter or elder. Ogilvie says: 'It would seem as if the writers were partly guided in choosing a title by the character of the community to which they were writing. To a Jewish Christian congregation the word 'presbyter,' denoting as it did an old office in the Jewish synagogue, was the more familiar and therefore in letters to such was more frequently employed; while, in correspondence with a Gentile congregation, the Greek word 'bishop' or 'overseer' drawn from Greek civic life, was usually adopted. But whether 'bishop' or 'presbyter,' the office in the earliest days was practically identical' (op. cit., p. 5).

In the foregoing we have not dealt with the founding of the order of presbyters or elders. It must be admitted that we do not have this indicated in the New Testament as we do for the order of deacons. The question must be asked, Why? The answer is to be

79

found in the unity of the Old and New Testaments and in the continuity of the people of God. It is often forgotten that in the apostolic times the majority of Christians were Jews (cf. *The Herald,* periodical of the The International Society for the Evangelization of the Jews, Vol. 130, No. 6. pp. 7–8, Rev. Baruch Maoz). Consequently it is reasonable to assume that as there was no command given to the contrary the order of administration in the Christian church would continue as in the Jewish synagogue. Lightfoot says, 'When he first, i.e. Luke, mentions the presbyters, he introduces them without premise as though the institution were a matter of course.' The office of presbyter was not a new office, for in the Jewish synagogues a body of presbyters directed the religious worship of the community. The first Christian congregations in Palestine were designated by the name of synagogues for some considerable time. They were in effect Christian synagogues and they were accordingly governed as the synagogue was governed. It was in countries outside Palestine that the term *ecclesia* or church was mainly used (cf. Leon Morris, *Ministers of God,* pp. 70 ff.).

What were the functions of the office of the presbyter? Did all exercise the same functions or were some peculiar to certain ones and not to others? From 1 Tim. 5.17 it would appear that all ruled, and from 3.5 they took 'care of the church of God,' which it is reasonable to assume means the same thing. When Peter commands the elders not to lord it over God's heritage it would appear that they were in a position to do so (1 Peter 5.3). *All the elders, therefore, it appears, had the power to rule.* (Some other passages do not mention the elders by name but most certainly refer to them, e.g., Heb. 13.17, 1 Thess. 5.12).

Another function which was common to all the elders, as no distinction was made, was *the pastoral duty of attending to the sick* (Jas. 5.14). It is not necessary to enlarge upon this.

The third function was common to all but was exercised mainly by some, that of preaching the word. That all could and should teach is seen from the desiderata required of all elders, namely, that they be apt to teach (1 Tim. 3.2). However, that it was the particular function of certain elders is also evident from 1 Tim. 5.17, 'Let the elders that rule well be counted worthy of double honour, especially they who labour in the word and doctrine.' The usage of the word 'labour' here implies the full-time engagement of the person in the task. This distinction is easily understood. There is a distinction between office and gift as we have already seen, but while they are distinct from one another they are not necessarily independent of one another. From the qualifications stated as necessary for the offices of deacon and presbyter it is apparent that gifts precede office, though it does not necessarily imply holding office. To occupy an office requires gifts but the possession of gifts does not necessarily imply holding office. All did not have the same gifts and some might have one gift more than another. In making this distinction between the ruling and teaching elder, John Owen says: 'Differing gifts are required unto the differing works of pastoral teaching on the one hand, and practical rule on the other, is evident—(1) From the light of reason, the nature of the works themselves being so different and (2) From experience. Some men are fitted for the dispensation of the Word and doctrine who have no ability for the work of rule, and some are fitted for rule who have no gifts for the discharge of the pastoral work in preaching. Yea, it is very seldom that both these sorts of gifts do concur in any eminency in the same person, or without some notable defect. Those who are ready to assume all things unto themselves are, for the most part, fit for nothing at all,' (Quoted in J. Moir Porteous, *The Government of the Kingdom of Christ*, pp. 218–219). Thomas Goodwin is of the same mind: 'Though to rule is the pastor's office as well as the elders', yet the elder is more especially said to rule because he is wholly set apart to it. It is his proper calling, which he is wholly appointed to mind' (Porteous, ibid., p. 218). The point is well made although both writers distinguish too sharply between the two functions. We must safeguard against the extreme of totally separating the two functions so as to exclude the function of one from that of the other.

The duties of the Presbyters were two-fold. It was required that they should both rule over and instruct the congregation. This appears from the usage in Eph. 4.11 of 'pastors and teachers,' where the form of the original indicates that the two words describe the same office under different aspects. It would appear that government was the first duty of the office and that teaching became their duty more and more as time went on. With the growth of the church the visits of the apostles and evangelists to any individual community must have become less frequent so that the burden of instruction would gradually be transferred to the officers of the local churches. Paul requires in two places (1 Tim. 3.2, Tit. 1.9) that the presbyter be able to teach; yet the distinction he makes in 1 Tim. 5.17 ('especially they who labour in the word and doctrine') would seem to indicate that the presbyter might decline the task of full-time instruction. Nevertheless there is no ground for supposing that the word of teaching and the work of governing belonged to separate members of the 'presbytery.' As each had his own particular gift, so he would devote himself more and more to one or other of these functions.

The two offices we have looked at, namely, that of elder and deacon, are the only ones recognized by the New Testament in the organization of the local church. However, in the presbyterian system there is a plurality of elders. This is a logical necessity arising from the last point, if there is a division of function amongst the elders (although that division is not absolute) there must be in all churches those who can attend to each part of the work. The scriptural evidence is substantial to support this. When Paul and Barnabas revisited the churches they had established 'they . . . . ordained them elders in every church and . . . . prayed with fasting, they commended them to the Lord in whom they believed,' (Acts 14.23). Titus ordained elders in every city, and in Philippi a few years after the founding of the church there, Paul writes to the 'bishops' in the plural. The writer to the Hebrews enjoins them to 'remember *them* that have the rule over you' (Heb. 13.7). 'Plurality is written in the boldest letters in the pages of the New Testament and singularity bears the hallmark of despite to Christ's institution' (J. Murray, *Collected Writings*, Vol. 2, p. 346). This plurality is the first essential element of the presbyterian system. Some seek to find traces of the later usage of 'bishop' in the New Testament. For example, Lightfoot quotes the example of James, our Lord's brother, as 'being regarded as a bishop in that more and special sense of the term.' However, it must be said that all James did as the spokesman and local representative of the church in Jerusalem could have been done just as easily by a moderator of a presbytery without the prerogatives of any episcopal authority.

The identity of bishop and presbyter emphasizes the second fundamental principle of presbyterianism i.e. the parity of presbyters. If there is not parity there can be no plurality. There is no superiority of one elder over another and there is no ground for believing that teaching elder ranks any higher than the ruling elder. This is a fact that has been jealously safeguarded in Presbyterian churches, at least in theory, if not always in practice. It is true that at certain times in the history of the church the exigencies of the day have required particular duties to be committed to certain

presbyters. For example, in Scotland, as is well-known, superintendents were appointed who fulfilled a semi-episcopal function
because of the scarcity of ministers. These duties particularly concerned the development of the church in areas where there was no
settled ministry. However, the principle of presbyterian parity was
never transgressed. They always remained answerable to the General Assembly. Modern pro-episcopal writers such as Gordon
Donaldson (*The Scottish Reformation*, p. 125) have sought in vain
to equate these superintendents with monarchical bishops. It is perhaps not so well-known that a similar situation existed in the presbyterian church in Canada when the popualtion was moving out to
the prairies in the late 19th century. Dr. James Robertson, whose
work has been portrayed in Ralph Connor's *Sky Pilot*, was typical.
Prof. W. Stanford Reid, Professor of History at Guelph University,
has stated in private correspondence that; 'My own father was
superintendent of missions for Alberta in 1910–1912 and my uncle,
A. S. Reid, was superintendent of missions for the synod of Mon-
treal and Ottawa and for the maritime synod after the union debacle
in 1925. His job was to found churches, help small congregations,
etc. He was answerable to the synods and to the General Assembly
for his work and was appointed by the General Assembly in consultation with the synods.'

Contrary to the popular conception of presbyterianism the system has always had an elasticity to meet peculiar circumstances and
particular problems while maintaining its essential principles.
There is a realm for the exercise of common prudence always acting,
of course, in accordance with the general principles of the word of
God. Historically there has always been a certain variety in the way
presbyterianism has been applied in different countries under
different circumstances. There is no obstacle in the way of the
church altering the details if it will be conducive to the good of the
church. In puritan New England under the Mathers and in Hun-
gary because of the peculiar problems confronting the church there,
developments similar to the superintendent system emerged.

It is a legitimate point of dispute whether the 'elders' in many of
the presbyterian churches today actually have the gifts and fulfil
the functions of the New Testament presbyter or whether they are
not deacons by another name. It may be argued with some cogency
that the plurality of elders in the New Testament was a plurality of
men who approximated more to 'ministers' in the modern usage of
that word and that the church in Corinth, for example, was several

'congregations' with a presbytery of elders presiding unitedly over them all. This is a viewpoint that has not been given sufficient consideration and a closer study of it may result for us discovering, in John Robinson's phrase, 'that God had yet more light to break forth from his word' on this question of the government of the church. We should be prepared to lay aside the spectacles tinted by several centuries of familiar practice and try and see what the scriptures actually teach. It may be that the older presbyterians from Calvin to Hodge on the one hand and Thornwell and the majority of presbyterians since, have divided the truth between them. The older presbyterians maintained that the ministers of the word alone were presbyters and that the so-called elders of their day were only 'governments' or representatives of the people. Thornwell and most presbyterians since then have maintained that our modern elders are presbyters. The viewpoint only touched on here may be the way to reconcile both these views equally strongly defended from the scriptures.

We have seen that the plurality of elders is 'written in the boldest letters in the pages of the New Testament.' Every church in New Testament times had over it several presbyters. Modern presbyterianism has sought to emulate the apostolic example by having with the teaching elder several ruling elders in each congregation. However, may it not be that we have wrongly identfied the 'congregation' with 'church?' A close study of the New Testament would seem to indicate that there was one church in each locality and that the elders i.e. presbyters, ministered to and ruled over the whole church whether it be the church in Jerusalem or Philippi or elsewhere. The identification of a 'church' with a 'congregation' i.e. a greater or lesser number of people meeting under one roof in a 'church building' may be the point of departure from apostolic example. An emotional response to what in modern terms may be called a 'team ministry' must not prevent us from making a serious study of the New Testament pattern. If so be that that was the pattern, namely, a number of teaching and ruling elders all of them presbyters in an equal sense, fully committed and devoted to the oversight of the flock of God in one city or locality, then we must be prepared to follow where the scriptures lead.

II The Unity of the Visible Church

The unity of the church of Christ is probably the most fundamental principle of presbyterianism. There is a necessary relationship between individual Christians. No believer stands alone. In the natural sphere no man is an island standing apart from the rest of humanity. He is born by the action of his parents and by his birth he becomes part of mankind. So in the spiritual sphere each Christian is born again from above, God is his Father. He is born 'not of blood nor of the will of the flesh nor of the will of man but of God,' (John 1.13). In this he is akin to all other believers; but there is a further kinship. As God is his Father so in a very real sense the church is his mother. No man converted by the grace of God is a partaker of the blessings of God's grace but through the instrumentality of the church of Christ. This is equally true of the heathen converted through the written word of God although he has never seen another Christian, for it is the church that has preserved, translated and distributed the scriptures. So from the very commencement of his Christian life the believer is caught up into the whole rich inheritance of the church of God. He is related to every other Christian in his participation in the sovereign grace of God and in the fellowship of the church of Christ.

This unity is invisible and already existing: it does not have to be brought into being. It must not, however, remain invisible and it is our duty to strive to make it apparent to men, 'that the world may believe' (John 17.21). Cf. J. Murray, op. cit., Vol. 2, pp. 321 ff.

The church of Christ is variously described in scripture. It is the body of Christ; it is a city, a household, a building, a temple. What is of significance in all these designations is that they imply a unity of complementation. Each part of the body has its own function and individuality but it is complementary to the functioning of the whole; so with the citizens of the city, the members of the household, and the parts of the building. Whatever gifts have been bestowed on individual members of the church have not been given for their own advantage only but for the good of the whole. How does this element of complementation become visible to the world, that each believer is pursuing the same end, has in view the same goal, is part of the same agency, is fulfilling his own part despite differences and functions, in the one great plan? How does this complementary unity, if we may so speak, that is between the Father and the Son find expression? Is it not in their unity in the work of salvation? (John 10.27–30). 'As thou hast sent me into the world even so have I sent them into the world' (John 17.18). So the unity which exists between all believers finds visible expression in their united participation in the work of salvation. The body of

Christ is a whole, a unity that is working together towards the great end of the ingathering of the whole elect of God. 'This principle of the unity of the church lies at the foundation of the Presbyterian polity and all its peculiarities are designed to bring this out and to give it a formal expression' (J. H. Thornwell, *Collected Writings*, Vol. IV, p. 136).

III   The Expression of This Unity

This fundamental principle of the unity of the church of Christ comes to expression in presbyterian polity through representative government, namely, that *the government and discipline of the church is conducted by the membership through presbyters ordained to rule and deacons appointed to serve.* This principle is applicable in the first place in the local congregation. It is the elders who rule. It must not, however, be assumed that the consent of the members of the church in her government is neglected. On the contrary every endeavour must be made to obtain the concurrence of the people, but their concurrence does not validate or invalidate the act of the elders and is not essential to it. The scriptural support for this method of government is quite considerable though for the most part it is indirect.

First of all the Divine appointment of an office of authority and government is itself strong presumptive support of such a procedure. If the office depends for its validity, not on human appointment, but on its Divine authority then the concurrence of the people is not essential to its function. Another indirect but nevertheless important consideration is the pattern upon which the office is based, that of the elder in Israel. The name and function of the elder corresponded to that in Judaism and the first Christian churches were without question based on the synagogue, (cf. Acts 18, 19, *passim*) so it would be very unexpected to find the ruling function of the Christian elder different from that of its predecessor unless a specific rule to that effect were laid down. When Christ gave directions for dealing with a brother who had wronged another He said that when private rebuke failed the complainer was to 'tell it to the church.' Now in view of the fact that the Christian church as an institution had not yet taken shape the command obviously implied that the mode of ecclesiastical procedure to be followed was that then existing, namely the procedure of the synagogue. According to that procedure the elders as the representatives of the people dealt with the offence, without the concurrence of the people. The use of the inclusive term 'the church' for the elders of the church has Old Testament precedent (Ex. 20.3, 21). God directs Moses, 'Speak ye unto all the congregation of Israel' and then we read, 'Moses called for all the elders of Israel and said unto them . . . .'.

Further with regard to Church admission to fellowship we never read of the concurrence of the people being sought. In the ordination of officers this concurrence is never shown as having been sought, but appears to have been by the elders meeting together, (1 Tim. 4.14). With regard to discipline the case is equally clear apart from the Corinthian matter. In other cases the directions for the discipline are directed to those who bear office, as in the case of the exhortations to Timothy: 'Against an elder receive not an accusation, but before two or three witnesses. Them that sin rebuke before all, that others may fear,' (1 Tim. 5.19, 20). 'A man that is an heretic, after the first and second admonition reject,' (Tit. 3.10). In directing Titus how to direct what appeared to be rather a difficult people Paul tells him to rebuke them sharply. The case of the Corinthian church is not quite so direct yet it must be looked at in the light of the whole of the Scriptures relating to the matter. This is but the application of the hermeneutical principle of the analogy of scripture. It is maintained that blame is attached to the whole of the church in Corinth for not having dealt with the offender, and so it is argued that it was the function of the church as a whole. This is a *non sequiter*. The fact that it was the responsibility of the church as a whole to maintain its purity does not imply that it was the function of the whole church to execute that responsibility. It was the duty of the church as a whole to see that those invested with that authority carried out their duty; a right that the people have in any form of presbyterian government.

It was essential to deal with this question because it is fundamental to the idea of representative government which, as we have said, is the most obvious characteristic of presbyterian polity. If the exercise of ecclesiastical authority is by the whole congregation then it is obviously impossible that there could be any representative government on any other level. It is of importance also because the local church is the unit of the system. In Scotland the kirk session was known for a time as the little presbytery. 'The presbyterian principle begins at the level of the particular flock or congregation and if, for good reasons, it does not extend further than one congregation, we are not to deem it unpresbyterian. To be concrete, to that local presbytery belongs all the functions that

Christ has accorded to presbytery,' (John Murray, op. cit., pp. 348, 349).

The expression of the unity of the church in representative government does not stop at the local level as, for example, in independent churches who govern through elders, but it also extends throughout the whole church. This does not mean that every office bearer has an equal responsibility for the government of each part of the church but his office bears a responsibility to the whole. This relationship is more apparent in the office of teaching elder. Every pastor or minister has a particular relationship to the whole church of Christ. This I think is maintained by us all, that our ordination to the ministry is ordination to the ministry of the Church of Christ and is valid for every branch of the church. We rightly refuse re-ordination when we transfer from one church to another. By the same token ordination to the office of ruling elder is an ordination that bears a relationship to the whole church of Christ. The ruling elder like the teaching elder has a particualr responsibility to the local church over which he is set, but that responsibility in virtue of the unity of the church extends to the whole church. For the doctrine of the unity of the visible church the most relevant Scriptures are Eph. 4 and 1 Cor. 12, and for a practical example of that unity Acts 15. Too much stress has perhaps been laid on this last passage but we must not under-rate its significance. This much is certain: the question that had arisen was referred to the apostles and elders, some of them from another assembly, if not from several assemblies, and the decision of that consultation was binding not only on the church which had remitted the question but also upon all the other churches, (16.4). 'And as they went through the cities they delivered them the decrees for to keep, that were ordained of the apostles and elders which were at Jerusalem'.

The presbyterian system is an attempt to give expression to this unity in a way that follows the apostolic precedent. It is interesting to note that many of the older independents granted this principle in conceding the right of synod and to my mind conceded the right of presbytery. This is especially true of the Westminster Independents. The concessions that they made and the ingenuity they showed in avoiding the implications of their concessions indicate that their resistance to the presbytery arose more from political or other motives than from an unbiased interpretation of Scripture. For example they say, 'Synods are an holy ordinance of God, and of great use for the finding out and declaring of truth in difficult cases, and for healing offences.' And, 'that all the churches of a province being offended at a particular congregation, may call that single congregation to account; yea, all the churches in a nation may call one or more congregations to an account; that they may examine and admonish, and, in the case of obstinancy, declare them to be subverters of the faith; that they are of use to give advice to magistrates in matters of religion. That they have authority to determine concerning controversies of faith; that their determinations are to be received with great honour and consciencious respect and obligation as from Christ; that if an offending congregation refuse to submit to their determinations, they may withdraw from them' (Porteous, op. cit., pp. 204, 205). Thomas Goodwin says: 'As we acknowledge elective occasional Synods of the elders of many churches, as the Churches have need to refer cases of difference to them; so in the case of maladministration, or an unjust proceeding in the sentence of ex-communication, and the like, we acknowledge appeals or complaints may be made to other churches and the elders of those churches met in a Synod, who being offended, may, as an ordinance of Christ, judge, and declare that sentence to be null, void and unjust; and that not simply as any company of men may so judge, giving their judgements of a fact done, but as an ordinance of Christ in such cases and for that end sanctified by Him to judge and declare in matters of difference.' John Owen is of the same mind: 'No church, therefore, is so independent as that it can always, and in all cases observe the duties it owes unto the Lord Christ, and the Church Catholic, by all those powers which it is able in itself distinctly without conjunction with others. And the church that confines its duty unto the acts of its own assemblies, cuts itself off from the external communion of the Church Catholic; nor will it be safe, for any man to commit the conduct of his soul to such a church. Wherefore, this acting in synods is an institution of Jesus Christ, not in an express command, but in the nature of the thing itself, fortified with apostolical example. That particular church which extends not its duty beyond its own assemblies and members is fallen from the principal end of its institution . . . . Synods are consecrated unto the use of the Church in all ages by the example of the apostles in their guidance of the first Churches of Jews and Gentiles which hath the force of a divine institution, as being given by them under the infallible conduct of the Holy Ghost,' (Both references Porteous, *ibid.*, p. 205).

The objection raised by some independents to meet this concession, namely, that such synods are only occasional and not regular, appears to be a mere cavil. Because of the complexity of life many difficulties and problems must inevitably arise and, therefore, make a regular meeting of synod necessary. The appeal of George Gillespie to the independents at the Westminster Assembly is still relevant. 'Brethren, we shall be one in heaven; let us pack up our differences in this place of our pilgrimage the best way we can. How much better is it that you be one with the other Reformed churches, though somewhat straitened and bound up, than to be divided, though at full liberty and elbow room! Better is a dry morsel and quietness therewith, than a house full of sacrifices with strife.'

The presbyterian polity can rightly claim to be undergirded by the government of the house of God in the Old Testament and to be the undoubted practice of the church of Christ in the New Testament.

In the foregoing we have only dealt with those matters that are essential to the polity. There are many other subjects that are germane to the discussion but we have not introduced them so that the distinctives of presbyterianism may be highlighted.

Bibliography

Gordon R. Balfour, *Presbyterianism in the Colonies*, MacNiven & Wallace, Edinburgh 1899.

D. D. Bannerman, *The Scripture Doctrine of the Church*, T. & T. Clark, Edinburgh 1887.

W. M. Campbell, *The Triumph of Presbyterianism*, The Saint Andrew Press, Edinburgh 1958.

Wm. Cunningham, *Discussions on Church Principles*, T. & T. Clark, Edinburgh 1863.

Robert L. Dabney, *Discussions: Evangelical and Theological*, Vol. II, Banner of Truth, London 1967.

Donaldson, *The Scottish Reformation*, Cambridge University Press, London 1960.

A. M. Farrer, *The Apostolic Ministry* (Ed. Kirk), Edinburgh.

George Gillespie, *One Hundred and Eleven Propositions Concerning the Ministry and Government of the Church*, Robert Ogle and Oliver & Boyd, Edinburgh 1844.

Charles Hodge, *The Church and Its Polity*, Thos. Nelson & Sons, London 1903.

T. M. Lindsay, *The Church and the Ministry in the Early Centuries*, Hodder & Stoughton Ltd., London 1903.

C. G. McCrie, *Public Worship of Presbyterian Scotland*, Wm. Blackwood & Sons, Edinburgh 1892.

John MacPherson, *Presbyterianism* ('Handbooks for Bible Classes'), T. & T. Clark, Edinburgh (re-issued 1949).

John MacPherson, *The Doctrine of the Church in Scottish Theology*, MacNiven & Wallace, Edinburgh 1903.

A. F. Mitchell, *The Westminster Assembly, Its History and Standards*, J. Nisbet & Co., London 1883.

James Moffat, *The Presbyterian Churches*, Methuen & Co. Ltd., London 1928.

Leon Morris, *Ministers of God*, IVF, London 1964.

Iain Murray (Ed.), *The Reformation of the Church*, Banner of Truth Trust, London 1965.

John Murray, *Collected Writings*, Vols. 1, 2, Banner of Truth, Edinburgh 1976–7.

J. N. Ogilvy, *The Presbyterian Churches of Christendom*, R. & R. Clark, Edinburgh 1925.

J. Moir Porteous, *The Government of the Kingdom of Christ*, J. Nisbet & Co., London 1888.

W. Stanford Reid, 'Knox's Attitude to the English Reformation,' *Westminster Theological Journal*, Vol. XXVI, No. 1.

Samuel Rutherford, *The Due Rightness of Presbyteries*, London 1644.

Thomas Smyth, *Presbytery and not Prelacy*, Wm. Collins, Glasgow 1844.

J. H. Thornwell, *Collected Writings*, Vol. IV, Banner of Truth, Edinburgh 1974.

Luder G. Whitlock, 'Elders and Ecclesiology in the Thought of James Henley Thornwell,' *Westminster Theological Journal*, Vol. XXXVII, No. 1.

J. R. de Witt, *Jus Divinum*, J. H. Kok N.V., Kampen 1969.

T. Witherow, *The Apostolic Church*, Free Presbyterian Church of Scotland, Inverness 1967.

T. Witherow, *The Form of the Christian Temple.*

The Practice of the Free Church of Scotland.

Miscellany, P.G.

Purity of Worship

HECTOR CAMERON, M.A.
Minister of Bon Accord Free Church, Aberdeen.

The Free Church service of worship, while distinctively a simple service, does of course share with the Christian Church universally the basic, formal elements of worship: the reading of Scripture, the preaching of the Word, the administration of the sacraments, the singing of praise, the offering of prayer. If the Free Church worshipper sits, for his part, to sing, and stands for the prayer, these peculiarities—or in Free Church eyes, refinements—are of little moment, relatively speaking, when the wider area of agreement is held in view. Confining the field for the present to Protestant practice, we can say that in one significant direction only, so far as matters of pure procedure are concerned, does Free Church worship diverge in a noticeable way from worship as discharged in the large majority of churches. But it does diverge in respect of the fact that neither uninspired hymns nor instrumental music are included in the church's order of congregational praise.

A Distinctive Position
With the twentieth century now three-quarters through its course, the position of the Free Church, which persists in avoiding the use in public worship both of uninspired songs and of instrumental music, is undoubtedly a highly distinctive one. And Free Churchmen themselves have tended on the whole to view this state of affairs with warm pride. It would be too much to expect the representatives of universal Christendom to see things in quite the same way. A certain admiration for the virtue of tenacity in the face of overwhelming odds may here and there be conceded to us. The general impression seems, however, to be that the Free Church's worship formula is distinctive in much the same way as operating with primitive domestic conveniences—tallow lamps and the like— would be distinctive. In other words, either it is in this day and age unenlightened of us, and in that case we should submit modestly to education, or else we are simply the children of misfortune, and therefore deserve, on compassionate grounds, a specially considerate mode of treatment. What cannot, it seems, be entertained is that the position itself has any element of right or reason attending it.

This does raise immediately a rather pointed question. How, after all, can people know what is right and reasonable in the realm of church worship? If it boiled down, as in politics, to majority taste and feeling, the complications would, one way or another, be much less forbidding. But the situation is not really like that. Issues of the type now discussed deserve to be heard, surely, in the exclusive forum of Christian taste and feeling. Even at that, unfortunately, we can be left too often with a considerable remainder of uncertainty.

The trouble stems to a large extent from this fact, that the descriptive word 'Christian' does not today possess that limpid clarity of meaning which marked its regular usage in the Pauline and Petrine churches of the first century. The assertion of being Christian can be applied quite intelligently to Roman Catholics, Baptists Brethren and Presbyterians alike. It is obvious, nevertheless, that each of these denominations may here and there be separated, and often widely separated, from one or more of the others, on what precisely the Christian thing is, which is required as a mark at any time either of belief or of practice.

Protestants, certainly, over a wide front, would be at least in theoretical agreement with the Westminster Shorter Catechism, which claims that 'the Word of God, contained in the Scriptures of the Old and New Testaments, is the only rule to direct us how we may glorify and enjoy Him.' Presumably they would agree, too, that this statement refers to the question of church worship along with other matters. The God who is to be worshipped takes a deep interest—could we conceive it differently?—in the worship which we may properly offer to Him, as our Lord was at pains to stress, in conversation with the woman of Sychar: 'They that worship the Father must worship Him in spirit and in truth. The Father seeketh such to worship Him.' What that may mean in detail is not obvious until Scripture at large has been searched, though it does plainly stress the interest God has that His worship should conform to a definite pattern. For an authoritative summary of what the Free Church believes the Bible to teach about worship, we have to refer to the Westminster Confession of Faith, together with the body of domestic procedure known as 'The Free Church Practice.' In this latter manual, to which it is convenient to refer first, the worship question comes to the fore in a paragraph bearing the somewhat cryptic title, 'Questions and Formula,' this being part of a suite of regulations by which the setting apart of ministers and other office-bearers is governed.

Questions and Formula

When ordinations and inductions take place in the Free Church, the candidate is required to put his signature to a paper known as the Formula, whose terms represent a condensed statement of answers given by the candidate to a standard set of questions. These questions lay out formally his official obligations to the Church. As well as declaring 'the whole doctrine contained in the Confession of Faith' to be the confession of his own faith, the candidate professes sincere approval of the 'purity of worship presently authorized and practised in the Free Church of Scotland.' To this doctrine and worship he gives, moreover, a commitment to conform, under all appropriate circumstances, his practice. 'Purity of worship' is not, needless to say, a self-explanatory phrase. Its meaning will emerge in the course of our discussion, during which, paying attention certainly to what is said in the Confession of Faith, we will examine an assortment of debates and decisions as well, which involved the Scottish Presbyterian Church at various times, from Knox's day and onwards. Very early the words 'purity of worship,' or their like, were already becoming familiar, presenting in a thoroughly challenging way a vital element in Scotland's Reformation witness.

It was almost if not quite inevitable, with generations of Presbyterian controversy about purity of worship lying behind, that the 1900 Free Church, entering now on a new phase of its confessional career, should have sought to crystallise its position in that particular direction. Crystallize that position, in any case, it did, first in 1905 and again, more elaborately, in 1910, by declaratory act of Assembly.

However, before coming to details we may go back just a little in time, to when, in the closing years of the nineteenth century, the union, involving the Free and United Presbyterian churches was nearing completion. A minority section of the Free Church at that time, having consulted their theological conscience about the projected union, saw it as their duty to abstain. It was this section which proceeded in due course to carry both the name, and what they took to be the principles, of the Free Church of Scotland into the twentieth century.

Two principles, especially, both being of front-rank concern to the church by any standards, were at stake: the civil establishment of religion and the confessional view of atonement. Many spectacular Assembly debates of the sort which agitated the three final decades of a much-agitated century, had these and related issues, almost without ceasing, as the centre of attention. Apt to be over-shadowed in the story of events, at the same time, is the fact that over much the same period there was deep contention within the Free Church about purity of worship. A vigorous clash of views kept occurring on whether uninspired songs might feature as materials of praise, or instrumental music as accompaniment, in the public worship of God.

The position that these admitted innovations were nevertheless allowable was advanced, not without some far-seeing calculations by its exponents (cf. G. N. M. Collins *The Heritage of our Fathers*, p. 71). Terms of union of a sort likely to pass muster with the United Presbyterian negotiating team were a first priority. The actual calendar of Free Church legislation on the subject of hymns and organs, when it is compared with the corresponding calendar of the United Presbyterian Church, has in this light a story of its own to tell. Hasty ecumenical adjustment, while it has had of course an exceedingly long and exquisitely various pilgrimage, carries with it into every period of the church's history the same unmistakable face. Permission for United Presbyterian congregations to make use of hymns was obtained in 1851, and to use organs in 1877: the corresponding Free Church dates being, predictably soon, 1872 and 1883. In the eyes of neither party, it would seem, did the ancient purity of worship clause have any special message for departures of this nature. Nor did the new denomination—the United Free Church of Scotland—fail to bind its office-bearers, as of yore in Scotland, to the maintainance specifically of 'purity of worship,' while there was the fullest possible readiness to make room, in the worship of the Church, for human hymns and instrumental music.

Such was the background of ecclesiastical events against which the Free Church Act of 1910, (*Act anent Public Worship*), is to be read. Evil effects had arisen, says the preface, 'from the introduction of uninspired materials of praise at variance with the Scriptural principles and usage regulating her (the Free Church's) worship, as also of instrumental music, by the late prevailing party in her judicatories.' On the secession of that party in 1900, however, 'neither of these innovations remained within her borders, and are now authoritatively proscribed by Act of Assembly, 1905, entitled, Act anent Public Worship.' The decision is then reached that 'the peace and harmony of this church ought to be safeguarded against disturbance, in all time coming from attempts to introduce these or similar innovations.'

With the blood stirred and the spirit of resolution braced for new action by such thoughts, the Assembly proceeded with no undue delay to the question of practical steps. From the archives of 1707 an Act, which answered to the truly formidable title, '*Act against Innovations in the Worship of God,*' was brought forth, reaffirmed, and included as part of the text of the new 1910 Act. Thus the Act of 1910, which abolished in express terms all use in public worship of hymns and instrumental music, went out to meet the world leaning on an ancient relative, whose distinctive and equally explicit objection was to innovations. The 1707 Act, of course, transports us backward in thought through the length of nearly three centuries to times, which although dim perhaps to the memory now, were uniquely stirring for the Scottish Nation, and which are, even yet, tinged with nostalgia for the Scottish Church. The Union of the Parliaments was the ideal which, despite the presence of a variety of sectional fears and forebodings, held fast for many in church and state their imagination, their mind, their heart and their will. Enthusiasm, however, as the looked-for goal came nearer, was not untempered with caution. The actual business of union, conducted as we know with courtesy, sagacity and mutual respect, was of such a nature from the start that the separate interests of each national church were guarded with the utmost expenditure of jealous care on both sides.

The Act of Assembly of 1707, while not scrupling indeed to refer to specific 'innovations of late set up' within the bounds of certain presbyteries, displays also an awareness of a remit which is very much wider. It objects significantly to 'any such innovations': to every imaginable innovation, that is, which would be typical at all of what the Assembly describes as 'the late prelacy,' and which would be moreover 'manifestly contrary to our known principle (which is, that nothing is to be admitted in the worship of God, but what is prescribed in the Holy Scripture).' The reference to 'our known principle' is an interesting one. C. G. Macrie says that 'the ritual value of this document lies in its explicit, although parenthetical, reassertion of that principle which gave distinctive character and form to Presbyterian worship, the principle so strongly affirmed in the utterances and writings of the Scottish Reformers and the Westminster divines—nothing is to be admitted in the worship of God but what is prescribed in the Holy Scriptures' (*Public*

Worship of Presbyterian Scotland, p. 260—referring to *Confession of Faith*, chap. 21, sect. 1 and Larger Catechism, pp. 108–9).

A Question of Relevance

Critics of the 1910 Act are not by any means wanting. So far indeed as its underlying purpose is concerned, it has not, at any time, been subject to question. It was a proper thing in every way, whether to make statements or to pass acts especially at that juncture, with a view both to clarifying, and also to placing beyond threat, the worship syllabus of the Church. If that was what the 1910 men believed they were obliged, surely, as well as entitled, to say so. Questions have in fact been raised, on the other hand, about the fitness for their purpose of those legislative measures which the 1910 Assembly were finally led to adopt. Were they indeed correct, in basing the act which they passed—hymns and organs being the offensive items—so very specifically and so very confidently on an act which, with 'innovations' for its special target, was passed in 1707? The immediate reference of the 1707 Act, after all, had to do with departures, of episcopalian origin, from the use and wont of rival presbyterianism.

We have an objection thus on our hands, and its merits it is only fair we should test. Take the matter of 'uninspired materials of praise' first. Did the 1707 Act against innovations have anything at all to do with uninspired materials of praise? In the contrasting expression, 'inspired materials of praise,' the 1910 men set forth, of course, their own standard of practice. They meant such songs of praise, presumably, as occurred in Scripture in the very form of songs of praise: this in distinction from 'human hymns,' or, from songs based upon passages of Scripture which, while making no claims themselves originally to being poetic texts, had been processed into metrical shape. Indeed, if Dr. Alexander Stewart can be taken as typical of the 1910 Assembly, it was the Book of Psalms itself, almost certainly, which was in mind. Dr. Stewart's history of the Free Church, from Disruption times till 1910, represented virtually the official version of this exercise. Of Free Church worship at that time (1910) he wrote: 'The Free Church confines herself to the words of Inspiration . . . the hymns of the Holy Ghost.' He then proceeds immediately to speak about 'objections to the Psalter as a manual of New Testament praise,' identifying in his own thought, the hymns of the Holy Ghost with the Book of Psalms, without including other Scripture songs.

But the Act of 1707 dealing with innovations, whatever else it intended to do, appears to have had no interest in protecting the status of the Psalter, as the Church's only manual of praise. The General Assembly of 1707, precisely on the day they legislated to purge the Church of innovations, passed also an Act dealing with 'Scripture Songs.' Background information on this latter act indicated, indeed, the Assembly's complete aversion to paraphrases. Even so, they were not apparently opposed in principle to considering songs taken from elsewhere in the Bible, alongside the actual Hebrew Psalter (cf. McCrie, op. cit., p. 277 ff.). The 1910 Act, therefore, if the intention really was to strengthen a case for the exclusive use of the Hebrew Psalter, in distinction from other Biblical songs, would not find the legislation put through in 1707 all that helpful.

A further point must be made. The Assembly of 1707 itself had clearly nothing on its hands by way of a hymn-singing problem of the sort to which its Act against innovations could in any obvious way apply: certainly nothing of the sort which made Free Church minds uneasy in 1910.

It is not for these reasons possible, then, to find any direct link between the anti-hymns clause of 1910 and the anti-innovations clause of 1707. The question, however, of an indirect link, of these two acts being related somehow in principle, is something altogether different, and certainly deserving to be explored. A brief excursion, therefore, into the previous century, with whose doings the meaning of the 1707 Act concerning innovations is very much involved, cannot well be avoided.

Seventeenth-century Presbyterianism and its Theology of Worship

Important above all else to remember, for a start, is how the 1707 Assembly was aiming at protection from any and every innovation which was typical in any way whatsoever of prelatic practices in worship. The word 'innovation' itself, deeply rooted as it was in the controversial diction of the National Covenant, was by no means carelessly chosen. It served as a link, the most natural link available, between the presbyterian holding-exercise of 1707 and presbyterian contendings at their classical best. By the renewed National Covenant of 1638, following the first overthrow of a prelatic church which had moulded itself obligingly to the Stuart dictum of 'the divine right of kings,' the subscibers had bound themselves 'to forbear the practice of all innovations introduced into the worship of God.' This sentiment, coupled with the very positive resolve 'to recover the purity and liberty of the Gospel,' was to claim the heart of Scottish presbyterianism throughout the entire covenanting period; far beyond it indeed; wherever, in fact, Reformation theology was allowed to pursue a normal course.

The Westminster Confession of Faith spoke firmly for all presbyterians in its statement: 'The acceptable way of worshipping the true God is instituted by Himself, and so limited by His own revealed will that He may not be worshipped according to the imaginations and devices of men, or the suggestions of Satan, under any visible representation; or any other way not prescribed in the Holy Scriptures.' Seventeenth-century prelacy, especially as controlled by the House of Stuart, operated by an altogether different principle, namely, that whatever is not forbidden in Scripture is allowable. The distinction is vital: on the one hand, clear prescription, on the other, arguable permission.

The Westminster principle relative to worship, moreover, was influential, in those very situations where, all through the seventeenth century, presbyterianism was obliged to come to terms with the special question of song praise. There were two streams of presbyterian concern—the one pretty fairly an outflow from the other—where the beginnings at least of discussion, for and against inspired materials of praise, can be distinguished. We may refer to these as, (1) Discussions about the doxology, and (2) More general questions about songs of praise.

DISCUSSIONS ABOUT THE DOXOLOGY

The earliest Scottish Psalter, published as a section of the first Book of Common Order (1564–65), contained no songs for church praise over and above the Psalms of David. With various subsequent editions over a period of years, however, a number of hymns, none of them belonging to the Book of Psalms, and some not even belonging to the Bible, began to make their appearance. Such appendices included, for example, the Magnificat, an assortment of doxologies, and the ancient hymn, 'Veni Creator.' There is no evidence, actually, that such songs received at any time the sanction of the Assembly. They appear to have owed their presence rather, in every case, to the doctrinal or other preference cherished by the publisher. And in this general connection a remark made by Livingston is worth bearing in mind: 'It must be remembered,' he says, 'that singing of compositions relating to religion—some more strictly devotional and doctrinal, others levelled at the abuses of Popery— was a conspicuous feature in the Reformation movement. But the distinction between use in worship and private ends seems to have been generally recognized. Even in Germany where hymns abounded, only a limited selection was admitted into the books prepared for the church. The 'Godly Ballates' may be regarded as including specimens of both sorts of material. The distinction being understood, it is not surprising that a few things intended for private instruction and edification should, for convenience sake, be appended to the Psalter' (*The Scottish Psalter*, Diss. 1, p. 4: quoted by Hay Fleming in '*The Hymnology of the Scottish Reformation*,' *Works*, II, p. 15). Thus Hay Fleming concludes that, 'Dr. Bonar (Horatius) is singularly illogical in holding that because certain songs and hymns were published with various editions of the Book of Common Order, therefore "there were hymns in the Church of Scotland." ' Bonar might as well have insisted, says Fleming, 'that the Alphabet and Multiplication Table are in the Church of Scotland now, because they have so long been printed with the Shorter Catechism!' (op. cit.) Nevertheless, with the political climate increasingly genial to its cause and the seventeenth century fairly under way, prelacy in Scotland gathered itself to make profit where it could. Doxologies, accordingly, began to venture forth from retirement. They were finding now a place, and as time went on an honoured place, in the open conduct of the church's worship.

Rank and file supporters of presbyterianism were for their part largely hostile. To the minds of Robert Baillie's 'four yeomen,' who were deputed, probably by the whole congregation, to visit their minister as protesters, the doxology figured, quite simply, as 'an humane popish invention.' And, according to the view of Livingston among others, scruples which were fully capable of matching these may have governed the attitude of a considerable portion of the Scottish people (Hay Fleming, op. cit., p. 38). The substantial opposition of many of the clergy, meanwhile, especially among men representing the south and west, is established beyond all question.

The Second Reformation, a decisive movement in every respect, excluded with unanimous consent, the use of doxologies from the worship of the church. Most important for a teaching influence which went to shape the convictions involved were the Westminster divines. Willing horses these men, all of them, they made space in a programme formidable as it already stood, for the production of a new metrical version of the Psalms. And in this, says Baillie, they 'kept punctuallie to the original text,' omitting the doxology in the process, as something 'whereupon the popish and prelatical party did so much dote' (Hay Fleming, op. cit., p. 38). The Confession of Faith itself and the Directory for Worship, of course, are both animated by the same chaste spirit. Each requires the singing of Psalms and neither makes room for additional singing material.

For the proverbial cat of nine lives, however, the seventeenth century doxology was a rival of no mean merit. As a direct practical consequence of the Restoration the re-instatement of the doxology in Scottish worship was widespread. That the practice was even then sharply contested is clear from the note made by Skinner, historian of the times, that the Episcopal clergy 'concluded their prayers with the Lord's prayer, and their singing with the doxology, both which the zealots of the other side decried as superstitious and formal.' In reply to Bishop Burnet's argument that the doctrine of the Trinity is better set out in the doxology than in any Psalm, and what was the difference, anyway, between saying it and singing it, McWard in characteristic presbyterian style offered this defence: 'We close our prayers ordinarily with praise and glory to the Father, the Son and the Holy Ghost: because it is warrantable from Scripture practice, to wit, in blessing; and agreeable to the truth and liberty of Gospel worship; and yet we refuse it in singing (mark it, not in praising) because for that exercise the Lord having instructed us with a sufficient plenty of divine composures, we think it neither needful nor acceptable that we should gratify an arbitrary imposition, in receiving the supplement of a human addition. It is true the words are Scriptural, but can you say that the Scripture bears any such allowance for their use in singing as it doth for the Psalms of David?' (op. cit., p. 43, ref. to McWard's *The True Non-Conformist*)

Such thinking was to hold an increasingly confident place in the Scottish Church right through to the next century. It was the view of Laing, the publisher of Robert Baillie's letters, that, at the Second Reformation, 'the doxology had been disallowed as prelatic practice.' Nor can there be any doubt that the type of presbyterianism which that circumstance clearly reflected was well and widely represented throughout Scotland up to, and including, the Union of the Parliaments. Principal John Macleod, making reference at one point in his book, *Scottish Theology*, to the martyrs of the Killing Time, sums the matter up in his own telling style: 'It was the plain, unadorned presbyterianism that had such a baptism of blood, which, without question, came to be recognized as the standard form of worship of the re-established Kirk' (*Scottish Theology*, p. 115).

MORE GENERAL QUESTIONS ABOUT SONGS OF PRAISE

Human hymns (Dr. Hay Fleming is convinced of this), did not figure at all in the Second Reformation conspectus of worship: the reason, he says, being 'that those who opposed the doxology would also have objected to them, and so they would have been specially mentioned.' The Westminster divines went actually much further than the mere laying of their canonical seal of approval on the existing worship of the Scottish Church. They put Scotland in their debt, most of all, for a whole theology of worship. Within that framework, furthermore, the intention seems certainly to have been that Psalms and only Psalms should be sung in the worship of the church. They were nothing if not practical, and there emerged speedily from their hands an entirely fresh translation of the Hebrew Psalter, which would in their plan function as the stated manual of praise across the kingdom. From this new book of praise they excluded, by deliberate and also common consent, even the doxology. Nor was that all. The explicit, and in no way qualified, instruction was proclaimed that psalms should be sung, this exercise being accredited, in forthright terms, as an essential 'part' of the public order of the church's worship.

It is impossible not to think, besides, that these steps were taken by the divines fully in view of their own regulative principle: and that, it will be recalled, required clear Biblical warrant as the minimum qualification for every article presuming to find a place in the church's worship. Hardly had the ink dried on the written statement of the regulative principle itself, than the quill returned once more to the sheet, entering carefully now by name the elements which can properly be said to belong to the worship of God. 'Prayer,' they wrote, 'the reading of the Scriptures, the preaching and hearing of the Word, the administration of the sacraments and the singing of Psalms are all parts of the ordinary worship of God.' Rare qualities of absent-mindedness must have been needed, surely, for any one of these elements of worship to have been insulated, in the thought of the divines themselves (and that is the point) from the natural effects of their regulative principle of worship.

Leading Scottish presbyterians who came later in the century were to carry the stamp, unmistakably, of a thorough schooling in the Westminster tradition. McWard for example: 'The Lord has instructed us with sufficient plenty of composures,' we remember him remonstrating with Burnet. His instinct drew him to songs which were 'warrantable,' and his objection centred, fairly and squarely, on 'the supplement of an human addition.' With McWard in fact, a developed theology is clearly already in motion. He is single-minded and unerring, in his insistence that divine authority alone should figure as the deciding factor for the content of Christian praise in the realm of song (*The True Non-Conformist*, p. 278).

Brown of Wamphray is worthy also of special mention. Covenanting exile and notable theological writer, he reveals a style of thinking about praise which is, in no essential respect, different from that of McWard. He comments, in his work against the Anti-Sabbatarians, on the 'psalms and hymns and spiritual songs,' to sing which the apostle Paul urges his Ephesiand and Colossian readers. These terms Brown does not hesitate to refer (summoning also an impressive battery of reasons) to the songs of the Hebrew Psalter (cf. Hay Fleming's *Works*, II, p. 46).

From the above brief summary of seventeenth century attitudes and events a number of facts have emerged:

(a) Debate did occur—rudimentary perhaps but substantial—about the type of songs which could suitably be employed in the public worship of God.
(b) There was discussion and division—presbyterianism versus prelacy—over the special issue of uninspired songs, of which the doxologies, undoubtedly, were typical examples.
(c) Doxologies and the like were bracketed by seventeenth century presbyterianism overall as 'prelatic innovations.'

Innovations, it will be remembered, of the type belonging specially to prelatic worship, were the distinct target of the Act of 1707. This act, we can now see, did have reference—at least in principle—to the precise question of uninspired songs. It is in this direction we need to look to justify the Free Church Assembly of 1910 and the claims which they made for the Act of 1707 as being strictly relevant to their cause. Reaching into the venerable law-book of the presbyterian establishment, they picked out the 1707 Act against innovations, in which they saw the readiest means available of linking up their own particular testimony about songs of praise with the testimony of Scottish Presbyterianism in its purest form. The essential purposes of 1707 and 1910, they believed, were identical. In this contention, it seems, they were right.

The 1707 Act and instrumental music

Is there good evidence, however, which would prove the claim pointedly made for the Act, that it covered instrumental music also in its brief? Two avenues of thought present themselves, each indicating strongly that it did. They are, (1) The Establishment of presbyterian practice, and (2) The circumstances of the Confession of Faith's production.

(1) THE ESTABLISHMENT OF PRESBYTERIAN PRACTICE

As important, probably, as any other circumstance which marked the programme of legislation put through the Assembly's books in 1707 was its ratification—performed actually in rather general terms—of a variety of earlier laws. Many of these earlier laws, certainly, leaving not a great deal to the imagination, had abolished prelacy, together with 'the whole train thereof.' Cautious feelings, prevailing on both sides at the Union, however, had produced within the Acts of Union themselves, a deliberate generality of expression, at all those points where practices which were not acceptable to one or the other church party came in for mention. Such generic terminology, at the same time, weakened in no way the applicability of these acts to what had received, in earlier circumstances of contention, the blunter treatment. Of undoubted interest for the organ question, this point deserves to be kept in special focus. Dr. Porteous says, having in mind especially the Claim of Right, that 'all denominations of Christians in England and Scotland did at that time consider instrumental music a characteristic of prelacy.' And to make the assumption, merely from the absence of an explicit veto statement, that instrumental music was not, in point of fact, banned, is to quibble. The men who legislated the exclusion of prelacy 'had no reserve on behalf of any one part of it.' They fairly and candidly intended that 'not only prelatical government, the liturgy and service-book should be abolished, but likewise that kneeling at the sacrament, the sign of the cross in Baptism, and instrumental music should share the same fate. Conversely, the formal affirmation of customary presbyterian styles of worship involved a clear-cut and highly conscious commitment to the practice of vocal praise alone' (cf. *The Organ Question*, Ed. R. S. Candlish, pp. 145–6 and 156).

In that very light and no other must the position held on this question by the Confession of Faith and the Directory for Worship be judged. Documents of critical authority at every stage, and given pride of place unmistakably in the Union legislation, they commend with one unfaltering voice the duty of vocal praise. Musical accompaniment, meanwhile, is conspicuous for the stark and eloquent reason that it receives no mention.

(2) THE CIRCUMSTANCES OF THE CONFESSION OF FAITH'S PRODUCTION

The Confession, like the Directory, was given to the world by the great mid-seventeenth century assembly of British divines which met, with every possible propitious omen for the kingdom, at Westminster. It is their views, rather than other views, to which reference needs, with each separate clause of the Confession's programme of teaching, to be made, if indeed we are to understand it. Three simple points bearing closely on the church–music issue can be stressed:

(a) The Westminster Assembly was commissioned by the Long Parliament. But already by the year 1644, as the Assembly got down to the preparation of their Directory for Worship, the Long Parliament had made summary work of 'extirpating prelacy and the whole train thereof.' The ministerial commissioners from Scotland, Robert Baillie and his party, reporting unanimously in these terms, declared they could see 'the good hand of God' in it all. Purgation and reform had been carried out, the report went on,' in a quiet manner and without tumult' and extended to 'the removal of the great organs at Paul's and Peter's in Westminster.' This particular thrust of the movement, actually, was to continue, And at the Revolution, says Dr. John Girardeau, 'most of the organs in Scotland had been destroyed' (John Girardeau, *Instrumental Music in Public Worship*, pp. 132–3).

(b) Two of the Scottish commissioners referred to above have elsewhere expressed opinions on this aspect of the worship issue. The presbyterian pastor, declares David Calderwood, 'loveth no music in the house of God but such as edifieth, and stoppeth his ears at instrumental music, as serving for the pedagogy of the untoward Jews under the law, and being figurative of that spiritual joy whereunto our hearts should be opened under the Gospel. The prelate loveth carnal and sensuous singing to the ear, more than the spiritual melody of the Gospel, and therefore would have antiphony and organs in the cathedral kirks, upon no greater reason than other shadows of the law of Moses' ('The Pastor and the Prelate,' p. 4, *Presbyterian's Armoury*, Vol. III).

Rutherford's 'Divine Right of Church Government' adopts the same point of view. 'Altars, organs, Jewish ephods or surplice, masse-cloths and Roman Crossing' are listed by Rutherford as being 'badges of Jewish and popish religion.'

(c) The English commissioners at Wesminster by and large, subscribed to views which were exactly similar. The Puritan movement disallowed the cathedral mode of worship. 'Nor did they approve,' says Neal the historian, 'of musical instruments, as trumpets, organs, etc., which were not in use in the church for above 1200 years after Christ' (*History of the Puritans*, Vol. I, p. 76, Choule's Ed.).

There is required, therefore, no more than a modest understanding of the issues between seventeenth-century prelacy and presbyterianism to decide in favour of the Free Church Act of 1910 in this connection also. Abjuring instrumental music in church worship, they based themselves, correctly and legitimately, on the 1707 Act dealing with innovations. The standard objection to using the 1707 Act against innovations as a lash for the back of instrumental music is put like this: 'But surely the 1707 Act had to do with prelatic worship!' It had, of course. But that, as we have seen, is precisely the point.

The Regulative Principle of Worship
Reaffirming the 1707 Act meant considerably more for the situation of the Free Church in 1910 than the mere symbolic shaking out and hoisting to the breeze of an ancient battle flag. Recent events had fostered a fresh sense of identity with Scottish Reformation positions. And it was vital now, as much for domestic morale as for public testimony, just as the Church was exerting itself to come to terms with questions affecting worship, to avoid by all available means an impression of upstart departure or of sectarian discord. Back to the foundations therefore they went.

As we saw earlier, the Act of 1707 proceeded with unerring directness to the regulative principle of worship, this being regarded as the acid test, with reference to which every question connected with worship must be decided. The regulative principle, moreover, has important practical, as well as strictly theological, points of value. Kept at the centre of the field of discussion, it helps to transfer the debate about worship from areas where emotional reaction is bound to enfeeble thought into the less impassioned atmosphere of theological exchange. For example, those churches in Scotland which happen to support the purity of worship ideal must reckon seriously with the image they have gained of dour and peculiar streaks of religious behaviour. It is here that the regulative principle of worship, if it once secures the attention which it clearly deserves, can help, by giving a strictly objective turn to any discussion dealing with worship.

The distinctly clannish temper of the Scottish mind, besides, operating even today in castle, in croft and in church, is of notable influence on this issue. The claymore itself indeed may be laid aside. But, the ecclesiastical shadow of that primeval weapon of the Gael has not surrendered wholly, even now, the age-old formula of militant strife. But the worship issue is a theological issue. The less, therefore, it figures as one more aspect merely of sectarian feud, the better the chances of truth itself being served by the christian church at large. And the aptest means by far of achieving that is to focus discussion steadily, on the regulative principle of worship.

Of the typical effects of the regulative of worship, when practised with any faithfulness in the life of the church, we have already obtained some glimpses. These rise up to the reader's eye in the historical records of the Scottish church mainly and regrettably, it must be said, in its earlier rather than its later pages. Nowhere, meantime, was a better *theoretical* statement ever achieved for the abiding substance of the regulative principle's requirements than in what the Westminster Assembly of divines have handed down to us, in the Confession and the Catechisms which carry their names. 'Nothing,' they teach, 'is to be admitted in the worship of God, but what is prescribed in the Holy Scriptures.'

The word 'prescribed' itself of course is ill-defined as the statement stands. The Confession, fortunately, has handled this question with care, well in advance. Chapter I states that 'the whole counsel of God, concerning all things necessary for His own glory, man's salvation, faith and life, is either expressly set down in Scripture, or by good and necessary consequence may be deduced from Scripture.' Such considerations as approved example and reasonable inference often have a prominent part to play. We are not, as a result, led to expect that any instruction, dealing either with instrumental music or with human hymns, for them or against them as the case may be, will necessarily be found to occur in Scripture, precisely in so many words. The principle holds good, actually, for a great variety of familiar and well-established doctrines of the Christian Church.

Scripture evidence for the regulative principle has been sought in several directions. The leading doctrine of Protestant theology, that the Scriptures are an infallible rule of faith and life is taken to imply it. Paul's statement to Timothy, claiming for all Scripture that is given by inspiration of God, 'being profitable for doctrine, for reproof, for correction, for instruction in righteousness, that the man of God may be perfect, thoroughly furnished unto all good works,' is often cited by way of illustration. Everything commanded in Scripture, by explicit or implicit statement qualifies on that account for entry into the doctrine, worship or government of the church: everything not so commanded is due for exclusion. The point is well demonstrated in Exodus 25.46. God's solemn charge to Moses, envisaging first the construction of the tabernacle, and next the attendant schedule of services, is focused with maximum clarity: 'And look that thou make them after their pattern, which was showed thee in the mount.' New Testament support is found in passages like Matthew 15.6, 'Thus have you made the commandment of God of none effect by your tradition'; and Matthew 28.19, 20, 'Go ye, therefore, and disciple all nations .... teaching them all things whatsoever I have commanded you.'

As helping to provide the regulative principle with enhanced solemnity, there are quoted a number of graphic instances of its special sanctions. Chief among the Scripture events concerned are: Cain and his offering; Nadab and Abihu; Korah; Dathan and Abiram; Moses striking the rock; Saul offering a burnt sacrifice at Gilgal; Uzzah and the ark; and Uzziah the king officiating as a priest. These all accentuate the principle, that what was not commanded in the worship of God was strictly forbidden. Stephen, defending his own Gospel position in the presence of the Jewish council, crystallized the deep guilt of his contemporaries by their breach precisely of this principle: 'As your fathers did, so do ye ... ye do always resist the Holy Ghost.' They had in fact retained, without a warrant for doing so, the typical ritual of the temple service, involving in the act, meantime, an outright rejection of Jesus Christ.

The Regulative Principle versus Uninspired Hymns

Many backwater points of view, variously claiming support from the Word of God, can be met with throughout the multi-channelled system of Psalm-singing conviction and theological belief. It is with the main river's main-stream, that for the time being we concern ourselves. The line of argument most commonly heard occurs, approximately, in the following form;

(1) The Church of God is one church, continuous from age to age.

(2) Certain songs of praise, divinely-inspired and divinely-appointed, were supplied to the church in the Old Testament stage of its course, and intended for permanent use in its order of worship.

(3) The New Testament Church, in turn, has been supplied with, and instructed also to use, those identical songs in its own order of worship.

(4) No songs additional to these appear, at any subsequent time, to have received the sanction of divine appointment.

(5) Divine appointment, however, is an essential feature of the regulative principle of worship, whose earlier relevance for the church's practice remains unchanged.

(6) Those songs, therefore, which were once given as praise material to the Old Testament Church, are the only songs possessing an arguable title to a place in the New Testament Church's order of worship.

The idea, forcefully canvassed from time to time, that the Christian Church possesses discretionary powers with respect to worship, which the church at an earlier stage did not enjoy, is lacking, simply, in proof. The Levitical system, of course, having served its day and reached its Gospel terminus, has now been dismantled. The Christian believer is certainly blessed with freedom, and freedom his older and Hebrew brother was never equipped to experience, the freedom of intimate access to God, without being in debt to earthly redemption, and without being obliged to an Israelite priest. That, however, is all.

The dismantling, moreover, in Christian times, of the Levitical system of worship, took place, emphatically, as did of course its erection, on the strength of divine commandment. It was, as we saw, expressly with defiance of the new regulation that Stephen,

the devout and zealous deacon of the Jerusalem church, was
to charge the great preponderance of his fellow-Jews. They
were clinging to Leviticus, and did not welcome the Gospel of
Christ.

The entire compass of what the Christian Church is expected to
do and to be is determined precisely by divine commandment. Paul
is never done, for example, of binding his readers to apostolic
commandment, as the authoritative reference point for every item
of the church's practice. 'Ye have received of us,' he reminds the
Thessalonian Christians, 'how ye ought to walk and to please God;
for ye know what commandments we gave you by Christ Jesus.'
That Pauline sentiment, besides, did no more than fulfil the intention of our Lord Himself, to which, when issuing the apostolic
commission, He gave special prominence: 'Teach them,' He said,
'to do all things, whatsoever I have commanded you.' No realm of
Christian duty is exempted, least of all, it is plain, the realm of
worship. The one unvarying factor is obligement to the Father's
will. 'They that worship the Father must worship Him in spirit and
in truth; the Father seeketh such to worship Him.' There was never
any suggestion that the regulative principle itself would be in any
way relaxed by the mere crossing of the border from Old to New
Testament. What in point of fact has happened, is that the regulative principle, besides being reaffirmed in impressive style, is
flanked, as it meets us in the Christian era, by a variety of reinforce-
ments, too many and too massive to be missed.

Most evangelical students of Scripture have no actual quarrel
with the facts. Support for human hymns has, as a usual thing, been
sought in other directions than casting doubt on the abiding relevance of the regulative principle of worship. The main claim put
forward has been that apostolic authority itself, no less, has sanc-
tioned the change, and has done so, indeed, by express and repeated
instruction.

The arguments met with, for all their number, fall pretty fairly
into one recognizable pattern. And, although the reasoning adopted
takes at one time a popular form, and at another a more scholarly
form, these tend to stress, each in its own way, Paul's enthusiastic
advice to the Ephesian and Colossian churches to employ, in communion and worship, a generous measure of 'psalms and hymns
and spiritual songs.' Meanwhile there is agreement between psalm-
singers, on the one hand, and hymn-singers, on the other, that even
if Paul, in the passages named is not referring necessarily to the

special question of public worship, his words do have a conclusive
bearing upon that activity.

(1) THE POPULAR ARGUMENT

Here there is no beating at all about the bush. In these Ephesian and
Colossian passages, it is said, Paul surely is recommending, in the
plainest of plain terms, that not only psalms should be used in the
worship of God, but hymns as well. If he says 'hymns,' after all,
what else can he mean but hymns.

The fact is of course well-known that, in modern times, the
English word 'hymn' refers usually to a human composition, and
the English word 'psalm' to one of the songs of the Hebrew Psalter.
The assumption is made, accordingly, that the apostle cannot but
be using these words—in the Greek of course—in the very manner
in which we, today, tend to use their English equivalents. But is he?
Almost certainly not, as we hope to show in the succeeding section
of the study.

(2) THE SCHOLARLY ARGUMENT

Taking rise, on the whole, from the middle of last century, various
exegetical efforts, dealing with the apostle's two words 'hymns' and
'songs,' have been made to link them either with classical Greek
vocabulary, or with certain forms and usages current in the Graeco-
Asiatic culture of Paul's own day. To this latter culture, of course,
the Ephesian and Colossian congregations both belonged. These
efforts, (surprisingly, in view of the overall scholarly treatment they
reveal) have tended almost to ignore a certain outstanding principle,
elementary indeed, of Biblical exegetical method. This principle is
one which discourages any special reliance being placed on the
force which any Greek word may originally have carried as a decisive factor for obtaining the meaning which, within the Christian
Gospels and epistles, is assigned to it. At best, the original meaning
of the word can figure as a junior handmaid only, where the critical
task must be to arrive at the true, contextual meaning of the word,
in the idiom used by the Bible itself. The Hebrew-Christian community had of course their own technical and religious understanding of what many of the words, borrowed freely from heathen
Greek contexts, denoted. Thus the Greek word for 'god,' handled
by Paul with distinctly Christian intent, in his Areopagus address,
held clearly for him a meaning which was quite abruptly and im-
mensely different from anything possibly conveyed by the word to

the Athenian gathering who heard him speak. For ancient Athens, in fact, the Greek word serving to denote 'god' implied a larger-than-life version of the human being, one among many indeed, whose moral qualities were not by a long way always commendable, but whose personal equipment, overall, was viewed as somehow infused with something divine. For Paul, the word 'God' signified no being whatsoever other than the one living and true God, creator and sustainer of all, and the judge besides of the whole inhabited earth; the God and Father of our Saviour Jesus Christ.

One is not by any means unprepared, therefore, for the idea that by 'psalms and hymns and spiritual songs' the apostle intended to refer to a class of songs which were totally private to the Hebrew-Christian community: not merely in the sense of songs which were tinctured with Christian as opposed to heathen sentiment, that being the least we would expect, but of an existing body of songs, well-known, well-defined, divinely-inspired indeed, and answering at once to the familiar and technical title of 'psalms and hymns and spiritual songs.'

The place of the Septuagint in this connection must not, on any account, be left untold. The Septuagint was intended to serve, much as the Gaelic Bible has served the Scottish Celt, those Jews especially who were, as Peter describes them, 'scattered abroad.' And during Paul's missionary journeys, 'when the Gentiles came into the church in large numbers,' says Berkeley Mickelson, 'the Septuagint became even more important. Hence the New Testament writings were originally written to a people who, for the most part, knew of the Old Testament through the reading of the Septuagint' (*Interpreting the Bible*, p. 125). The Septuagint was, without question, the Bible of the synagogue at Ephesus, whose converts to the Christian Faith figured as the early nucleus of the Christian Church in that city. This must have been true, fully as much, of the extensive Jewish community who are known to have settled the Colossian district. So thoroughly did the Septuagint translation become the Bible of the apostolic church that the bulk of Paul's quotations taken from the Old Testament appear in his writings as Septuagintal translations. The Septuagint fulfilled, in fact, a highly influential role in giving to the technical or theological language of Gospel and Epistle its distinctive shape. With that circumstance, as a matter of decided priority, the reader of the New Testament must not, at any point, be slow to reckon.

The psalm-singing fellowship by and large, accordingly, tend to see in these terms a reference almost certainly to the Hebrew Book of Psalms. The very Greek terms employed (psalmoi, humnoi and hodai) figure one or another of them—and on occasion all three together—in the Septuagintal titles of the Psalter, as they figure in addition, from time to time, in the actual body of the Psalter's text. The same thing precisely is true of the historical books of the Septuagint version. In sixteen distinct places, throughout the books of Samuel, Chronicles and Nehemiah, the Psalms, considered as a collection, are called 'hymns' and 'songs' indifferently, while the exercise of singing these songs is described as 'hymning' them. This was, as we say, the Bible of Paul, as it was also the Bible of the Christian communities in Asia Minor for whom the apostolic letters were first intended, and in whose frequent meetings for worship, besides, the Greek version of the Psalter must have functioned, as it regularly functioned in the Jewish synagogue, as the standard congregational manual of praise.

There are indeed claims made, with no more than speculative reconstruction to support them, to the effect that additional songs, of which traces are fairly apparent to the practised eye, did hold some place in the worship service of the apostolic church. Certain writers from as far back as Michaelis down to Ralph Martin, have seen in the rhythmical flow and special vocabulary of, for example, Ephesians 5.14, Colossians 1.15–20, I Timothy 3.1–16, and II Timothy 2.11, a degree of evidence for viewing these passages as the bits and pieces of former apostolic church hymns. 'If by rhythmical flow,' says Dr. James Gibson to the contrary, 'is meant euphonious Greek, we cordially assent. But we engage to find hymns in every chapter, if not verse, of Paul's epistles, if we indulged in such a fancy' (*Public Worship of God: Its Authority and Modes*, p. 50). More recently, William Hendriksen—and he makes special reference to Colossians I—has adopted the following view: 'These characteristics do not prove, whether, on the one hand, we are dealing here with a hymn or other liturgical unit or whether, on the other hand, we have here an example of Paul's own preaching concerning the glory of Christ. A hymnal unit is obtained only after considerable reconstruction of the text.' (*Exposition of Colossians and Philemon*, p. 68). James Pennington's conclusion is the same: This passage represents simply 'a great Christological confession, composed by the apostle Paul, and not intended for use in public worship as a hymn of praise to God' (An Exposition of Colossians

I.15–20. Art. Symposium: *The Biblical Doctrine of Worship*, Reformed Presbyterian Church of North America).

Another important point ought certainly to be mentioned. No divine commission and no divine gift seem ever to have been conferred in apostolic times, with the enlarging of the song praise repertoire of the Christian Church as its distinctive assignment. Old Testament precedent would, as a matter of course, lead us to expect that much. David, distinguished in his own day as 'the sweet psalmist of Israel,' was both specially ordained and appropriately inspired to satisfy the minimum fitness requirement for the specific duties of hymnodic office. Unique functions and gifts of this nature were as mentionable in their proper place, it would seem, as those which belonged specially to the kingly, priestly, or prophetic class of offices. Yet in the listed diversities of Christian gifts, whether ordinary or extraordinary, as given to us by Paul, there is no hint of any endowment which would have for its specific task the composition of a new range of hymns, with whatever supposed adjustment to whatever supposed special requirement of the worship of the Christian Church. Everything considered, the impression left with us from the apostle's references to 'psalms and hymns and spiritual songs' is that of a pre-existing stock of songs. This moreover is something which fits, as nothing whatever otherwise seems to fit, the well-understood function of the Book of Psalms in the worship of the apostolic church.

It is the biggest soldier in the squad whose absence from parade is the least easy to conceal. What strikes one at once on any reading of the literature associated with the 'hymn fragment' way of thinking, is the lack of any obvious theology, certainly of any structured theology, of Christian worship. Neither technical competence on the language side, nor possession of imaginative literary insight—both of these excellent gifts being available almost to a fault with the school of thought now in mind—can themselves compensate for a serious deficiency of this nature. There are, all in all, two main criticisms from which the 'hymn fragment' theory has not succeeded in freeing itself:

(a) Ingenious conjecture in whatever quantity is a distinctly different thing from reasonable evidence. And that we still await.

(b) The regulative principle of worship, if it is in fact seriously entertained, is certainly not noticeably applied.

Professor John Murray, writing in partnership with Dr. William Young, sums up the case for inspired psalmody, as Young and he see it, in the following set of propositions:

'(1) There is no warrant in Scripture for the use of uninspired human compositions in the singing of God's praise in public worship.
(2) There is explicit authority for the use of inspired songs.
(3) The songs of divine worship must therefore be limited to the songs of Scripture, for they alone are inspired.
(4) The Book of Psalms has provided us with the kind of compositions for which we have the authority of Scripture.
(5) We are therefore certain of divine sanction and approval in the singing of the Psalms.
(6) We are not certain that other inspired songs were intended to be sung in the worship of God, even though the use of other inspired songs does not violate the fundamental principle in which Scripture authorization is explicit, namely, the use of inspired songs.
(7) In view of the uncertainty with respect to the use of other inspired songs we should confine ourselves to the Book of Psalms.' (*Minority report: O.P. Church committee.*)

The two points which conclude the list contain a certain degree of special interest, and Professor Murray has developed the viewpoint they express in another context. This, for the sake of completeness, may be stated briefly in the following way:

(a) The offer to us, by the Holy Spirit, of a specific book of psalms may well indicate that there is no need to choose our songs of praise from other portions of Scripture.
(b) The Book of Psalms includes a number of songs which occur elsewhere in the Old Testament, but excludes certain others in the same category. This itself may supply the caution that the Christian Church is not free to select its materials of praise, except from a book which has been specially designated, and whose component parts have been specially gathered, for that identical purpose (Offered in private conversation).

The Regulative Principle versus Instrumental Music
Main-stream views must limit once again the breadth of treatment it is possible, in the space remaining, to provide. Considerable agree-

ment exists, in fact, certainly on the claim itself that Scripture excludes instrumental music from the church's worship, but also on the type of evidence which Scripture is believed to supply by way of support.

The governing principle, as before, is that 'nothing is to be introduced in the worship of God but what is prescribed in the Holy Scriptures.' One slight adjustment only, occurring where the principle is actually applied to the case, falls to be noticed. For, while there is, no hint of genuine warrant present in Scripture for the use in the Christian church of human hymns, there is at least, the appearance of support for instrumental music. This practice did, after all, enjoy a function in the Old Testament order of public worship which was quite meticulously covered by approving sanctions. Any argument, therefore, presuming to decide that the practice has no legitimate place today in the church's worship, must reckon strictly with the earlier state of affairs. The logical skeleton of the case which is raised against the practice of instrumental music can be stated briefly, as follows:

(1) Instrumental music considered as an element in religious worship was:
   (a) instituted by divine commandment;
   (b) practised as a branch of Levitical service in tabernacle and temple;
   (c) performed by the Levitical order exclusively.
(2) But the distinctive features of the Levitical system, the type giving place in Gospel times to the correlative anti-type, have been abolished.
(3) Instrumental music, being strictly a part of the self-same system of worship, has also, therefore, now been abolished.
(4) No New Testament prescription, effectively restoring instrumental music again to the church's worship, can be distinguished.
(5) The practice has no legitimate place, accordingly, in the worship of the Christian Church.

Churches who hold to these views or similar ones pick their way, it would seem judiciously, through a variety of occurrences of instrumental music in the national history of Israel. Thus Miriam's timbrel-players (who also incidentally danced) and the minstrel element in the school of the prophets, are not seen to be associated in Scripture in any way with the ordinary worship of the Jewish

Church. The sound of the silver trumpets, which were specially designed for marching and military occasions, for the calling of public assemblies, and for marking the onset of festal occasions, was not in any familiar sense, of course, instrumental music at all. The trumpets, besides, were priestly items of equipment.

It is the priestly and Levitical links, especially, of those Old Testament musical services, devised at first by David in response to divine command, that Christians who favour a service without such music tend to bring up. There is, for example, that supremely impressive ceremony at the dedication of Solomon's temple. The Levitical families of Asaph, Heman and Jeduthun are described as 'arrayed in white linen, having cymbals, psalteries and harps,' and as standing 'at the east end of the altar,' in company with a hundred and twenty trumpet-sounding priests. Repeatedly, indeed, in various other places throughout the books of Chronicles, there is this coupling of Levitical musical performances and trumpet-blowing with the distinctly sacrificial programme belonging to the temple. The instruments involved in this, therefore, for all we are ever told to the contrary, were as thoroughly Levitical in their function as altar, or incense, or priestly washings of hands and of feet.

John Girardeau, who writes with impressive learning on this subject, distinguishes (1) the generic or essential elements of worship in the Jewish system from (2) the typical and symbolic elements. Under class (1), which were intended for permanent observance, he lists, the reading and exposition of God's Word, exhortation, prayers, the singing of psalms and the giving of alms. These were especially characteristic of the worship of Israel out in the country, in whose various districts, from very early times, synagogal worship was the established practice. Professor Girardeau invokes Psalm 74.8 at this point, which laments the burning up of 'all the synagogues of God in the land,' as one thread of evidence for his claim that such meeting-places did in fact exist, far back in Israel's national history. He further comments that 'the well-ascertained practice of post-exilic synagogues clearly established the absence of instrumental music from those weekly assemblies' (Instrumental Music in Public Worship, pp. 41–49).

Under class (2), comprising the typical and symbolic elements of worship, Girardeau places the various specifications which belonged uniquely to the temple service. Strictly temporary functions of the Jewish system of worship, these filled out the entire Levitical programme of pageantry, ritual and symbolic act. And instrumental music, distinct as one component among the many which served the temple order of public worship, not only fulfilled an eminent ritual function, but carried a degree of typical significance, above and beyond. It foreshadowed, as a symbol standing in its own right, some feature or other of those ultimate Gospel arrangements, which, in respect of actual history, were yet to come.

Irrespective of one's viewpoint, Girardeau's analysis of the type-inspired anatomy of the Jewish temple is a fine effort, and highly instructive. He points out, interestingly, a number of temple-types which had Christ specially in view, others which had the Holy Spirit, and others yet again which had both Christ and the Holy Spirit, at one and the same time, in their view. Referring miscellaneous instances of washing with water and anointing with oil, specifically as types, to the Holy Spirit, he brackets instrumental music firmly together with them, as possessing the same general significance. The temple music he regards as generally typical of 'the joy and triumph of God's believing people, resulting from the plentiful effusion of the Holy Ghost in New Testament times.' The Spirit could not be given in such copious measure to the church of God, until the reconciling sacrifice of Christ had actually come to pass. And it pleased God, Girardeau adds, 'to typify the spiritual joy to spring from a richer possession of the Holy Ghost, through the sensuous rapture engendered by stringed instruments, and the clash of cymbals, by the blare of trumpets, and the ringing of harps. It was God's instruction in a lower school preparing them for a higher.' And the fact that the apostolic church, evangelical and spiritual of settled intent in their worship of God, did not incorporate instrumental music at all as an element in the new christian code of practice, is seen as the ultimate item of proof which this particular view of the question would certainly need to support its case.

Calvin, commenting on Psalm 92, would regard it as 'burying the light of the Gospel, should we introduce the shadows of a departed dispensation.' He is referring especially to instrumental music. It belonged to the worship of the Old Testament, and that, he adds, 'was figurative and terminated with the Gospel.' The basic assumption which is being countered by those who hold Calvin's view is, as Girardeau says, that 'what God has approved at a certain place, at a certain time, and in certain circumstances, He approves at all places, at all times, and in all circumstances.' The assumption plainly is not true (*Instrumental Music in Public Worship*, pp. 49–64).

The 150th Psalm

Psalm 150, which contains that joyful summons to the church to worship the Lord, and to employ in the sacred process a whole orchestra, it would seem, of musical instruments, has traditionally figured as a ready-to-hand device for presbyterian-baiting. 'How can you do it?' it is exclaimed. 'How can you sing, with any integrity of heart, a psalm which cheerfully canvasses support from timbrels and harps and organs, and yet exhibit, as you always do, the most dogged resistance to their actual use in the public worship of the church?

The dilemma, while a perfectly fair one to pose, is not actually viewed, by those who defend the simple service, with any particular qualms, of mind or of conscience. Their system of thought has ample capacity, so they believe, for absorbing the dilemma, quite without trace. For in terms of that system. the musical references of the 150th Psalm are held to be carrying, for Gospel times, an exclusively figurative force. The place of symbolic turns of speech and of spiritualized echoes of meaning, in any case, is too well and widely accredited as normal, in the language and literature of the Christian church, for this idea to be scouted simply as absurd. Nor is the problem seen to be specially complicated by the fact that the musical references in question bespoke, at one stage in the life of the church, certain actual musical performances, though they are taken to imply now, with the coming of the Christian era, matters that are of strictly spiritual significance. Instrumental music, it is believed, does no more than share, in these respects, a distinction which belongs to every separate item of Old Testament typical ritual. Nobody has any problem, in fact, when the Epistle to the Hebrews calls upon Christians to 'go forth, therefore, unto Jesus without the camp', or when it asserts that we Christians 'have an altar whereof they have no right to eat that serve the tabernacle'. Nobody is puzzled at the advice 'to offer to God continually the sacrifice of praise, the fruit of our lips.' Nor does the same epistle's insistence that Christian believers 'are come to Mount Zion, the city of the living God' provoke the retort, 'But only a few Christians surely have ever visited the Holy Land!' And it lies in the same evangelical formula, to adopt language of that nature, as it does to sing of hyssop and cherubim and evening sacrifices, or, as it does again, to sing of cymbals and psalteries and organs.

To be literalistic with respect to the 150th Psalm, or any such psalm, would pose some serious difficulties for the Christian use of Isaiah 35, 53 and 55, or for the extraction of any Christian meaning from such things as white stones, golden candlesticks, stars, trumpets, harps, incense and foundations of jasper, which meet one in quite glorious profusion everywhere in the Book of Revelation. The use of figurative language is a supremely useful aid, actually, as the whole history of poetry will avouch, where the higher reaches of thought, imagination and feeling impose their distinctive claims upon a man.

This is true, undoubtedly, of Christian praise and worship. Take the Book of Revelation again. A conspicuously Christian document from beginning to end, it presents to the reader's eye, at one superb climax in the succession of resplendent visions given to John, a heavenly scene with which there is associated for the ear of the observer 'the voice of harpers harping with their harps.' In simple but masterly brush-movements the prophetic canvas is portraying at this point the full development of a capacity for both joy and praise in equal measure, which properly belongs to those who as the vision itself states, 'were redeemed from the earth.' Clearly from the Christian reader there is expected no unusual subtlety of mind to be able to grasp the essentials of that situation. Indeed, to be a fully proficient visitor to such a gallery, he would require no more than an average man's acqaintance with the type of imagery which regularly figures as the natural and looked for accompaniment of all Hebrew language and literature. He would not, as a Christian interpreter, experience the hint of a difficulty when confronted by those Johannine harpers if he had encountered in the Old Testament little more than the corresponding troupe of Davidic tympanists and harpists of Psalm 150. It is their joyous procession across the picture which enlivens the Psalm immeasurably, as a salvation song of purest praise. 'He only understands Virgil's *ECLOGUES*,' says Luther, 'who has lived with the shepherds: and he who will understand a poet must travel to the poet's country.'

The alleged negotiable 'circumstances' of the Confession of Faith

Chapter I, and section 6, of the Confession of Faith states that 'there are some circumstances concerning the worship of God . . . common to human actions and societies, which are to be ordered by the light of nature and Christian prudence, according to the general rules of the Word, which are always to be observed.' And the attempt has been made, from time to time, conjointly with a full acceptance of the regulative principle of worship, to obtain confessional coverage for human hymns and instrumental music on the ground that they belong to the negotiable 'circumstances' envisaged above. The argument is not, however, a valid one, and for at least two straightforward reasons:

(1) The Bible, as we saw at an earlier stage, has itself coupled up the questions, both of instrumental music and hymnodic composition, with the principle of divine commandment. It becomes, therefore, a matter of man not being free to put asunder what God Himself has joined together. The position is not negotiable.

(2) Neither instrumental music nor the singing of hymns falls into the category of circumstances which are 'common to human actions and societies.' The proof texts for this particular section of the Confession (I Cor. II.13–14; 14.26–40) indicate that the circumstances referred to are, as Professor James Thornwell says, 'those concomitants of an action without which it either cannot be done at all, or cannot be done with decency and decorum' (*Collected Writings*, Vol. 4, pp. 244 ff. Quoted by Girardeau, op. cit., p. 151).

Conclusion

Luther's note about 'the poet's country' indicates in principle what most of all colours the attitude of the Free Church to the whole question of public worship. The overruling concern is for the Bible itself to be its own interpreter, so that conceptions and considerations that are foreign to it are not, on any account, imported into it. Laurentius Valla, who was one of the very earliest contributors to the Reformation movement in Europe, vigorously challenged, as an all-important first step, the system of Biblical interpretation which the mediaeval church had anciently maintained. It was Valla's earnest wish to eliminate 'the clamour of strangers in the presence of the Word of God.' A miracle of hearing had taken place in Europe, and men were listening with new-found intentness to what the Bible itself was actually teaching. The Church of Engalnd formularies were to say the essential thing: being determined very specially, 'never to expound one place of Scripture so that it be repugnant to another.'

Assuming then, to go back at this point to the main thesis, that the Bible genuinely does teach a regulative principle of worship, it is the Bible itself, and no other, which turns the question of 'hymns and organs' into something which is insistent and acute and urgent, instead of being routine, pottering and far down the scale of possible questions. It is the Bible itself which gives to the question a compelling twist and demands of Christians, whether 'hymns and organs' are not, in point of fact, repugnant to its own regulative principle of worship: hymns, since there is no evidence they were ever authorized: organs, since they belonged, as Calvin says, to 'the shadows of a departed dispensation.'

Most people within the Free Church, if we may hazard that guess, are content that its present practical position on worship should remain. Not anything like so many, it seems certain, believe that a principle is involved, according to which this position is lifted from the lower level of acceptable tradition to the higher one of mandatory Christian commitment. It is in fact sometimes argued by Free Church people that what may be safe or expedient, or binding on the Free Church as its documents stand, does not necessarily place the Christian conscience under any changeless obligation to it. In the same vein of questioning ancient assumptions attention is drawn to the claim, officially made for Free Church worship, that it is 'founded on the Word of God, and agreeable thereto.' This, it is suggested, may mean no more than it is a Biblically laudable thing for church-people to offer to God in worship the singing of Psalms, and to opt, if they wish, not to have music. And who could question such practice so far as it goes? What remains unanswered, is whether hymns or organs or both together may not equally be found to agree with the Word of God. Considered in this light, it is argued, the present practice of the Free Church may carry no necessary implications for what is practised outside: no necessary implications, if it comes to that, for Free Church people themselves, who are likely to worship, from time to time, in other fellowships which have other practices.

On the face of it this appears reasonable. The trouble is, though, that the expression 'founded on the Word of God and agreeable thereto' cannot be interpreted in isolation. It has to be understood contextually, which certainly means reading it in the closest possible connection with the regulative principle of worship already noticed, and to which we are confessionally bound. It equally compels us to come to terms with those inferences which, rightly or wrongly, our Presbyterian forefathers considered that principle to require. The conclusion they arrived at, we may recall, envisaged the exclusive use of inspired songs, without instrumental accompaniment, as the one authentic medium of public praise.

But if this stringent interpretation be accepted, where then do we stand when it comes to holding church fellowship among Christian bodies whose mode of worship diverges significantly from our own? Well, why not attempt, as a first step, to assess the status of the externals of Christian worship (to which category of obligation congregational praise belongs) in relation to all other types of Christian obligation that there are?

It is of course a Biblical axiom that the various laws which are imposed upon us by God differ from one another in relative dignity and importance, and that, wherever a conflict may occur, the law which lies lower down on the scale must yield precedence to the one higher up. Positive and ceremonial duties, for example, must defer to those that are of moral significance. Students of Scripture are well aware that the normal rule for Sabbath-keeping could be breached, or some external observance of the temple's worship be suspended, wherever the demands of mercy might render it necessary. The retrieval of one's animal from a pit on the Sabbath day, and the eating by David, in the extremity of hunger, of the hallowed shewbread, are well-known cases in point. 'I will have mercy' said God 'and not sacrifice.' With that in mind, we could go on to ask whether the presumed obligation to use only inspired materials of praise, unaccompanied by instruments—this being a prescription which blends both positive and ceremonial elements—may not on occasion be suspended, in the interests let us say of promoting the communion of saints (an ongoing moral obligation), or to satisfy some other sufficiently presing dictate of love in the context of inter-church relations.

In the interval, and assuming the Free Church's standpoint relative to worship to be the correct one, we would owe it to our brethren to 'teach them the way of the Lord more perfectly.' To proclaim the bare facts of our distinctive position is hardly the same thing as patient demonstration. At any rate, the suggested turn to the debate which has just been indicated, and which assumes the classical presbyterian application of the regulative principle, may very well repay a closer look.

To sort out the implications of the regulative principle of worship means coming to grips with a variety of confessional, exegetical and theological matters of importance. Meantime, whatever our remaining differences of opinion over this subject, the temptation to distrust one another ought to give way to mutual respect, dogmatism to dispassionate research, party spirit to co-operative effort, and the fascination of the quick verdict to the cool and sober reflection that real progress in theology has never been easy. Given these conditions, and with due dependence on the divine help, we may reasonably hope to reach some decent consensus of viewpoint in the end of the day.

Bibliography

D. Calderwood, *The Pastor and the Prelate*, Presbyterian's Armoury, Vol. 3.

J. Calvin, *Commentary on the Psalms*.

R. S. Candlish, *The Organ Question*, Johnstone & Hunter, Edinburgh 1866.

G. N. M. Collins, *The Heritage of our Fathers*, The Knox Press, Edinburgh 1974.

H. Cooke, *The True Psalmody*, James Gemmell, Edinburgh 1883.

D. H. Fleming, 'The Hymnology of the Scottish Reformation,' *Works*, Vol. 3, Edinburgh 1884.

J. Gibson, *The Public Worship of God*, James Nisbet, London 1869.

J. L. Girardeau, *Instrumental Music in Public Worship*, Richmond 1888.

J. Macleod, *Scottish Theology*, Free Church Publications Committee, Edinburgh 1943.

J. MacNaughter, *The Psalms in Worship*, United Presbyterian Board of Publication, Pittsburgh 1907.

R. P. Martin, *Worship in the Early Church*, Marshall, Morgan and Scott, London 1964.

C. G. McRie, *The Public Worship of Presbyterian Scotland*, William Blackwood, Edinburgh and London 1892.

A. B. Mickelson, *Interpreting the Bible*, Eerdmans, Grand Rapids 1972.

J. Murray and W. Young, *Song in the Public Worship of God*, undated, Minority Report of Committee of Orthodox Presbyterian Church, U.S.A.

D. Neal, *History of the Puritans*, New York 1844.

——, *The Practice of the Free Church*, Knox Press, Edinburgh 1964.

——, *The Biblical Doctrine of Worship*, Symposium R.P. Church (N.A.) 1974, published by Reformed Presbyterian Church 1974.

Skinner, *Ecclesiastical History of Scotland*, 1788.

A. Stewart and J. K. Cameron, *The Free Church of Scotland*, Hodge Edinburgh and Glasgow 1910.

J. H. Thornwell, *Collected Writings*, Vol. 4, (Ed. J. B. Adger.) Richmond 1971–73.

——, *Westminster Confession of Faith* and *Directory for Public Worship*.

The Lord's Day

FERGUS A. J. MACDONALD, M.A., B.D.
Minister of Cumbernauld Free Church.

In Scotland Sunday is traditionally known as 'the Sabbath,' as well as 'the Lord's Day,' because the Scottish church, for at least three hundred years, has recognized the Lord's Day as the continuation into the New Covenant of the Old Testament Sabbath, albeit with certain modifications. This position is summed up by the Westminster Confession of Faith as follows: 'As it is of the law of nature, that, in general, a proportion of time be set apart for the worship of God; so, in His Word, by a positive, moral and perpetual commandment, binding men in all ages, He hath particularly appointed one day in seven for a sabbath, to be kept holy unto Him; which from the beginning of the world to the resurrection of Christ, was the last day of the week; and from the resurrection of Christ, was changed into the first day of the week, which in Scripture is called the Lord's Day, and is to be continued to the end of the world, as the Christian Sabbath' (XXI.7).

Recent years have seen a gradual, but radical, shift from this position, culminating in 1964 in the acceptance by the General Assembly of the Church of Scotland of the report prepared by its Church and Nation Committee on *The Christian Use of Sunday*. This report drew a fairly sharp distinction between the Jewish Sabbath and the Christian Sunday concluding that, 'the evidence of the New Testament for observing the Lord's Day as a day entirely distinct from the Sabbath, both in origin and purpose, is very strong.'

This growing tendency to regard the Sabbath as exclusively an Old Covenant institution and altogether different from the Lord's Day is by no means confined to Scotland or the British Isles. For several years a Committee of the Reformed Ecumenical Synod which embraces 36 churches with a world-wide membership of some five million, has been studying this problem. The majority of the Committee which reported to the 1972 Synod introduced their section of the report as follows: 'We as members who sign this report have been reared in churches which regarded Sunday as the Christian Sabbath. And we are not asking Synod to reject this view. But we feel compelled to point out that there are certain weaknesses in this doctrine which should make us hesitant to impose it upon the churches as the will of the Lord.'

This tendency leads, in turn, to a more liberal form of Lord's Day observance. The majority of the RES Committee went on to assert that, while Christians will desire to interrupt all their ordinary activities on the Lord's Day, 'nevertheless, ordinary activities do not become sinful because they are performed on the Sunday.' The Westminster Confession takes a different view: 'This Sabbath is then kept holy unto the Lord, when men after a due preparing of their hearts, and ordering of their common affairs beforehand, do not only observe an holy rest all the day from their own works, words and thoughts about their worldly employments and recreations; but also are taken up the whole time in the public and private exercise of his worship, and in the duties of necessity and mercy' (XXI.8).

In the face of this growing tendency to question the Westminster view of the Sabbath within churches which have traditionally upheld it, we must ask what is to be the reaction of the Free Church of Scotland which, from its inception in 1843, has unambiguously upheld the Lord's Day as the Christian Sabbath?

First of all, we must resist the temptation to resort to censorious criticism as a substitute for courteous Christian debate. To yield to it would be to repeat the mistake of the Pharisees who so devastatingly belie the simplistic equation that strictness equals correctness.

Secondly, and more positively, we must look again at the Scriptures in an effort to study the whole problem afresh, praying that the Holy Spirit, whom Jesus has given to his church to lead her into the truth might make clear the will of the Lord in this matter. The Scriptures alone are our ultimate authority.

Thirdly, we must recognize that this difference of opinion regarding the Sabbath arises from what appears to be a tension within the New Testament itself. On the one hand Paul calls it a shadow of things to come now fulfilled in Christ, while on the other, the apostolic church followed a seven-day week and observed the first day as belonging specially to Christ.

Fourthly, it should disturb us that Christians are divided in their understanding of the mind of Christ in relation to one of the ten commandments. The fact that some aspects of Scriptural truth are not immediately clear is no reason for abdicating our responsibility to seek a common understanding of them. Should we not see this, then, as a divinely-given challenge to our faith to claim the guidance of the Spirit according to Jesus' promise?

Principles of interpretation

Our first task is to define the basic principles of interpreting the Bible, with special reference to its division into two distinct testaments or dispensations, with their differing religious orders and institutions. Under the old covenant the church was a nation, and it looked forward to the coming of the Messiah (or the Christ). In contrast, under the new covenant the church is no longer a nation but a voluntary society composed of those from all nations who profess faith in Jesus as the Christ. This contrast is sharpened by the discontinuation in the New Testament church of many of the Old Testament forms of worship.

The difference between the old and the new dispensations must not, however, be exaggerated. When the New Testament speaks of the *new* covenant it nearly always uses the Greek word meaning 'renewed,' rather than that meaning 'completely different.' There is continuity as well as discontinuity. For example, the simple form of synagogue worship became the pattern for Christian worship, and the Old Testament institution of the eldership was adopted by the Christian church, even in Gentile areas.

But the line between what was to be discontinued and what was to be carried over was not always clear. How then are we to approach this area of uncertainty? Are there any criteria by which we may distinguish the permanent from the merely preparatory, commands of the Old Testament?

A Commentary on the Confession of Faith by A. A. Hodge offers some very helpful guidance here: '(1) When the continued obligation of any commandment is asserted or practically recognized in the New Testament, it is plain that the change of dispensations has made no change in the law . . . . On the other hand, when the enactment is explicitly repealed, or its abrogation implied by what is taught in the New Testament, the case is also made plain. (2) Where there is no direct information upon the question to be gathered from the New Testament, a careful examination of the reason of the law will afford us good ground of judgment as to its perpetuity. If the original reason for its enactment is universal and permanent, and the law has never been explicitly repealed, then the law abides in force. If the reason of the law is transient, its binding force is transient also' (p. 255). These two principles rightly assume that the New Testament, as the later and fuller revelation, is to interpret the Old for us.

Let us see how Hodge's principles work. On the basis of the first principle, we are, for example, to regard the eighth commandment as still binding because of Matt. 5.21–26, but the prohibition of 'unclean' food as having been relaxed because of Mark 7.19b (RSV 'Thus he declared all foods clean'). On the basis of the second principle, the requirement of Deuteronomy 22.8 to build parapets on the roofs of houses, while no longer literally obligatory, does impose on us the duty to ensure personal safety on our property. However, many of the civil laws of Israel—e.g. the prohibition to wear garments of mixed cloth (Deut. 22.11)—and all the cere-monial ritual regulations, relate only to the historical setting and religious circumstances of the time, and, therefore, are not binding on the Christian.

We must now apply these two criteria to the Sabbath. So, first of all we must ask, Does the New Testament ratify or abrogate the Sabbath? And, if this question cannot be answered with certainty, we will have to go on to ask a second, Was the original reason for the Sabbath commandment permanent or transient?

The New Testament
In order to ascertain the New Testament's attitude to the Sabbath we shall have to look, in turn, at the teaching and practice of Jesus, and the teaching and practice of the early church.

JESUS AND THE SABBATH
The conflicts between James and the Scribes and Pharisees over the Sabbath are prominently reported in all four gospels. Obviously the evangelists were of the opinion that this was an important matter on which young converts (for whose instruction the gospels were originally written) should be informed. These conflicts re-volved round two issues. First, the incident in the cornfields when the disciples plucked the ears of grain on the Sabbath (Mark 2.22–28; Matt. 12.1–8; Luke 6.1–5). And second, the various healing miracles performed by Jesus on the Sabbath. There are seven such miracles recorded—the cripple at the pool of Bethesda (John 5.1–6), the demoniac in the synagogue at Capernaum (Mark 1.21–28), Peter's mother-in-law (Mark 1.29–31), the man with the withered hand (Mark 3.1–6), the blind man at Siloam (John 9.1–41), the woman with the spirit of infirmity (Luke 13.11–17), and the man

with the dropsy (Luke 14.1–6). In the cornfields incident it is the disciples who were accused of Sabbath breaking; in the case of the Sabbath miracles it is the Lord himself. These events, along with the sayings of Jesus which they gave rise to, provide us with a considerable amount of evidence on which to decide whether Jesus ratified or abrogated the Sabbath.

DID JESUS ABROGATE THE SABBATH?

The article on *sabbaton* in Kittel's *Theological Dictionary of the New Testament* maintains that the dialogue between Jesus and the Pharisees following the healing of the cripple at Bethesda (John 5) affords conclusive proof that Jesus abolished the Sabbath. Verse 18 is regarded as crucial: 'therefore the Jews sought the more to kill him, because he not only had broken the Sabbath, but said also that God was his father, making himself equal with God.' The Greek verb *luo*, which literally means 'to loose,' and is translated here as 'broken,' sometimes means 'to abrogate,' as, e.g. in Matt. 5.19 (RSV 'relax,' NEB 'set aside'). It is contended that this must be the meaning here since Jesus justifies his healing on the Sabbath by asserting that God the Father works on the Sabbath, 'My Father worketh hitherto and I work' (v. 17). The argument is that Jesus revokes the Sabbath commandment by declaring that God is working on the Sabbath, and not resting as the commandment assumes. This repeal of a divine commandment led to the Jewish charge of making himself equal with God.

However, this interpretation of John 5 is open to very serious question. Let us look at the facts in turn. First, the meaning of the verb *luo*. Most English translations understand it here in the sense in which it is used in 7.23—also in relation to the Sabbath—of 'to infringe.' The use of the imperfect tense ('was breaking') supports this, and suggests that the verb refers to Jesus' habitual action of healing on the Sabbath rather than to the saying in the previous verse specifically spoken on this occasion.

Secondly, the statement that Jesus broke the Sabbath is not the opinion of the Fourth Evangelist, but of the Jews.

Thirdly, the charge that Jesus claimed equality with God should probably be distinguished from that of breaking the Sabbath ('not only . . . but also'). The saying in v. 17 in which Jesus puts his activity on a par with the Father's would have provided sufficient grounds in the Pharisees' eyes for formulating the charge of blasphemy.

Fourthly, had Jesus abrogated the Sabbath we would expect him to have been charged with this offence at his trial. But in fact his enemies found it impossible to sustain a genuine charge of any kind.

Fifthly, if Jesus did abrogate the Sabbath on this occasion, then the manner in which he did this is in sharp contradiction to his declared relationship to the Old Testament law. He came to fulfil the law, not to destroy it (Matt. 5.17). When this messianic fulfilment took the form of rendering the ceremonial aspects of the law unnecessary and obsolete, it was always on the grounds that with his coming their preparatory role had been exhausted, and never that he questioned or denied their original divine authorization. Surely, then, it would be most surprising to find him here abrogating the Sabbath in terms of contradiction rather than of fulfilment! But in fact there is no contradiction. Jesus is simply reminding the Pharisees that God's Sabbath rest involves his preserving and governing the completed creation, and that in consequence he himself is perfectly justified in sustaining created life on the Sabbath day.

This dialogue in John 5 illustrates well the fundamental rift between Jesus and many of his contemporaries on Sabbath observance. For them Sabbath observance was essentially cessation from all avoidable activity. But Jesus saw it as a day for doing the work of God. Deliberately and regularly he defied the scribal law by tending non-emergency cases of illness on the Sabbath. His quarrel was with the Scribes and Pharisees, not with the fourth commandment itself.

DID JESUS RATIFY THE SABBATH?

We must now enquire whether there is positive evidence that our Lord ratified the Sabbath. It is clear that he and his disciples regularly attended the synagogue on the Sabbath and that he often preached during the service (Mark 1.21–22; 1.39; 6.2; Luke 4.16–21; 13.10; John 6.59; 18.20). And his several sayings about the Sabbath suggest that this practice involved much more than religious convention and evangelistic opportunism.

The climax of the group of Jesus' sayings which arose out of the cornfields incident is undoubtedly the sentence, 'the Son of Man is Lord of the Sabbath.' It is recorded by all three synoptic gospels and may be alluded to in the fourth (John 9.35). Closely associated with it is the well-known saying (recorded only by Mark), 'The Sabbath was made for man, and not man for the Sabbath' (Mark

2.27). The sayings found in the Sabbath healing accounts are perhaps summed up by that uttered immediately before the healing of the man with the withered hand, 'It is lawful to do good on the Sabbath' (Matt. 12.12 RSV). These three sayings encapsulate Jesus' teaching on the Sabbath, and a close study of them in their contexts will show that he believed that the Sabbath possessed both a divine authority and a humanitarian purpose.

First of all, Jesus' emphasis on the *divine authority of the Sabbath*. His declaration that 'the Son of Man is Lord of the Sabbath' was made in order to explain by what authority he had pronounced his disciples 'guiltless' (Matt. 12.7) after the Pharisees had accused them of doing 'that which is not lawful to do on the Sabbath day' (Matt. 12.2). He asserts his messianic Lordship of the Sabbath over against the authority claimed by the Scribes to determine what is lawful and what is unlawful on the Sabbath. According to the Scribes, the disciples were guilty of Sabbath-breaking on four counts—they were reaping, they were threshing—for they plucked the ears of grain (Matt. 12.1)—they were winnowing ('rubbing them in their hands,' Luke 6.1), and they were preparing a meal. They argued that the Mosaic prohibitions of these activities on the Sabbath, by implication condemned the disciples' action.

Clearly our Lord rejects this legalistic form of casuistry. But he does much more. He is in fact challenging the right of the Scribes to take it upon themselves to legislate for conscience. It is not they, but the Son of Man, who is Lord of the Sabbath, he reminds them. By adding to what was divinely written they were usurping the divine sovereignty over the Sabbath. So as God's special representative (the term 'Son of Man' is a messianic designation) Jesus asserts the *divine* sovereignty over the Sabbath.

Furthermore, Jesus found support for his acquittal of the disciples in the Scriptures. He cites three Old Testament passages in support of his more liberal interpretation of Sabbath observance. First, he refers to the account in 1 Samuel 21.6 of David's eating the shewbread when in dire hunger (Matt. 12.3). The incident was relevant not only on account of the parallel between David's hunger and that of the disciples (Matt. 12.1), but also because it, too, probably took place on the Sabbath. According to Leviticus 24.8 the supply of shewbread was to be replaced with fresh bread every Sabbath, and the 1 Samuel reference suggests that this had been done on the day of David's arrival. Next, Jesus alludes to passages such as Numbers 28.9–10 which prescribed extra sacrifices for the

Sabbath involving the priests in additional Sabbath work (Matt. 12.5–6). Thirdly, he quotes Hosea 6.6, 'I desire mercy and not sacrifice' (Matt. 12.7). This three-fold appeal to the Word of God underlines Jesus acknowledgment of the divine authority of the day of rest.

Jesus' second emphasis was on the *humanitarian purpose of the Sabbath*. 'The Sabbath was made for man, not man for the Sabbath' (Mark 2.27). 'It is lawful to do well on the Sabbath days' (Matt. 12.12). Divine in origin, the Sabbath is humanitarian in purpose.

Our Lord is recalling that the Sabbath was given to help man in his physical weakness. Our physical constitution is such that we cannot live without the rest and recuperation which the Sabbath affords us. It is God's gift to us in our frailty. Thus the Pharisees are condemned by Jesus for perpetuating hunger by their Sabbath observance. It should be noted that the Greek verb *peinao* used in Matthew 12.1 indicates that the disciples were famishing, not merely peckish. The quotation of Hosea 6.6 makes it clear that in our Lord's view the Sabbath for the Pharisees was no longer an instrument of mercy, but a ritual in its own right, an end in itself, just as the sacrifices had become in the prophet's time.

Similarly Christ's deliberate choice of the Sabbath as a day particularly suited to healing, confirms this humanitarian aspect. It is a day for doing good. We fall into the error of the Pharisees if, when thinking of the Sabbath observance, we place 'works of mercy' on a level with 'works of necessity.' Works of necessity are unavoidable, but the works of mercy in which our Lord engaged were not. For him the Sabbath was a day particularly suited to performing works of mercy. He declared that the woman with an infirmity for eighteen years 'ought' to be loosed from her bond on the Sabbath day (Luke 13.16). To do well on the Sabbath is lawful not because it is permitted, but because it is commanded.

However, Jesus did not view the humanitarian purpose of the Sabbath only—or even principally—in terms of physical rest and healing. After all he taught that man cannot live by bread alone (Matt. 4.4). So we find him commending not only work which mediates mercy to the hungry and the ill as appropriate to the Sabbath, but also the work which is involved in worship. In the temple the priests profane the Sabbath, but, like his disciples in the cornfields, they are 'guiltless' (AV 'blameless'; the RSV preserves in English the link between verses 5 and 7 by translating the same Greek word 'guiltless' in both instances). A related saying is found in John 7.23 where Jesus reminds his enemies that the work involved in circumcising male infants born eight days previous to any Sabbath is justified in order that the ceremonial law be fulfilled.

The worship aspect of Sabbath observance played a relatively minor role in the Sabbath conflicts of Jesus not because Jesus considered it to be of lesser importance, but because it was not in dispute.

The keynote of Jesus' teaching and practice on the Sabbath seems to have been 'reform' rather than 'repeal,' for again and again he sought to purge it of Pharisaic distortions and restore it to its original spiritual purpose.

Of course, some would argue that the evidence of the gospels is of little importance to us, since, in his conflicts with the Jews, Jesus was simply meeting men on their own grounds. While it is conceivable that Jesus may have done this on occasion, to claim that this technique played a prominent role in his teaching method is surely to make him guilty of the slick oratory and mental adroitness which Paul shunned as utterly unworthy of the Christian message (1 Cor. 1.17 ff.). In fact Jesus relied no less on the authority of the Scriptures in his Sabbath teaching than in his own spiritual life, whether when facing the devil in the wilderness, or bearing the wrath of God upon the cross.

THE CHRISTIAN CHURCH AND THE SABBATH
Turning from the gospels to the Acts and the epistles, we find that the seventh day appears not to have been generally observed in the Christian Church. The general rule in all churches – Jewish and Gentile – was for believers to meet together for worship and fellowship on the first day. The questions we must seek to answer is this: Does this abandonment of the seventh day in favour of the first indicate the end of the Sabbath?

SEVEN-DAY WEEK
In reply we must, first of all, bear in mind that the new arrangement retained the Sabbath principle of one day in seven. The Lord's day was observed once every seven days, not once every three or every ten. This is more significant than it may appear at first sight, for it indicates that although the Jewish seven-day Sabbath was not laid upon the Gentile churches, the Jewish seven day week was. In the New Testament era the seven day week was not observed outside of Semitic and Egyptian spheres of

influence. The Romans had for centuries followed a clumsy three-fold division of the twenty-eight day month and the evidence available to us suggests that the seven day week was not adopted throughout the Roman empire until late in the first century. So H. P. Porter is almost certainly correct in his assertion that, 'The Corinthians would not have known what the First Day was unless he (Paul) had taught them' (*Day of Light*, p.18). Apparently the churches of Galatia were similarly instructed (1 Cor.16.1).

The seven-day week was determined by the Sabbath, and it is difficult to see why the week should be retained if the Sabbatic principle of one day in seven specially dedicated to the Lord was not still valid. If, as will be argued later, both the Sabbatic principle and the seven-day week are creation ordinances and, therefore, valid for all men in all ages of history, then Paul's action makes sense. On the other hand if these were not creation ordinances, as some maintain, we are presented with the very tricky problem of explaining why Paul should arbitrarily foist a purely Jewish convention on the Gentile churches, thus contradicting all that he said against the Judaizers.

It is possible, of course, that the adoption of the seven day planetary week throughout the Roman empire may have been earlier than known sources indicate. If so Paul's action could readily be understood in terms of prevailing custom. But even if this were the case we must ask why in Gentile churches—in Galatia, Corinth, Troas—the *Jewish* designation 'first day' was used instead of the Gentile designation 'Sunday'? Furthermore, Sunday was not the first, but the second, day of the planetary week which began on Saturday,—Saturn being regarded as the most powerful planet. Although the Christian church very soon accepted the names of days from the planetary week it resisted tenaciously that week's sequence, insisting that Sunday, and not Saturday, was the first day.

Although the New Testament has no explicit command to worship on the first day, this was undoubtedly the custom of the apostles and the early church. Their example should be sufficiently authoritative for us. Almost certainly an apostolic command lies behind this early practice. In Luke's account of Paul's visit to the church in Troas (Acts 20.6–12) we read that 'upon the first day of the week when the disciples came together to break bread, Paul preached unto them.' The vocabulary—'came together,' 'to break bread,' 'preached'—implies Christian worship. The reference in the

Corinthian letter to the collection for the famine-stricken Christians in Judea indicates that the Christian use of the day focused on service to one's fellows as well as on the worship of God—a striking correspondence with our Lord's use of the Sabbath. This is surely more than coincidence and warns us against dismissing out of hand the possibility of a connection between the Sabbath and the Lord's Day simply because this is not explicitly made by the New Testament.

LEGALISTIC SABBATARIANISM

Other evidence in favour of regarding the Sabbath as obsolete is allegedly found in Paul's teaching that for first-generation Jewish Christians, Sabbath observance is a matter of indifference (Rom. 14.5–6), and that for Gentile Christians it is tantamount to apostasy (Col. 2.16; Gal. 4.10).

One cannot be absolutely certain that Paul is here referring to the weekly Sabbath. The Colossian reference is to sabbaths in the plural, and in Galatians and Romans the more general term 'days' is used. Accordingly, some maintain that the references are to Jewish holy days other than the weekly Sabbath. But, although these days may have been included, it is more likely that the seventh day Sabbath is principally in view. The Greek plural *sabbata* signified a single Sabbath day when it reflected the Aramaic singular *sabbatha'* (cf. Mark 1.21; 2.23; 3.2–4), and its singular coordinates *'feast'* (AV 'holyday') and 'new moon' in Colossians suggest that this is the case here. Therefore, Fairbairn, Lightfoot and many others are probably correct in seeing the primary reference to be to weekly Sabbath days. There are, however, certain factors which make it precarious to read into these apostolic condemnations of Sabbatarianism the end of the Sabbath.

There is, for example, their background. Judaizers were seeking to impose Jewish customs on Gentile converts to Christ as conditions of their salvation. So what Paul is dealing with in these passages is not so much Sabbath observance as Sabbath perversion, which, we must recall, was as much a heresy under the Old Covenant as under the New (cf. Isaiah 1.13). Again, the general term 'days' in Galatians and Romans might be used with equal force against Lord's day observance as against Sabbath observance. But these passages can hardly mean that no day at all was to be specially observed in the churches, for Paul instructed the Galatians and the Corinthians to assemble on the first day (1 Cor. 16.1–2), and, although he was in Troas for seven days, it was on the first day that he and the disciples there met together for worship (Acts 20.6–7).

SHADOW OF THINGS TO COME

Colossians 2.16–17 classifies the Sabbath along with the dietary laws and ceremonial festivals of the old covenant as 'a shadow of things to come.' On the most natural reading of his words, Paul is saying that the Sabbath has been fulfilled in Christ. For him to say this of Jewish food and festivals is readily understandable in the light of our Lord's teaching on these matters. But not so his inclusion of the Sabbath, for, as we have seen, Jesus reaffirmed its divine authority and its humanitarian purpose. Are Jesus and Paul then in disagreement? Not if we see in Colossians 2.16 a reference to the Seventh-day Sabbath only. 'The Sabbath is here regarded not as it was primevally (Gen. 2.3) 'made for man' (Mark 2.27) . . . but as it was adopted to be a symbolic institution of the Mosaic Covenant, and expressingly adapted to the relation between God and Israel (Exodus 31.12–17). In that respect the Sabbath was abrogated.' (H. C. G. Moule, *Cambridge Bible, Colossians and Philemon*, pp. 109 f.). Because of its role as a sign of the old covenant 'it became necessary to assign to such Sabbaths—the Jewish seventh day of rest—a place among the things that were done away, and so far to change the ordinance itself as to transfer it to a different day, and even call it by a new name' (Patrick Fairbairn, *The Typology of Scripture*, Vol. 2, p. 147).

This interpretation of Colossians 2.16 is confirmed by the terms of Hebrews 4.9 which suggest that Christ's fulfilment of the Sabbath is not yet absolute and final. 'There remains a Sabbath rest for the people of God' (RSV). The great day of rest—the eternal Sabbath—although come in Christ, is not yet fully come.

When we look back over the ground we have covered in this section, what pattern emerges? First, that the Christian church adopted the seven day week of the Jews. Second, that it observed one day in seven—the first day—as the Lord's day. Third, that what we know of the church's activities on this day corresponds strikingly with the twin emphasis on worship and service of our Lord's Sabbath observance. Fourth, the Sabbath has been fulfilled in Christ, but is not yet consummated in the eternal rest of the people of God.

We feel that the cumulative effect of this evidence points towards the identification of the Lord's day with the Christian Sabbath. But it would be a rash person who would claim that thus far the case is proved. Nowhere does the New Testament explicitly record the Fourth commandment. Nor does it command Christians to rest from work on the Lord's day. This silence may well be explained by the impracticability of first day Christian rest in a hostile society. But we cannot be sure. For this reason it is impossible, from the New Testament itself, to assert with certainty that the Lord's day is the Christian Sabbath.

The Old Testament

It is for this reason that we must now go back to Hodge's second principle and ask, What was the original purpose of the Sabbath? The answer the Bible gives to this question is crucial to our enquiry, for as the Reformed Ecumenical Synod Committee observes, 'all problems relating to our subject hinge on the question whether or not the Sabbath is a creation ordinance.' If it is, it has a universal significance and continuing obligation. If not, it is merely a statute belonging exclusively to the ceremonial ritual and civil order of the Jewish nation.

IS THE SABBATH A CREATION ORDINANCE?

On the face of it there seems to be little doubt as to how the Old Testament answers this question for it traces the origins of the Sabbath back to the creation of the world. This is the case in both the creation narrative in Genesis 2 and the fourth commandment in Exodus 20. Genesis 2.3 tells us that it was at the foundation of the world that, 'God blessed the seventh day and sanctified it.' Along with marriage it was revealed as an integral part of God's will for men from the very beginning. In passing it might be noted that the seven-day week, as well as the Sabbath which defined it, seems to have been regarded as a creation ordinance. (The Hebrew word for 'week' comes from the same root as 'seven' and means 'a period of seven days'). The rhythm of six days of work followed by one of rest is the divine blueprint for mankind's activities for it reflects God's own activity during and after the work of creation. The rhythm of divine activity is to be reflected in the rhythm of human activity. The Sabbath commandment rests on the same fundamental premise of all biblical ethics,—viz., that man's duty is to imitate God (cf. 1 Peter 1.16; Matt. 5.48).

The fourth commandment also regards the Sabbath as a creation ordinance. It commands us to keep the Sabbath holy. Why? Because 'in six days the Lord made heaven and earth and all that in them is, and rested the seventh day' (Exodus 20.11). The point could scarcely be made more clearly. Furthermore, the introductory phrase 'remember the Sabbath day' assumes that the Sabbath was instituted before Sinai.

If the Sabbath is indeed a creation ordinance we would expect it to be found in the *moral* law of Israel. And this is in fact the case, for it is an integral part of the decalogue which was clearly demarcated from the purely ceremonial and civil laws in the Mosaic code in the following ways:

First, the ten words alone were spoken by the Lord directly to the people 'And the Lord spake all these words, saying . . .' (Exodus 20.1–19; cf. Deut. 5.22). Secondly, of all the Mosaic legislation only they were engraved on tables of stone (Exodus 34.28; cf. 32.19; Deut. 4.13; 5.22; 10.4). Thirdly, only these two tables were accorded the honour of being placed within the Ark of the Covenant below the mercy seat in the most holy place of the sanctuary. The decalogue is thus differentiated from the other Mosaic laws because it is the *moral* law of God, a republication of the creation ordinances or life-norms given to the human race at the beginning of history. And this differentiation led the Westminster Assembly to regard the Sabbath as 'of the law of nature' and its sanctification as 'a positive, moral and perpetual commandment, binding men in all ages.'

However, there are many who maintain that Genesis 2 and Exodus 20 only *appear* to teach that the Sabbath is a creation ordinance, and that in fact it was a later and purely Jewish rite.

Some arrive at this conclusion as a result of questioning the integrity of the text in both passages. Neither passage, they contend, is a literary unity, but rather an interweaving of several different sources brought together nearer the end than the beginning of Old Testament history. This view, known as the documentary hypothesis, identifies Genesis 2.2–3 as belonging to a source originating sometime after the exile in Babylon in the sixth century B.C. On this view the presentation of the Sabbath as a creation ordinance in Genesis and Exodus is no more than a pious reconstruction in which doctrines, later associated with the Sabbath, were read back into the narrative of ancient events. The documentary hypothesis seeks to accommodate the Pentateuch to pre-conceived theories of the evolution of Israel's religion, and raises fundamental issues which we do not have time to go into here. We shall, therefore, restrict our survey of arguments against the Sabbath as a creation ordinance to those which respect the integrity of Scripture.

Some regard the account in Genesis 2.2–3 of God's blessing and sanctifying the Sabbath as a prospective reference to the fourth commandment to be imposed on the Israelites later. There is, we are told, no specific command in the passage to observe the Sabbath. However, this interpretation does not take the passage in its most natural sense, which surely is that man is to follow God's example by observing Sabbath rest. Further, the divine example would have been sufficient ground of obligation for unfallen man. Before the Fall it was not necessary for all divine commandments to be formally enacted. And finally, it is surely highly unlikely that God would have ordered his whole method of procedure at the creation of all things simply to facilitate the later establishment of a temporary ritual.

Others maintain that the creation narrative cannot be taken as normative in any universal sense for the observance of weeks and the consecration of one day in seven, because, according to them, the creation week of God's work and rest is not of the same order as our calendar time. Genesis 1.1–2.3 simply casts its description of the divine activity into the 'conceptual mode' of a week. But surely whether or not the creation week can be regarded in exactly the same terms as our calendar week is beside the point which is that the pattern, or rhythm, of the creation process is, by divine arrangement, reflected in the pattern, or rhythm, of our calendar week. The seventh day of God's post-creation rest need not be identical with the seventh day of our weekly cycle in order to be the prototype of the latter. The most natural reading of the passage would suggest that the seventh day of Genesis 2.2 belongs to the creation week and the seventh day of Genesis 2.3 is that of the calendar week.

For some, a strong argument against the creation ordinance doctrine is the absence of all reference to the Sabbath commandment in the biblical record covering the centuries between Genesis 2 and Exodus 16. It is true that we are not explicitly told that the Patriarchs observed the Sabbath, although there is evidence that they divided time into periods of seven days (Genesis 7.4–10; 8.10–12) and that weeks were known in Padan-Aram (Genesis 29.27–28) and in Egypt (Genesis 50.10–11). But arguments from silence are unreliable and, in this case, by no means conclusive, for any disregard for the Sabbath on the part of the patriarchs would no more dis-prove its divine appointment than their polygamy would deny that monogamous marriage was a creation ordinance. The unsatis-factory nature of this kind of argument can also be demonstrated from later history, for the accounts of the period from Sinai to the days of Elisha—which covers several centuries—contain no refer-ence to the Sabbath either.

None of the evidence we have cited so far would justify us in interpreting Genesis 2.2–3 in any other way than in its most natural sense—viz. that God instituted the Sabbath for man at the creation of the world. However, we have still to consider two further argu-ments often cited against this conclusion. They concern the clear ceremonial overtones in the Mosaic legislation about the Sabbath and the typological use of the Sabbath in both testaments. We shall now turn to each of these in turn.

A COVENANT SIGN

It cannot be denied that the Sabbath was a covenant sign between the Lord and Israel (Exodus 31.13), a mark distinguising the Jews from other nations. As such it celebrated the deliverance of Israel from slavery in Egypt to become the people of God (Deut. 5.15). However, this later adoption of the Sabbath as a sign of God's covenant with Israel does not contradict the creation ordinance doctrine any more than the adoption of the rainbow as the sign of the Noahic covenant implied that sunlight refracted differently through water before that covenant was made. Nor does a practice require to be exclusive to Israel to become a sign of God's covenant with her, for circumcision, the sign of the Abrahamic covenant, was widely practised in the ancient world by other nations.

To regard the Sabbath purely as a sign of God's covenant with Israel is to isolate one of the ten commandments as possessing a different *genre* from the other nine which are universally regarded as being moral and permanent. But surely this is to put asunder what God has joined together! As we have seen, the decalogue was clearly distinguished from the ceremonial laws. How strange then that the Sabbath should have been misplaced! The fact that Script-ure tends to regard the moral law as an organic unity—to keep one commandment is to keep all and to break one is to break all—should warn us against imposing arbitrary divisions.

To regard the fourth commandment as possessing the same moral *genre* as the other nine is not to deny that there were aspects of Sabbath legislation which were indeed purely ceremonial or civic and, therefore, of temporary validity. There were, after all, ceremonial and civic ramifications of most of the ten commandments, e.g. the Mosaic regulations governing the offence of adultery. Into this category fell the regulations governing the Sabbath sacrifices, new moon Sabbaths, the Sabbatical year, and the sanction of capital punishment for Sabbath-breaking (Exodus 35.2; cf. Numbers 15.35). Indeed some of the Sinaitic legislation surrounding the Sabbath probably fell into desuetude after the nomadic life of the wilderness years had passed, The prohibition to leave one's tent (Exodus 16.29) was specifically related to the gathering of manna which ceased at the conquest, and the prohibition to kindle a fire (Exodus 35.3) should probably also be understood against the background of life in the desert. Apparently not even the Sadduccees and the Pharisees considered it applicable in the cold wintry conditions of the Judean highlands, for Josephus, the Jewish historian of the first century, informs us that only the Essenes regarded Exodus 35.3 as perpetually binding.

SABBATH TYPOLOGY

We must now consider the argument that the typological use of the Sabbath implies its temporary validity. It is alleged that this places it in the same shadowy and preliminary category as the levitical sacrifices and laws on diet and hygiene. Now, as we have already seen, there are aspects of the Old Testament Sabbath which indeed have been fulfilled in Christ and are in consequence, no longer binding. But this cannot be said of the Sabbath institution as such, on typological grounds, for two reasons. First, in its original authorization there was nothing shadowy or typical of salvation. Man was unfallen, so as yet there was no need of salvation. Originally Sabbath typology was exclusively eschatological; only after the Fall did it assume soteriological significance. Second, while the writer to the Hebrews argues strongly that the sacrificial types have been completely fulfilled and done away with once for all in the death of Christ, in contrast he insists that the spiritual rest symbolized in the Sabbath still falls short in this life of complete fulfilment—'So then, there remains a sabbath rest for the people of God' (Hebrews 4.9, RSV).

It is helpful to compare the Sabbath with marriage in this regard. Both are creation ordinances, and, therefore, instituted before there was any need of redemption. Both were later taken as types of the end of salvation, the Sabbath of the eternal rest purchased for the people of God by Christ, and marriage of the union between Christ and his church (Ephesians 5.32). On the principle that the type remains until the antitype has come, both have continued and will continue as spiritual, viable institutions until that rest and union are consummated in the new order.

The prophets and the Sabbath

No survey of any aspect of Old Testament morality would be complete were it to ignore the prophets of the eighth century B.C. onwards. Fearlessly they denounced all legalistic reliance on form and ceremony, insisting that if men did not do justice, love mercy and walk humbly with God, then all their religious observances would be of no avail. The Sabbath, like the sacrifices and festivals, had become for many a religious end in itself. So inevitably its abuse was denounced by Isaiah along with the abuse of the sacrifices: 'To what purpose is the multitude of your sacrifices to me? saith the Lord . . . . Bring no more vain oblations; incense is an abomination unto me; the new moons and the sabbaths, the calling of assemblies, I cannot away with; it is iniquity, even the solemn meeting' (Isaiah 1.11–13).

In contrast one cannot but be impressed how Isaiah upholds the observance of the Sabbath as an integral part of the great *moral* responsibilities of man. 'Thus says the Lord: "Keep justice, and do righteousness . . . . Blessed is the man who does this, and the son of man who holds it fast, who keeps the Sabbath not profaning it, and keeps his hand from doing any evil" ' (Isaiah 56.1–2, RSV). Note how the prophet cites Sabbath keeping along with doing justice and righteousness.

Perhaps the best known Sabbatic passage in Isaiah is chapter 58.13–14 where the prophet urges us to honour the Sabbath and call it a delight. The Sabbath could not have been given a more elevated moral context, for these verses form the climax of the chapter which contains one of the most powerful moral appeals in all Scripture. The prophet 'places the keeping of the Sabbath on a level with the practice of love' (George Adam Smith, *The Book of Isaiah*, Vol. 2, p. 420). The older prophet Amos similarly gives the Sabbath a strong moral focus, albeit in a negative way, when he tells us that the merchants who found its strict observance unbearable were those who trampled on the needy, who dealt deceitfully with false balances and sold the poor for a pair of shoes

(Amos 8.4–6). This prophetic emphasis on the moral nature of the Sabbath commandment follows on logically from what we have already learned of the Sabbath as an integral part of the creation order and the moral decalogue. Of course, as we would expect the prophets—especially Ezekiel—also underlined the ceremonial aspects of the Sabbath as a sign of the old covenant (see Jeremiah 17.19–27; Ezekiel 20.12, 16, 20, 24; 22.8, 26; 23.28; 31.13, 17; 44.24), but this does not detract from the Sabbath as a moral commandment.

SIGNIFICANCE OF THE SABBATH

Thus far we have established that the Sabbath was a primitive and important moral commandment in the Old Testament. We must now go on to ask what was its significance? For it was no meaningless taboo, but a 'sign' which was intended to be understood helpfully by man.

First of all, the Sabbath was a reminder of man's origin as the creation of God. Its recognition of the need for physical rest reminds us that we are made from the dust and derive our physical life from God. Along with the seven day week it reflects the rhythm of the work of creation itself, regularly reminding us that we live in an ordered cosmos.

Secondly, the Sabbath is a pointer to man's duty as the creature of God. If its provision for physical rest reminds us of our finite nature, its insistence that this rest take the form of acts of worship and service reminds us of our spiritual nature. It tells us not only that we are dust, but also that we are made in the image of God. It asserts that the worship of God is our highest human function—and that we are to worship him in the totality of our being, with our body as well as with our mind. Further, its humanitarian motif (Deut. 5.15) insists that we worship God in the totality of our relationships.

Thirdly, the Sabbath is a pointer to man's destiny. The weekly rhythm for human activity of six days of work followed by one day of rest reflects the pattern of human history. Long before it assumed a soteriological significance, the Sabbath was an eschatological symbol. It symbolized the *telos*, or the end, of time, reminding us that history is not an aimless existence—either as a blind chaos or an endlessly recurring cycle—but a linear development which will climax in a great consummation. Before the Fall Adam would have been reminded by the weekly Sabbath of the eternal life which he and his race were promised should they live by faith and obedience. After the Fall the Sabbath did not lose this significance, for God in his grace promised to save his people and give them, through the work of Christ, the eternal life forfeited by Adam. Had Adam's probation been successful, 'then the sacramental Sabbath would have passed over into the reality it typified, and the entire subsequent course of the history of the race would have been radically different. What now is expected at the end of this world would have formed the beginning of the world-course instead' (Geerhardus Vos, *Biblical Theology*, p. 157). This eschatological dimension of the Sabbath lies behind the prophetic vision which saw the new heavens and the new earth as a perpetual Sabbath (Isaiah 66.22–23), and is taken up in the New Testament by the writer to the Hebrews.

SABBATH OBSERVANCE IN THE OLD TESTAMENT

It is a logical step to pass from consideration of what the Sabbath symbolized to how it was observed. Most commentators agree that it was observed both by rest from work and by special religious worship, but there is no unanimity as to which aspect had priority. Patrick Fairbairn argues that physical Sabbath rest, however needful and beneficial, was never meant to be an end in itself: 'It is no part of the fourth commandment, fairly interpreted, to prohibit ordinary labour, excepting in so far as it tends to interfere with the proper sanctification of the time to God' (op. cit., Vol. 2, p. 143). On the other hand, the majority Reformed Ecumenical Synod report (1972) reckons that we must understand the Sabbath command 'first of all as an order to refrain from working.'

The question at issue is, could the Sabbath be kept merely by resting? Or was participation in worship also essential to its observance? This is not a quibble, for it has an important bearing on whether the Lord's day is basically continuous with the Sabbath. If the Sabbath was a day of rest rather than of worship, and the Lord's day one of worship rather than of rest, then the case for discontinuity is strong. But if, on the other hand, the Scriptures regard both days as primarily days of worship, then there is more likelihood of a connection between them.

While it is true that the fourth commandment is consistently stated as an injunction to cease from working (Exodus 16.29, 30; 20.10; 23.12; 31.12–17; 34.21; 35.2–3; Numbers 15.32–36; Deut. 5.12–15; Nehemiah 13.15–22), it hardly follows that the day is hallowed merely by cessation of labour. We must not forget that most of the ten commandments are couched in the negative form, and that the same principle of interpretation which covers them must also surely apply to the fourth—viz., that the prohibition of one kind of works is made with a view to works of an opposite kind being performed. For example, the commands not to commit adultery or to bear false witness are truly obeyed by loving our wives or husbands, and telling the truth. Not for a moment do they imply that avoiding adultery is more important than loving one's marriage partner, or that not bearing false witness is more important than telling the truth.

Furthermore, there are many passages where Sabbath observance is inextricably bound up with worship. For example, in Leviticus 23 the Sabbath stands at the head of the list of the religious festivals of Israel. It is one of the 'appointed feasts' (RSV) and is described as a 'convocation' (verses 2–3). Numbers 28.9–10 prescribes special sacrifices for the Sabbath in addition to the normal daily offerings (cf. 1 Chron. 23.31; 2 Chron. 2.3; 8.13; 31.3), as did also Ezekiel's vision (Ezekiel 45.17; 46.41). The Sabbath—designed to be a joyous festival (Hosea 2.11)—is desecrated by unethical worship (Isaiah 1.12–17) as much as by unnecessary labour. The Sabbath was considered an appropriate time to consult a prophet (2 Kings 4.23).

Finally, and most significantly of all, the divine rest upon which the Sabbath rest was patterned was certainly not a rest of inactivity. When God ceased from the work of creation immediately he was actively rejoicing over it, sustaining and governing it. The *raison d'etre* of the Sabbath institution was to give man a special opportunity every seventh day to enter into communion with God, sharing in his rejoicing in the works of creation (and, later, of redemption). Hence our Lord's insistence that his Father 'is always at work to this very day' (John 5.17 NIV).

So the worship of God seems to have been the primary aspect of true Sabbath observance. However, cessation from work, was also an integral part. The works proscribed on the Sabbath included jobs essential to Israel's economy, such as sowing and reaping (Exodus 34.21), treading the winepress, trading and carrying burdens (Nehemiah 13.15–22; Jeremiah 17.19–27).

On the other hand, the prohibition of work was not absolute. As our Lord reminded the Pharisees, the priests did extra work on the Sabbath—offering special sacrifices (Numbers 28.9–10), preparing fresh shewbread (Lev. 24.5–9; I Chron. 9.32) and circumcising infants (John 7.27–28). Such work obviously helped to sanctify the day to the Lord and was not merely permitted, but positively commanded. The same principle seems to have operated in the case of ordinary Israelites travelling to consult a man of God (2 Kings 4.23). 2 Kings 11.4 ff. indicates that a state of military alert was maintained on the Sabbath, and the writer tacitly commends the action of Jehoiada the priest in organizing the *coup d'etat* on the Sabbath which saw the young Joash crowned, his evil grandmother assassinated and the temple of Baal razed to the ground. However, military actions such as this and the conquest of Jericho cannot be taken as indicative of normal Sabbath observance in Israel. They merely demonstrate that the Old Testament made allowances for emergency situations.

One further aspect of Old Testament Sabbath observance remains to be discussed—that is, whether the prohibition of work was extended to include cultural and recreational activities. The fact that the cultural mandate of Genesis 1 and 2 is regarded as part of man's work as steward of the creation strongly suggests an affirmative answer to this question. So does Isaiah 58.13–14, for there the prophet warns the people against seeking their own pleasure on the Sabbath. To do this is to tread the Sabbath underfoot. Clearly, in the prophet's view, self-centred pleasure is inconsistent with the Sabbath ethos. The delight of the Sabbath is rather to come from taking delight in the Lord Himself. The Hebrew word *hephets*, translated 'pleasure' in the AV and RSV, is sometimes rendered by 'business' or 'affairs' (see RSV margin and NEB), but there is no justification for departing in this passage from the primary meaning of the root which is 'to delight in.'

Our study leads us to conclude that the Westminster view of the Lord's day as the Christian Sabbath still remains the most consistent and satisfactory interpretation of all the biblical evidence available. It does not solve all the problems, but it leaves us with fewer and less serious questions than does the contrary view. Although the New Testament evidence is inconclusive, the Old Testament does explicitly assert that the Sabbath is a creation ordinance. This assertion is not contradicted in the New Testament and it helps to make both our Lord's positive approach to the Sabbath and the Gentile church's attitude to the Lord's day more intelligible than they would otherwise be.

THE SABBATH TODAY

This study would be incomplete were it to end without some attempt to approach the practical implications of Christian Sabbath observance today, so we shall try and outline briefly three biblical lines of approach.

First of all, our Lord's day observance should be characterized by *obedience*.

Today the predominance of Sunday work in many industries throughout the greater part of the country makes obedience to the Lord of the Sabbath no easy matter for a large number of people. Most Sunday work is done purely for economic reasons. Management wants a quicker return on its investment and workers grasp at the double pay. As a result Christian worship and service tend to be accorded a low priority. This surely illustrates why unnecessary Sunday work is considered sinful by the fourth commandment.

However, some secular work on Sunday is unavoidable. Works of necessity have multiplied both with the growth of vast connurbations and their web of supporting services, and with the establishment of modern industrial plants featuring continuous processes. In these complicated situations Christian workers will seek to bear a clear witness to the Lord's day. This will not be as simple as it may appear, for if Christians are ready to benefit from the system they should be prepared to play their part in maintaining it where and when this is necessary. On the other hand, where the work is unnecessary, Christians should be prepared to stand up and be counted for the Lord of the Sabbath regardless of the economic sacrifice this may involve.

The growth of Sunday entertainments also militates against our observing the Lord's day in modern society. Commercialized amusements and sports on Sundays are inconsistent with the Christian Sabbath. Private forms of entertainment and recreation are more problematical because many regard them as a form of relaxation. However, the fact that the Sabbath rest is to be distinguished from self-centred pleasure has convinced many Christians that they should abstain from what the Shorter Catechism calls 'worldly recreations' (Answer 61) on the Lord's day in order to demonstrate in a special way their love for God and for their neighbour.

The second feature of our Sabbath keeping should be *love*. Jesus and Paul taught that love is the fulfilling of the law. The clear implication is that mere respect for the commandments which does not spring from grateful love to God and neighbour is fleshly legalism, not Christian obedience. This point must be made with considerable emphasis for, traditionally, in Scotland an external obedience to the fourth commandment has been regarded as the measure of the community's acceptance of the Christian way of life. Too often we may have repeated the error of the Pharisees in thinking that the commandment is honoured in some measure by sheer inactivity. We must never forget that the Sabbath commandment demands from us a response of love. A total love to God expressed in private and public worship. And a sacrificial love to our neighbour demonstrated in acts of thoughtfulness and kindness.

Thirdly, our celebration of the Lord's day should be characterized by *joy*. It is the day of resurrection and ascension on which the Son of God entered into his rest after completing his work of redemption. Easter Sunday is every Sunday! Along with the Lord's Supper, the Lord's day shares the unique distinction in the New Testament of being given the Greek adjective *kuriakos*, meaning 'belonging to the Lord' (i.e. Jesus). The Lord's Supper commemorates the Lord's death, and his day, his resurrection, and both are to be observed with the joy of sharing in Christ's triumphant rest as the early church did at Pentecost. The Christian Sabbath thus fulfils in the deepest sense Isaiah's challenge to call the Sabbath a delight (Isaiah 58.13).

The Sabbath's purpose is similar to that of all the commandments. It is to bring us to Christ (Galatians 3.24). So it becomes truly the Lord's day for us when our observance of it brings us to a greater obedience to Jesus' Lordship, to a more ardent love for his person, and to a more exquisite delight in his creation and redemption.

Bibliography

Standard commentaries on the appropriate passages of Scripture.

Acts of the Reformed Ecumenical Synod, Australia, 1972
Biblical Theology, by Geerhardus Vos, Grand Rapids, 1948.
Christian Graduate, September 1973, 'Sunday, puzzling Sunday' by John Wesson.

Christian Graduate, December 1974, 'A Reply to John Wesson' by
William Still.
Class Book on the Confession of Faith, by A. A. Hodge, London,
1870.
Confession of Faith, Edinburgh, 1955.
Foundations of the Sabbath, by B. B. Warfield, London.
Sunday, by Willy Rordorf, London.
The Christian Use of Sunday, a report by the Church and Nation
Committee of the Church of Scotland, 1964.
The Covenantal Sabbath, by Francis Nigel Lee, London, 1969.
The Day of Light, by H. B. Porter, London, 1960.
The Lord's Day in History, Theology and Life, by an inter-denomin-
ational group of Scottish Ministers, Edinburgh.
The Sabbath Institution, by John Murray, London, 1953.
The Typology of Scripture, Vols. I & II, by Patrick Fairbairn,
Edinburgh, 1870.
The Westminster Journal of Theology, XXII.2, May 1960, 'The
Two Tables of the Covenant,' by Meredith G. Kline.
Theological Dictionary of the New Testament, ed. R. Kittel, Grand
Rapids, articles *sabbaton* and *kuriakos*.

The Ordination of Women

JAMES W. FRASER, M.A., B.D.
*Professor of Hebrew and Old Testament Literature,
Free Church College, Edinburgh.*

This subject has become topical not only because of the emancipation of the modern woman and her infiltration into what were, until recently, the exclusive preserves of the male; not only because of legislation, too, in her favour against sex discrimination and the woman's liberation movement; but also because several denominations, including the Church of Scotland, have legislated in favour of the ordination of women, while the Church of England is vacillating over the issue. If the present trend advances we in the Free Church of Scotland, and other small denominations with a similar theological viewpoint, will be in the minority—apart, of course, from the Church of Rome, for while it may have feminine orders and mothers superior it has no women priests, much less a female pope! The matter, then, is one which deserves ventilation. Why do we not allow women elders and women ministers? Is it due to prejudice, conservative tradition, or are there weightier reasons for the exclusion of women from ordination? Can it be that, in a matter like this, the concensus of modern Christian opinion is wrong? Are the churches 'all out of step but our Jock'?

The tendency today is to treat all things after a pragmatic fashion Does it work? If it does then it is right. This same rule is often applied to the ordination of women and by its criterion there does not seem to be any insuperable, practical objection to their being set apart to the office of elder or minister. Women, it is agreed, are just as dedicated as men, often more so. Is it not a fact that the Church down through the ages has been supported largely by women, devout and honourable not a few? The bulk of our communicant membership is made up of the female sex. They are not lacking in gifts. Indeed some may be able to preach better than the majority of men! Their zeal is not under question; in most cases it puts men to shame. They are particularly understanding in social contacts and so may be of special value in pastoral and counselling matters. They have shown themselves the equals of men in every realm into which they have entered, monarchs, prime ministers, lawyers, judges, business executives, literateurs, professors in college and university. You name it, they excel in it! Besides, do we not employ them on the mission field as Bible women and in other ways? What hinders, then, that they should not be ordained to full office in the church, elders of Kirk-Sessions, ministers in charge, moderators of Assembly and professors in theological seminaries?

If it were merely a matter of pragmatical criterion then it could be left to the vote of the brethren. Even then the matter would have to be reviewed in the light of the difference—the mental and temperamental as well as the obviously physical difference—between the sexes. A superficial pragmatical approach, even here, would be too trivial. But there is a positive guidance on this subject given in the Scriptures, not only in the practice of the Church of God, both in its Old Testament and New Covenant forms, but also in explicit references to the matter in the Pauline epistles, particularly. For a church committed to the leading of the Word of God, a church which accepts unquestioningly the Scriptures as its sole primary standard, the verdict of Scripture is final. 'To the law and to the testimony; if they speak not according to this word it is because there is no light in them.' (Isa. 8.20) A little city in Israel boasted of its ability to settle controversy, 'They shall surely ask counsel at Abel: and so they ended the matter.' (II Sam. 20.18) With far better credentials we may affirm the same of the Word of God as the arbiter of all questions of theology, religion and morals. In this instance we ask, 'What does God's Word say on this issue of the ordination of women?' Has it any pronouncement on the question? If so it is final and must be obeyed.

Before, however, we consider the Scriptural passages bearing on this matter, we might, perhaps, be advised to look briefly at the place of women in the church and so to get the question under review in its proper perspective and in a wider context. We affirm that so far as status and privileges in the church are concerned, men and women are on equal footing. All are one in Christ Jesus. In Him there is neither male nor female; as Christians there is no distinction of the sexes. Women have full rights to all the privileges of believers. They have equal rights with men to the sacraments of the Church, baptism and the Lord's Supper. Their soul's salvation is just as precious in the eyes of Christ as the salvation of men. Exclusion from the office of rule and teaching in the Church is not a diminution of their standing as Christians. So far therefore, as rights and privileges are concerned there is no discrimination of sex, for God is no respecter of persons. Besides, in the after-life the distinction between the sexes appears to be abolished, for in the resurrection they neither marry nor are given in marriage, but are as the angels of God in heaven (Luke 20.36).

Where the charismatic gifts of the Spirit are concerned women have shared in them as well as men. The gift of prophecy has been bestowed on them. Witness Miriam the sister of Aaron and Moses, Huldah in the reign of Josiah, Anna at the time of our Lord's presentation in the Temple and the four daughters of Philip the Evangelist. There were no women priests under the Levitical law (a significant fact we shall advert to later) but there were prophetesses in the church both under the Old and New Testament dispensations. Paul speaks of women praying and prophesying (I Cor. 11.5) whatever this may mean exactly.

Besides, Christian women, far from being excluded from service in the Church have their own distinctive contribution to make. First, there is the obvious and all-too-often unappreciated rôle as mothers in Israel. The women's-liberation movement tends to brush aside the bearing and rearing of children and contemptuously dismiss mothers of large families as little better than brood mares. But Scripture places great importance on the maternal function: 'nevertheless they shall be saved in child bearing . . .' (I Tim. 2.15) It was to a woman that the honour was given in rearing the greatest leader of Israel, albeit, unknown to Pharoh's daughter, she was the mother of the abandoned babe! Our Lord Jesus himself traces His immediate descent as man exclusively from a woman. To the female sex alone was this honour given, for the Virgin Birth excludes any earthly father. Women ministered loyally to our Lord in the days of his sojourn in Galilee and came with him on his last visit to Jerusalem. Phoebe was the servant of the church in Cenchrea. Dorcas plied her needle in the interests of the widows and their children belonging to the church in Joppa. Eudoia and Syntyche were helpers of the apostle in the work of the Lord as were other Christian women mentioned in Romans 16. The church of God has been enriched down through the ages by the service of devout and honourable women. This paper does not try to demean their contribution or depreciate their status as Christian believers. We would generously acknowledge their work of faith and labour of love.

Our scope of enquiry is therefore limited to what is commonly called 'Office in the church,' in the Old Testament the priesthood, in the New Testament church the ruling and teaching ministry.

The Word of God gives us explicit guidance on this matter and we shall consider this in greater detail later. But the history of office in the church, both in the Old and New Testament dispensations, has also something to teach us on this issue. There were no women priests under the Levitical law. Scripture has something to say about the wives and daughters of the priests but they never on any occasion exercised the sacerdotal function. Women, devout and godly, prophesied, gave guidance (Huldah), bore rule (Deborah) and exercised a spiritual ministry (Hannah) but never on any occasion did they approach the altar to offer sacrifice. Miriam the sister of Aaron, the high priest, prominent and influential as she was, never assisted at the altar. This is significant. Again in the New Testament, while we have a woman as the honoured mother of our Lord, He did not number any among his apostles, not even the spiritually aware Mary of Bethany or the devoted Mary of Magdala. The women of the Gospels often put the men to shame with their zealous devotion and spiritual insight, but this did not qualify them for office as apostles, not even after our Lord's resurrection and the outpouring of his Spirit at Pentecost. No women are numbered among the presbyter-bishops, not even among the ordained diaconate of the New Testament church. It is by no means proved that Phoebe was a 'deaconess' in the modern accepted sense of the term, or that the women mentioned in the Pastoral Epistles were anything other than the wives of office-bearers, administering the bounty of the church among destitute women and children, where it would be indelicate and undesirable for men to enter, as was the case, in modern times with the zenana missions in Moslem India. The fact of the exclusion of women from the priesthood of the Levitical church and their non-participation in the ministerial orders of the Christian Church is one that cannot lightly be set aside. Nor will it do to explain it away in terms of the prejudices of these respective ages. As 'second class citizens' in the eyes of a male-dominated society, it might be agreed, they were scarcely eligible as candidates for office; the ecclesiastical suffrage was no more theirs than the political one. Now that women have won the right to hold any political office, what doth hinder the modern emancipated woman from exercising her gifts in the pulpit, the Kirk Session and General Assembly? But the Biblical history of women holding or usurping office in state or church is not encouraging as precedents. Deborah exercised the office of judge in Israel in times which were out of joint but no one supposes that the era of the Judges was normal or gave us a valid precedent to follow. Athaliah, the daughter of Jezebel and Ahab, usurped office and began her heathen rule in Judah with a palace pogrom. In the New Testament Paul censures the women in Corinth for their forwardness in assuming functions that were not theirs. Our Lord rebukes the church in Thyatira for suffering 'that woman Jezebel, which calleth herself a prophetess, to teach and seduce my servants . . .' (Rev. 2.20). Altogether any reference to women in the Bible bearing rule is far from encouraging. But we have a more sure word of prophecy to which we do well to take heed on this subject. And to this word we must now turn, bearing in mind that her exclusion from office in the Church does not diminish the status of a Christian woman or deprive her of her rightful privileges.

The classic Biblical passages which give explicit guidance on the subject of the ordination of women (or rather non-ordination!) occur in two of the Pauline letters—1 Cor. 11.7–9, 14.34, 35 and 1 Tim. 2.11–14. The first of these refers, specially, to the demeanor of women at worship in the church assembly, particularly with reference to the covering of the head during worship (a rule which, incidentally, has not been abrogated or repealed). The second passage is, perhaps, more material to our consideration. The third passage cited bears more explicitly on the subject before us.

But while 1 Cor. 11 has to do primarily with woman's conduct at worship it puts the matter on a principial basis—her subordination, in the creation-ordinance of the sexes. This is not just a subordination in time—Eve having been created after Adam—but a subordination of functions as well. (Paul obviously accepts the historicity of the Genesis account of Creation as he also does of the Fall). Now this subordination does not imply inferiority. Woman is not inferior to man. The very purpose and mode of her creation proves this. Eve was not taken out of Adam's feet, a symbol had it been done, that she might have been trampled upon, as indeed happened in the society of fallen man. Nor was she taken, as good Matthew Henry points out, from his head for her to lord it over him. She was taken from his side, near his heart to be loved and to be cherished and to be a worthy help-meet for him. She is not inferior but she is subordinate, according to Biblical teaching. The head of every man is Christ and the man is the head of a woman (1 Cor. 11.3). The man is the glory of God for he was made in the image and likeness of God, but woman is the glory of man from whom she is derived: 'For man does not originate from woman, but woman from man. For indeed man was not created for the woman's sake but woman for the man's sake' (1 Cor. 11.8–9, New American Standard Bible). But the male may not, for that reason, look down on the female, for the epistle goes on to say: 'However in the Lord neither is woman independent of man, nor is man independent of woman. For as the woman originates from the man, so also the man has his birth through the woman; and all things originate from God' (1 Cor. 11.11–12). The Corinth assembly appear to have tolerated an obliteration of this distinction between the man and the woman. In this they were 'odd man out' where the worship of the church as a whole was concerned: 'But if one is inclined to be contentious we have no other practice, nor have the churches of God' (1 Cor. 11.16) The creation-ordinance of the subordination of the woman to the man remains in the Christian church.

The apostle applies this specifically to the subject in hand in 1 Tim. 2.11–15. He excludes women from the office of rule and of teaching on the two grounds of man's primacy in creation and woman's priority in sin (vv. 13 and 14). He thus adds to the original ground referred to in I Cor. 11 the notorious forwardness of Eve in the tempation and the Fall. 'For it was Adam who was first created, and then Eve. And it was not Adam who was deceived, but the woman being quite deceived fell into transgression.' However ungallant this statement may appear it is factually true and theologically of paramount significance. (We must not attribute it to any misogynistic bias which has been wrongly alleged against Paul. Neither must we dismiss it as merely his own private opinion. Paul here is speaking in the Spirit. It is the word of God given by inspiration, infallible and authoritative. We may not pick and choose but accept the verdict as the teaching of God the Spirit.)

These two grounds for the exclusion of women from office in the church—man's primacy in creation and woman's priority in sin—are not 'dated' in the sense that they belong to a specific age of the church's development. They do not apply only to an age when women were under bondage. It will not do to say that the New Testament church was just adapting itself to the conditions of its own age. They are primeval and primary and all the most advanced women's lib. in the world will not alter them in the slightest degree. This is the Biblical and historical basis on which Paul, speaking by the Spirit of inspiration, excludes women from the office of rule and teaching in the church of Christ.

Of the two reasons just quoted the first is principal—man's primacy in creation and women's derivation from man. Man heads the team and woman is at his side a help-meet. She was not made to rule, but to be in subjection to her husband and so fulfil the function as a suitable companion for man. The divine order for woman is not the bachelor business girl but the married wife. Her rule is in the home to guide well her own household (Prov. 31.10; 1 Tim. 5.14). Within that sphere she occupies an honourable and highly influential position. The trite old adage has a lot of truth in it, 'The hand that rocks the cradle rules the world'. A godly woman as wife and mother has exercised incalculable influence for good down through the ages of the church of God. The modern underrating of the status of wife and mother, together with the economic necessity of the married woman having to go out to work, has done immeasurable harm to the family. Her work as wife and mother is a full-time job and eminently worth while. Her status as such is not inferior to any.

The second reason alleged—woman's priority in sin, 'and Adam was not deceived but the woman being deceived was in transgression'—appears to be cited to show what happened when woman took the lead. The serpent showed his subtilty in striking at the vulnerable part of the Adamic partnership. He plied his temptation with the 'weaker vessel' and through Eve got at Adam. It was a back-door attack. This is not the place to enter into a lengthy discussion of the psychology of the Fall, but the Genesis account, on which the apostle bases his argument, does seem to demonstrate woman's inherent unfitness to take the initiative on a grave matter like this. At best she should have repudiated, without parleying, the serpent's suggestion. At least she should have referred the matter to her husband and her head, with whom the Covenant arrangement was made by God.

Not inferior in human qualities to man, Eve, as Adam declared, was 'bone of his bone and flesh of his flesh' and so just as human as Adam, yet there are psychological nuances to the female make-up, her instincts and intuitions, which distinguish her from the male. Capable of a variety of exercises, her main function, as the apostle notes here ('she shall be saved in childbearing,' a statement we regard as referring to parturition in general and not here to the Virgin Birth of the sinless Son of Man), her main function is maternal within the context of marriage. It is not that of head of the household, still less is it head in the church courts.

The apostle is very explicit on the subject of woman's place in the church. 'I suffer not a woman to teach or to usurp authority over the man but to be in silence.' (1 Tim. 2.12) The wording of the Greek original makes it emphatic—'A woman to teach I do not allow . . . .' Praying and prophesying in the exercise of charismatic gifts she might do, but from authoritative teaching in the assembly she is explicitly debarred. With this also agrees 1 Cor. 14.34, 35 which Paul declares is also the pronouncement of the Law of God. He backs up his own pronouncement by the words 'the things that I write unto you are the commandments of the Lord'. The function of teaching belonged to male members of the church duly elected and set apart to office. The ruling function is also exclusively a male preserve, and these two—leading and rule—constitute the fundamental work of the bishop-presbyter (one order) and the main office for which ordination is required.

The exclusion of women from ordination was not just a local enactment for the church in Corinth with its bold and immodest female members. Paul declares that his judgement whereby women should appear in church dressed becoming their role and status as women, is according to the practice of the churches everywhere else. (I Cor. 11.16) Besides, the reasons for which he makes the exclusion, belong not to any one period or place, but are derived from first principles affecting the creation and nature of man and woman.

For us, therefore, the Scriptural pronouncement is final—it is the end of all strife and controversy. The Biblical position is the non-ordination of woman, derived both from precept and practice. We refuse to ordain women to the ministry, not because *we* wish to keep it a male preserve, but because God's word appears to us clearly to debar them from the office of teaching and rule in the Christian church.

This of course, as we have been at pains to show, does not demote women or deprive them in any way. Office in the church may be an honour and a privilege, but it is essentially a service, a ministry in the strict sense of that term. Even the Papacy pays lip service to this in spite of the triple crown—the Pope professes to be 'the servant of the servants of Christ.' The elder, according to Peter, who gloried in the title for himself, was not a lord over God's heritage but an example to the flock as under-shepherd. Office in the church is, therefore, not something to be coveted for personal vain–glory. Duly called and orderly ordained and diligent in the pursuit of his high calling the Christian minister, or elder, (the office is essentially one) may look forward to the reward of the eulogy of his Master—'well-done good and faithful servant,' but servant he is and not master. The members of the church who have not been ordained to office are not deprived of any real privilege in the Christian life. They are not in the least inferior. Any proud coveting of position in the church savours of the spirit of the sons of Zebedee who wanted the chief places in the kingdom of heaven for personal glory.

The scope of this paper is limited—if limited be the right word— to the Biblical teaching on the subject. We have not gone into the history of the ordination of women except as it relates to the practice under both Testaments. What the church, ancient and modern, has done, or is doing, is no criterion for us. We are subject to the verdict of scripture only and so of apostolic practice. The fact that not a few churches in modern times have opened both pulpit and session-door to women places an added obstacle in the way of union with them. It may also raise the question even with our own membership as to why we do not concede what others have done. But we must take our stand on God's Word, which we have shown is explicit and clear on this issue, however embarrassing it may yet become. With Luther we must say, 'Here I stand, I can do no other. So help me God.'

The Unity of the Church

JAMES MACKINTOSH, M.B.E., M.A., B.D., M.Ed.
Professor of Systematic Theology,
Free Church College, Edinburgh.

From the first quarter of the present century the world Church has concentrated on the question of unity in a quite unprecedented way. The Communist bloc had taken its stand against Christianity, a revitalized nationalism had filled the religions of the East with a spirit of independence, while, as far as men could see, the advance of Christianity was halted in the Afro-Asian continent and in the West the enemy was at the gates. The church on the defensive felt there might be hope of safety in uniting separate churches, but the cold record of history is that unions in England, Scotland, Canada and South India have to the present failed to bring spiritual renewal or evangelical advance.

Modern theological writers have shown a marked interest in the unity of the Church, sometimes with a socializing trend, based on the new universalism. Salvation, it is maintained, is corporate and is found in the solidarity of the new humanity of which Christ is the head. A second motif would call for unity by secularization of the Church. The world is Christ's kingdom inasmuch and in the same sense as the Church is. 'Can we not say that where the world is left to be the world, the secular left to be secular, thus being at the free disposal of men, Christ is at work.' (*The Church for Others*, p. 11, Geneva 1967). A third tendency does not confuse the Church with the world but with Christ. The church is sacramentalized and fulfils a mediatorial role in the world. On the one hand it actualizes the presence of Christ and on the other hand it is a sign and seal of the incorporation of all men into Christ. It may appear an over-simplification of the position held by admittedly competent scholars to say that their views on the doctrine of the church are vitiated by their radical stance in theology. Our view-points in ecclesiology must be consistent with what we have learned from other and more central areas of God's revealed truth. To study the church we require the fullest Biblical description of our subject that we can attain.

While we may isolate the Church as a separate topic for study we should note that the Bible does not treat this doctrine except as an integrated part of the revelation of grace. The church does not derive from below but from above. Both the source and the goal of the church are in the eternal purpose of God. It owes its being to the quickening it derives from union with Jesus Christ. It comprises all who are united to him in the bonds of true faith. To the church belong all the elect of the past, of the present, and of the future. In the words of the Westminster Confession (Chap. 25): 'The catholick or universal church, which is invisible, consists of the whole number of the elect that have been, are, or shall be gathered into one, under Christ the head thereof; and is the spouse, the body, the fulness of him that filleth all in all.' In other words the purpose of the election is the creation of an organism, which in turn involves the redemption, renewal and glorification of a regenerated mankind which proclaims the excellencies of God. When God carries out this election in time He does this only by way of the covenant of grace; and He never in that covenant includes anyone in independence from all the others. He establishes His covenant with Adam, Noah, Abraham and with their seed from generation to generation. The believer, therefore, never stands apart by himself. He is born from above out of God, but he receives the new life only in the fellowship of the covenant of grace of which Christ is the head and at the same time the content. From the moment of his regeneration he is incorprated into the great whole, the '*communio sanctorum.*' In this rich fellowship he is a member of a new nation and citizen of a spiritual kingdom whose king is glorious in the multitude of his subjects (Prov. 14.28). We must see the church's unity, then, in terms of its union with God. The church is one because Christians share a common relationship to the three Persons of the one Godhead, a relation that is common, not merely in the sense of being similar in every case, but in the further sense of being a single, communal relation whereby God, Father, Son and Holy Spirit, holds all Christians, every moment, in saving union with Himself. God's relation to the whole church is numerically one, just as a father's relation to his family is numerically one, as it embraces the group and each individual in it. Later we hope to show from Scripture that it is this unitary action of God causing sinners to stand in His grace that makes and keeps the church one. The church as the creation of God is bound to reflect the unity and integrity of the divine being as His eternal purpose becomes actualized.

The Church as Invisible and as Visible

Many modern writers on the doctrine of the church oppose the use of the above terms, *invisible* and *visible* because, they hold, an invisible church is not a fellowship but a *numerus electorum* and fundamentally individualistic. The Reformers needed the awareness afforded by this distinction to support their conviction that they were still in the true church of God although they had withdrawn from the Church of Rome. Justification by faith, Luther declared, is the article by which the church stands or falls, but regeneration and faith are in themselves spiritual and invisible. It is beyond human power to determine infallibly who are regenerate and who are not, who have faith and who have not. The union of believers with Christ is a mystical one; the Lord alone knows them that are His. While the term 'invisible' is not predicated in Scripture as an attribute of the church there are occasions when the distinction invisible–visible is indicated. 'They are not all Israel, which are of Israel' (Rom. 9.6), 'He is a Jew which is one inwardly; and circumcision is of the heart, in the spirit and not in the letter' (Rom. 2.29); and our Lord Himself distinguished between those who professed to be his disciples and yet were not (John 8.31). We conclude, then, that the Scriptures teach that the invisible or true church of God both does not include some who belong to the visible church and does include some who are not reckoned by men as members of the visible congregation of God's people. This distinction has sometimes led to misconception and Murray is surely right when he says, 'It is more proper to speak of the church as invisible or the church as visible or of the aspects of invisibility and visibility attaching to the church rather than of the visible church and the invisible church' (*Baptism*, p. 35). The danger is found in separating the two aspects into two churches, so destroying the church's essential unity. Bannerman says: 'When we speak of the church invisible and the church visible, we are not to be understood as if we referred in these designations to two separate and distinct Churches, but rather to the same Church under two different characters. . . . We do not assert that Christ has founded two different Churches on earth, but only one; and we affirm that that *one* Church is to be regarded under two distinct aspects.'

When we turn to consider the visibility of the church we observe that it is as a society, an assembly, a congregation, a visible, observable entity that we meet the church in the New Testament. Faith that unites with Christ must find expression in word and action and the divine Head of the church has appointed His church visible in the world the place of worship, testimony and fellowship. Murray states this well: 'The very constitutive idea of the church, namely, union with Christ and union of believers with one another in the body of Christ, as an idea realised in the history of this world, necessarily involves visible union and communion. We cannot think of the church invisible as anything that exists in abstraction or apart from the overt expression which the spiritual and invisible facts of union and communion with Christ demand' (*Baptism*, p. 37). Thus the unity which characterized the church of the New Testament was a visible unity. We shall discuss this further when speaking of the duty of Christian unity. The subjects of God's kingdom do God's will. The presence of the unifying Spirit is manifested by its fruit. The light is not to be put under a bushel, but in love, joy, peace, long-suffering, kindness, goodness, faithfulness, meekness and temperance to beam forth that men might glorify God.

The Scripture gives a series of figures which state the nature of the church: the people of God, the kingdom and body of Christ, the fellowship of the Holy Spirit among others. No one of these alone summarizes the whole of ecclesiology and in this study we shall limit ourselves to a review of some of the lines of New Testament teaching on the unity of the church.

The People of God

The meaning of the New Testament word we translate as church (*ecclesia*) can best be understood by reference to the Old Testament. The Septuagint, a Greek version of the Old Testament, was known and used by the New Testament writers. The Hebrew word used for assembly (*qahal*) is regularly, though not invariably, rendered by *ecclesia*. It may be taken as established that the Christian church is ascribed the title of the Old Testament people of God as the *Qᵉhal-Yahweh*. Paul's frequent use of the phrase 'church of God'—bearing in mind that the word *ecclesia* means 'called out'—points directly to 'assembly' or to 'summon an assembly' and is seen to have particular relevance to Deut. 9.10; 10.4; 18.6, which speak of the 'day of the assembly.' This use of a name by the early Christian church was an expression of confidence that in its existence the true people of God, the Messianic congregation of the great end—time (Matt. 16.18) had been revealed, and that the privileges and qualities attributed to ancient Israel in the making of the covenant in the wilderness had found their God-ordained application in this church. The assembly was the covenant people of God gathered to Him as God's 'own possession from among all peoples . . . a kingdom of priests, and a holy nation' (Exod. 19.5–6), 'the people which I have formed for myself, that they might set forth my praise' (Isa. 43.21). Peter weaves these and other passages together when, without actually mentioning the church, he describes it: 'But ye are an elect race, a royal priesthood, a holy nation, a people for God's own possession, that ye might show forth the excellencies of him who called you out of darkness into his marvellous light: who in time past were no people, but are now the people of God: who had not obtained mercy, but now have obtained mercy' (1 Pet. 2.9–10). Moreover, the assemblies of Israel had special divinely-communicated significance. The gathering of Israel in 'the day of the assembly' (Deut. 4.10) marked a climax in redemptive history and constituted the people as the people of God. There were assemblies for worship, for war, for the renewing of the covenant and when the restoration of the people is promised by the prophet Joel the image of an assembly is used again. The great ingathering of the Gentiles is to a festival assembly of God (Isa. 2.2–40; Psalm 87). Here heaven met earth, God was present on Mount Sinai in the midst of the heavenly assembly (Deut. 33) and 'all His holy saints' are those who stand in God's assembly. When we turn to the Epistle to the Hebrews, chapter 12, we find the New Testament Church described as an extension of those assemblies. 'Ye are not come unto the mount that might be touched, and that burned with fire. . . . But ye are come unto mount Sion, and unto the city of the living God, the heavenly Jerusalem, and the innumerable company of angels, to the general assembly and church of the first-born . . . to God the judge of all . . . and to Jesus the mediator of the new covenant. This assembly is the Christian church and the idea of the people of God assembled in the heavenlies with Christ dominates the New Testament conception of the church. In Exod. 29.42–46 we see that the tabernacle of assembly was the place where God met with His people, spoke to them and dwelt among them. Here is what is central in the covenant blessing: 'I will be your God and ye shall be my people' (Rev. 21.3). The assembly of God exists wherever God is in the midst of His people and it is the presence of God Himself that makes them one for He is one. The unity of God held before Israel in the *Shema* (Deut. 6.4) is for Paul the proof of the divine redemptive will calling his people, both Jews and Gentiles (Rom. 3.29–30; 1 Tim. 2.4, 5–6).

Because many seem to hold that the church found its inception only after the outpouring of the Spirit at Pentecost, let us call attention to the very important truth that, according to Scripture, there is only one true seed of Abraham, and that these are the elect, the believers, the spiritual children of God, both of the old and new dispensations. There are children of Abraham according to the flesh and according to the promise, but this is true of both dispensations and only believers are the true seed of Abraham. In Romans 9.6–8 we see that the word of promise had come to Israel and now with Christ's coming she had entered into its literal fulfilment; yet the majority of the Jews did not receive the promise and were lost. Did that mean that the promise had failed? No! Because all the descendents of Abraham are not counted as Abraham's seed. There is an 'Israel' within the ethnic *Israel*. 'The Israel distinguished from the Israel of natural descent is the *true Israel*. They were indeed "of Israel" but not coextensive with the latter' (Murray, *The Epistle to the Romans, ad* 9.6). Again in Romans 4.11–16 Abraham is presented as the father of only one seed, whose sole distinguishing characteristic is faith. Literal descendents of Abraham are not counted for seed but only in as far as they follow in Abraham's faith; and to this spiritual seed, both Jew and Gentile, there is only one promise (cf. Gal. 3.7–9). In Hosea 1.10–11 there is a promise for the children of Israel that they shall be as the sands of the sea which cannot be measured. To them the Lord had said 'Lo ammi, ye are not my people,' and, 'Lo ruhamah, ye are not the objects of my mercy.' In the Epistle to the Romans the apostle refers to this passage (9.24–26) with reference to the church of the new dispensation as it is called from Jews and Gentiles. In other words the promise to Israel was fulfilled when God called His church from all nations. It is clearly inferred from these passages that the church is one, no interim gathering, as dispensationalists seem to hold, but one flock under one Shepherd, one body of Christ called out of the world in every age. The church cannot be separated from Israel. The one line runs through the one, holy catholic church. The unity of the Old and New Testaments cannot be broken.

Turning now to the use of the word church (*ecclesia*) in the New Testament and excepting one occasion where there is no reference to the church (Acts 19.32, 39–40) we find that local assemblies are frequently referred to: Jerusalem, Antioch, Ephesus, Cenchrea, Corinth, Laodicea, Thessalonica and those mentioned in Revelation 2 and 3. There are also many references to churches in the plural, e.g. Cicilia, Galatia etc., and Paul has four references to the church in a house. Now although there is plurality all are truly and fully the church of God. The word *ecclesia* is uniformly used in the

New Testament in reference to the company of believers, the called, the churches of God or of Christ or of the saints.

There is, however, an inclusive use of the word church in the New Testament which must be studied. Jesus spoke of all his disciples taken together as His church (Matt. 16.18 and 18.17) and the apostles talk in the same way of the body of believers. The church is the bride of the Lamb adorned for her husband (Eph. 5.32; 2 Cor. 11.2; Rev. 22.2), the house and the temple of God built by the apostles on the foundation of Christ (1 Cor. 3.10–16) or, according to another application of the same figure, built upon the foundation of the apostles and prophets, Christ Himself being the cornerstone and believers the living stones. One local assembly could not fulfil the conditions and qualities predicated of these churches and we are forced to think of the whole actual church. 'When Jesus speaks of "my church," he is thinking of those gathered and knit together after the pattern provided by the Old Testament as the people for his possession, as the community which he is to constitute, and which stands in a relation to him comparable to the congregation of the Lord in the Old Testament' (Murray, *Nature etc. of the Church*, p. 3). In Matt. 18.17 taken along with Matt. 16.18 we see in our Lord's own teaching the inclusive and the particular use of the word. It throws light on the subject of our study, the unity of the church, to consider how Paul used the term in both the particular and inclusive senses. He often refers to particular churches in the plural and he also uses the singular in the inclusive sense. In Acts 8.3 it is said that 'He laid waste the church.' He regrets how he 'persecuted the church of God' (1 Cor. 15.9) and directed not to give offence 'neither to the Jews, nor to the Gentiles, nor to the church of God' (1 Cor. 10.32). In Acts 9.31 we read that '(*he ecclesia*) the church throughout all Judea' had peace, while in Gal. 1.22 Paul says that he was unknown to 'the churches of Judea which were in Christ.' Here we have the notion of the catholicity of the church, a universalizing that brings into sharp focus the simultaneous unity and plurality of the church. While the inclusive use of the term 'church' certainly implies a corporate unity it is of the utmost importance to observe that the New Testament dignifies each community, however obscure, that confesses the Lord, as the church in its own place, an 'outcrop' of the total church. There is the church of God with all the promises, rights and powers which the Lord has conferred on His church. 'For where two or three are gathered together in my name, there am I in the midst of them' (Matt. 18.20) and this promise Jesus gave is as true of those meeting in a private house as it is of the people of God in their great assemblies. The New Testament writers appear ignorant of the tensions we feel, between the church as inclusive and the church as particular. Their common calling, faith and baptism united them through the work of the Holy Spirit in one Christianity.

The concept of assembly stresses the idea of the *immediacy* of God's presence with His gathered people and the idea of a house stresses the *permanence* of the Lord's presence. The tabernacle or temple symbolized God's dwelling among His people: 'And I will set my tabernacle among you: and my soul shall not abhor you. And I will walk among you, and will be your God, and ye shall be my people' (Lev. 26.11–12). E. P. Clowney expresses this truth very clearly when he writes, 'The assembly and dwelling figures are intensely theological, for they show God as present in the midst of His people. The people of God are not an already existing nation brought into relationship with Him. They are constituted by God's assembling and God's dwelling. Nationalism became a sin to the theocratic people, but the theocracy was not founded in nationalism. God's people are united to each other only because they are united to God' (*The Doctrine of the Church*, p. 15).

As we have already shown the idea of unity enters fundamentally into the New Testament doctrine of the church; one kingdom of God, one mediator, one Holy Spirit who unites the elect to one Christ. It is also important to note that the idea of unity is prominent in all the images used in Scripture to reveal the nature of the church as God's family, God's kingdom, God's flock or as a vine, a temple, a body to mention only some of them. We shall select one, the body, for special study as it is generally considered the most typical description of the church in the Pauline epistles and also because it gives a further and fuller explication of the church as the people of God.

The Body of Christ

Although there is an extensive and growing literature at present on the designation of the church as the body of Christ there is a marked lack of agreement among New Testament scholars. In the main they may be divided into two groups, those who regard the qualification 'body of Christ' in a figurative, collective sense and those who take it in a real personal sense.

The physical body of our Lord is, of course, the subject of the references to his crucifixion, lying in the tomb and rising again on the third day. When we come to the references that speak of the Lord's Supper we find a secondary or symbolical sense appended and developed. A most important passage is I Cor. 12.12–27. After treating of the disunity of the congregation at the time of the Lord's Supper (11.17–34) there follows a discussion of the various gifts given by the Spirit to the different members of the church. In 12.12 an equivalence is claimed: 'For as the body is one, and hath many members, and all the members of the body being many, are one body: so also is Christ.' Calvin, dependably apposite, comments: 'The name of Christ is here used instead of the Church, because the similitude was intended to apply not only to God's only-begotten son but to us. It is a passage that is full of choice consolation, inasmuch as he calls the Church *Christ*.' It is not merely that Christ is seen as the unifying principle of his people, nor that the Body of Christ is like a body, but Christ is like a body. It is the first part of the verse quoted above that sets the note of the passage: unity and diversity; one body and many members. This is in line with Rom. 12.5, 'so we being many are one body in Christ, and every one members one of another.' The root idea of *the many* represented by the *one* shall be examined later. The distinguishing feature of the figure *body* however, is that these *many* (because together they belong to Christ) form in him a new unity with each other. Now returning to our Corinthians passage (10.16–17) where the exegesis is not easy, we see that v. 16 refers to the physical body of our Lord, for the cup is a 'communion of the blood of Christ' and the bread a 'Communion of the body of Christ!' The idea is that of *partaking*, while verse 17, though it admittedly does not say that we are the body of Christ, cannot be read to mean that we *partake* of the one body of which we the many are part. The term 'one body' here must refer to believers (cf. I Cor. 12.27) and this truth is symbolically represented by the one loaf. There is, of course, the closest relationship between 'the body of his flesh' and his body the church (Col. 1.18–22) 'It is because we are partakers of Christ's body that we are one body in him. It is because we are the beneficiaries of the offering of the body of Christ once for all, because he bore our sins in his own body upon the tree, that we are constituted the body of Christ. It is because, representatively, and by mysterious identification with Christ in his death and resurrection, yea even in his ascension to the heavenlies

(Eph. 2.4–7), and thus identification with him in that which he accomplished in his own body, that we are one body in him. Indeed, it is because he was obedient unto death even the death of the cross that he is head over all things to his body the church' (Murray Op. Cit., p. 6). So the unity is not one that is imposed from the outside; Christ is Himself in the unity and not distinct from his body. Believers have unity with each other on the ground of their unity in him. We shall see more precisely how this mutual unity is to be understood when we come to examine certain statements in Ephesians and Colossians.

Before leaving this aspect of Scripture teaching on the relation of Christ to his church we may look at the relation of the Holy Spirit to the church. In 1 Cor. 12.13 we read that 'in one Spirit we are all baptized into one body.' This does not mean that the Holy Spirit is the soul of Christ's Body nor that He constitutes the Body; the Spirit adds members to the body and waters them. The Spirit that builds them also refreshes them. Thornton compares the members of the church to dry soil that will not hold together, but damp soil does. So 'the unity of the church is established by the water of the Spirit and each new member, or piece, is made to cohere with the main body.' But the church cannot exist by itself as a special creation of the Spirit nor does it have an independent life of its own. It is the kingdom and body of Christ and exists solely because of its organic relation to him. The church is not a kingdom of the Spirit but only a kingdom of Christ in and by the Spirit. The church is not the body of the Spirit. It is indeed quickened and born of the Spirit; it is filled and directed by the Spirit but to the end that it may be rooted and grounded in Jesus Christ, in His incarnate being and mission.

Before concluding this note on 1 Cor. 12.13 it is to be observed that the apostle, in employing these words, does not say that the unity of the body comes into being by baptism. He is indeed pointing to a unity that lies *behind* this unity of the Spirit, the unity of the body. Believers are baptized *into* one body, they are incorporated by the baptism of the spirit into the body of Christ. We find a parallel thought in 1 Cor. 6.15 f. underlying the profound warning against fornication. He who is joined to a prostitute becomes one body with her; he who is joined to the Lord is one Spirit with him. To be a member of Christ's body means to be one Spirit with him and he must be so guided by his relationship with that body and Spirit that he must not be one body with a prostitute. The fellowship of the Spirit is inferred from incorporation in the body and not vice versa.

Here we must make a short digression in order to indicate the grounds on which we consider the term 'body of Christ' to be metaphorical language. Several recent expositors would apparently deny this and plead for a realistic and ontological interpretation of the words. 'We are members of that body which was nailed to the cross, laid in the tomb and raised to life on the third day' (L. S. Thornton, *The Common Life in the Body of Christ*, p. 298). E. L. Mascall and J. A. T. Robinson hold similar views. The church is viewed as an extension of the incarnation. To quote Robinson, the church is 'the risen organism of Christ's person in all its concrete reality.' In a very useful book on the subject, *One Body in Christ* (S.P.C.K., 1955) E. Best meets this position very adequately. He argues that both the Old and the New Testaments have a wealth of metaphor we should never be so absurd as to interpret literally. Then he points out the variation within the figurative usage: e.g. in 1 Cor. 12.21 the head is an ordinary member of the body; in Col. 1.8 and 2.19 the head is Christ. Both cannot be realistically true. The figures change in Paul's hands e.g. Christ can be the foundation and the coping stone of the temple. More cogent still is Paul's choice of one figure after another to describe various aspects of the church's life. To take one of these ontologically and realistically is to put the others out of court. Christ does not speak of the church as his body but he does declare that he is the *vine* and his disciples the *branches*—a closely related concept that could in no way be literalized. So we conclude that the phrase 'the body of Christ' is, on the analogy of scripture, a metaphor. But when we give up the claim to realism we must be careful that we do not think of a 'mere' metaphor. A metaphor can have a very firm grip on reality.

In the epistles to the Ephesians and the Colossians there is a further unfolding of the idea of the church as the body of Christ. There is a variation of the figure and Christ is said to be the head of the body: 'He is the head of the body, the Church '(Col. 1.18); 'he put all things in subjection under his feet, and gave him to be the head over all things to the Church, which is his body' (Eph. 1.22; cf. Eph. 4.15; 5.23; also 1 Cor. 11.3). Ridderbos (*Paul* p. 380) seems correct when he reasons that Paul uses the word 'head' (*kephale*) to describe the supremacy of Christ and had his thought influenced in this particular by its use in the LXX to translate the Hebrew '*rosh*' which means primacy, honour, authority or origination. All things were created by him and all things are 'headed up' in him. The primacy of Christ rather than the priority is in view here. He who is head of all powers in heaven and on earth, every angelic power or Satanic dominion is also head of the church (Col. 2.10; 1.18).

The figure of 'head' should not be understood in terms of physiological conceptions derived from the relationships within the human body rather as an independent metaphor. It would be difficult to understand the representation of a body nourished by the head and growing up toward the head (Eph. 4.15–16; Col. 2.19) in terms of a composite metaphor. When Paul states (1 Cor. 11.3) that the man is the head of the woman, that Christ is the head of the man and that God is the head of Christ, or when in Eph. 5.23 ff. the husband is called the head of the wife and the wife the body of the husband it is clear that we have to do with an independent metaphor where the figure 'head' though closely related on different occasions to the 'body' figure is nevertheless independent. The head figure does not demand a body for its completion. Having said that however it must be evident that the two figures are very closely associated in the thought of the apostle and at times seem to merge gradually into one composite metaphor. Our interest is in the teaching of these epistles on the unity of the church. In Ephesians and Colossians the organic figure is approached with special emphasis on the union of life between Christ and the church. There must be harmonious functioning in the body and the link with Christ who is the head must be preserved (Col. 2.19). Indeed the relationship is complementary. Christ fills the church with the power of his grace. The head of the church is Lord of the universe and His body need not, dare not, fear any other power while at the same time 'mediatorially He interlinks Himself with His spiritual offspring, bereft of whom He would be dismembered. To them He assumes a relative office and they are indispensible to its discharge. A physician cannot practice without patients nor a guardian exist without wards. Thus the church forms the integration or complement of Christ's saving mission, requisite to His fulfilment of the work, inasmuch as He has been pleased to identify His interest with hers' (E. K. Simpson, *Commentary on the Epistle to the Ephesians, ad.* 1.23). It is also to be noted that Christ's cosmic sovereignty, while springing from the fact that 'He is before all things, and in Him all things hold together,' is a primacy established by His victory over all the power of evil. His mediatorial dominion is conditioned by his headship of his church: 'And he is the head of the body, the church: who is the beginning, the firstborn from the dead, in order that he might be preeminent in all things, because it pleased the Father that in him all the fulness should dwell' (Col. 1.18–19). There is no uniting of the church and the powers. Paul's language makes it difficult to understand the confusion of contemporary theology at this point.

We shall now look at the figure of the body against the background of covenantal headship and see the unity of the 'one' individual messianic servant with the 'the many' as the servant people. The Gentiles (Eph. 2) were separate from Christ, aliens from the commonwealth of Israel and strangers from the covenants of the promise. But in Christ the new covenant is made, both Jew and Gentile have access in one Spirit to the Father, they are no more stangers but fellow-citizens with the saints and of the household of God, reconciled 'in one body unto God through the cross.' The Messiah unifies by representing the people of God and gathering them to himself. Christ's person comprises the new humanity into a unity in Himself—in Christ. This identity of representation is clearly the basis of the reasoning in Rom. 5.12–21 and an analogous way of thinking appears in the concept of Christ as 'Abraham's seed' in Galations 3. The promises are given to Abraham and to the seed of Abraham (v. 7) on the ground of faith. Believers are justified by faith in the redeeming work of Christ. As the chief representative of the collectivity of faith and of the righteousness of God, Christ is called Abraham's seed: 'That is, Christ unites in himself the believers and in him, that is, in his body, christians are Abraham's seed. So on the one hand Christ is Abraham's seed (v. 16) while on the other the church is Abraham's seed. There is unity between the sons of faith and Christ because He has 'redeemed them from the curse of the law.' The covenant stands in objective redemptive history. He represented the church in his death and resurrection, the enmity is slain through him, our reconciliation is accomplished in the crucified body of Christ, our covenant head the one for the many. E. P. Clowney says, 'Covenant representation offers the key for understanding the body of Christ figure. Since the one physical body of Christ dies and is raised on behalf of the saints, they are united representatively in that body. From this conception a figurative extension is a small step. If the many are all reconciled in Christ's body, then the unity of their new position may be pictured as a body' (op. cit., p. 41).

Covenant representation, where Christ's own body is central, giving meaning to all he is and does in his body, helps to explain variations in the use of the body figure. While the earlier epistles have the physical body of Christ and him crucified in view the Colossian and Ephesian emphasis is generally on the risen and glorified body. Here we see Christ as the triumphant Lord. False teachers in Asia Minor had no place to speculate concerning heavenly hierarchies. Christ, Paul asserts, is over all things now and always. He was before all things and in the good pleasure of God is appointed heir of all things (Col. 1.15–17; Eph. 1.10, 20–22). The triumph of Christ, the covenant representative, is the culmination of the history of redemption. He rose from the dead and ascended to the right hand of God where His people, His chosen heritage, chosen before the foundation of the world, are seated with him in heaven. His exaltation is theirs for He is their covenant representative. From this exalted head and covenant representative the church as the body derives life, the fulness is being bestowed—the pleroma. However we interpret the notoriously difficult verse, Eph. 1.23, it is the church that is being filled as a receptacle out of Christ's fulness (cf. Psalm 68.18) 'until we all come in the unity of the faith and of the knowledge of the Son of God, unto a perfect man, unto the measure of the stature of the fulness of Christ' (Eph. 4.13). The fulness of Christ is communicated to a dependent church. The one life vitalises both as the branches in the vine. So the status of the church is determined by representative covenant union with Christ (Col. 2.10) in whom she is complete and from whom she is also being filled. There is no contradiction here, but an apparent tension that arises from the imperfection 'that still inheres in the church and awaits for the consummation as the day when it will be finally eliminated' (Murray, op. cit., p. 8).

There are very many passages that treat of the church as the body of Christ but we shall conclude this discussion by marking some points that have special bearing on the idea of unity.

1. The unity of the church with Christ has its real ground in the church's belonging to Christ in the redemptive historical sense, in the inclusion of the *many* in the *one*.
2. The organic figure of the body relates the individual believer to the church as a whole, to Christ the head who Himself relates to His chosen directly and not through mediating institutions. It follows that all the members are united to one another and that the body is a unit.

3. As Christ is one so the church is one in the most inclusive and universal sense; now in the sense that the church is catholic and at the end-time, when the kingdom will be completely fulfilled, in the unity of God who will be 'all in all!'

Other figures besides the body indicate the living union between the church and Christ. Reference has been made to the vine and the branches. The union of the temple with its foundation or corner-stone (Eph. 2.20–22; 1 Pet. 2.4–5; and Psalm 118.22). This figure teaches the wholeness of the church. A temple is not a mere pile of brick and wood and other building material, but a planned and orderly whole. Each part, however small, has its own place, fitting into the whole and serving for the beauty of the whole only in its own place; to exchange, withdraw or insert a part when all is finished would mar the architecture. Like the body the temple shows a complete and perfect unity, a 'wholeness' in Christ's church. Since both the individual and the church corporately are regarded as the temple and body of Christ then the very existence of the church must be in terms of Christian witness and communion. We may not relate the duties and privileges that arise from the oneness of the church to the church as invisible only. The unity of the faith must be confessed by living men and women. It is the unitary action of God, saving sinners by His grace, that makes and keeps the church one in an existential sense. When Paul says to the church at Corinth, 'we the many are one body,' he referred to the church in a concrete situation of witness where the members were to keep themselves inside harmonious relationships and avoid schism and strife in the Christian fellowship. Their divisive attitude elicited the question, 'Is Christ divided? Was Paul crucified for you? or were ye baptized in the name of Paul' (1 Cor. 1.13)? Clearly, God's people should make conscience of seeking to be governed and regulated in their behaviour by the unity of the body of Christ, giving it all possible expression by word and action in the here and now.

Unity as the Church's Duty
We turn now to consider the church as the fellowship of the Spirit. It is the Spirit of the Living God proceeding from the throne of Christ that actualizes and seals the blessings of the New Covenant to God's elect children. He is the vital bond between Christ and his body from whom all the grace by which the church is constituted

HOLD FAST YOUR CONFESSION

and equipped proceeds: 'In one Spirit were we all baptized into one body . . . and were made to drink into one Spirit' (1 Cor. 12.13). There is a double relationship here, the Giver and the Gift. The third Person of the Trinity gives not only the gifts of His grace but He gives Himself as the personal, living Seal of the bond between God and His people. As the Spirit of Life (Rom. 8.2) He created the church; as the Spirit of Truth (John 14.17) He guides the church. 'Those whom he guides, he guides into the knowledge of the truth, and as he cannot contradict himself those under his guidance must in all essential matters believe the same truths. And as the Spirit of love, he leads all under his influence to love the same objects, the same God and Father of all, the same Lord Jesus Christ; and to love each other as brethren' (Hodge, *The Church and its Polity*, p. 43). But this rich endowment of the gifts of the Holy Spirit does not end with individual enrichment, it becomes corporate, a *common* life in Christ. There is a 'dividing' of gifts that should make for the harmony of the fellowship. There is one Spirit as there is one Lord (Eph. 4.4–5). We see provision made for the Church assuming the form of a visible society when we recall exhortations to believers to unite together for worship, for instruction, for the administration of the sacraments and for mutual watch and care.

The first five chapters of the Acts of the Apostles describe the earliest period in the history of the Christian Church. It was a period of spiritual enthusiasm and brotherly unity. Membership was as yet confined to the Jews. A fair picture is given us in Acts 2.41–42: 'Then they that gladly received the word were baptized: and the same day were added unto them about three thousand souls. And they continued steadfastly in the apostles doctrine and fellowship, and in breaking of bread and in prayers.' Under the Apostles' teaching they were as one family. All who were wealthy gave lavishly of their goods and lands for the benefit of the poor, there was daily care of widows and those in need. Self-sacrifice, unity and generosity displayed what must be abiding characteristics of the church of Christ. As they grew numerically and Gentiles were brought into their fellowship they saw themselves not as a new structure but as the seed of Abraham, the true Israel, the one olive tree from which unbelieving Jews have been pruned and into which the Gentiles who believe are grafted (Rom. 11); one building resulting from the abolition of the barrier which had previously excluded the Gentiles (Eph. 2); it is the enlarging of Shem's tent that Japheth might dwell there. Tensions there might be, but the Hebrew Christian church acted as one through the apostles as their recognized leaders, or on occasion through the elders as responsible representatives. In other cases action is simply spoken of as taken by the church, so that united church action was an expression of church unity.

The seat and centre of unity for the Hebrew Christian church was at Jerusalem first of all. From here, according to Christ's appointment His witnesses were to go to 'all Judaea and Samaria and to the uttermost parts of the earth.' In Jerusalem the advent of the Spirit took place and the disciples were first clothed with power from on high. The strong church in Jerusalem became the nursing mother of the faith throughout the Holy Land and beyond. Here the sense of oneness with all the brethren in the Lord and responsibility for their welfare was strongly developed and united action taken for the benefit of new converts wherever they might be found. Peter and John are sent to Samaria. The founding of the church there was not left to Philip. It was incumbent on the twelve to see that a branch church, formed among an alien and hostile people, should not fall out of the unity of brotherhood with the mother church at Jerusalem. The Samaritan converts were brought into the church on a footing of complete equality with the brethren in Jerusalem and Judaea. When the 'apostles and brethren that were in Judaea heard that the Gentiles also had received the word of God' Cornelius and his friends stood before the barrier of racial prejudice and the matter was taken up at once by the whole community of believers. No deputation was sent to investigate the situation; Peter, having come from Caesarea, related what had taken place, defended his conduct and regarded the interest of the brethren as proper and representing the care of the church as a whole. The sending of Barnabas to Antioch was a measure taken to maintain harmony and good relations. His selection for the mission was described as the action of the church as a whole. When Agabus came and announced the great famine all over the world, the disciples at Antioch sent relief to their brethren 'by the hand of Barnabas and Saul.' Thus by reciprocal giving and receiving, by interchange of messengers and by brotherly help both in material and spiritual things, the unity of the Apostiolc Church, from its centre in Jerusalem to its farthest outpost in the midst of heathendom was from the first manifested and strengthened.

Referring to the Gentile Christian Churches some scholars

affirm (D. D. Bannerman, *The Scripture Doctrine of the Church*, pp. 520–52) that in towns like Corinth and Ephesus more than one congregation was included in the designation, 'the church in Ephesus' or 'the church of God which is at Corinth.' Although it is true that it is in reference to those Gentile churches that the word *ecclesia* is first used in its plural form it was, as we have seen earlier, also used in its inclusive sense. The church was spoken of as one, felt itself to be one and acted as one. We see that the 'brethren who came from Judaea' interested themselves in the affairs of the churches at Antioch, Galatia, Corinth or Rome and we have no record that their right to do so was ever questioned. As the church grew outward and prominent leaders arose, the distinctions of race, philosophy, cultus and culture were not sufficient to divide the church. There remained a tangible unity, finding expression in the ministry, in finance and especially in government (Acts 15).

The attribute of unity continues to receive emphasis in the early centuries, Ignatius relating it very closely to being present at the Lord's Supper and Cyprian seeing in it a safeguard from the Devil. As the episcopal church developed its doctrine the unity of the church came to be based on the unity of the bishops. The visible organized church was identified with the kingdom of God, where the Pope became an absolute monarch and the idea of the church as the communion of saints was generally disregarded.

The Reformers, as we have seen, broke with the Roman Catholic view of the church. Instead of an infallible, hierarchical church dispensing salvation by means of the sacraments they regarded the church primarliy as a *communio sanctorum*, a communion of saints. They distinguished the church as invisible from the church as visible, not to present two churches but to clarify that the church is essentially a fellowship of believers; that where saving faith is the church is; and that in the Visible New Testament church as in Old Testament Israel there may be those who have no rightful place because they are alienated from God. Although the Reformers rejected the Roman Catholic view of the unity of the church as expressed in a visible hierarchical organization they did not at all deny the New Testament teaching of the unity of the visible church. They turned from the imposed unity of an outward organization and found their bond of union in the true preaching of the word and the right administration of the sacraments. Tensions and divisions among the Reformers are amply recorded in history. What is sometimes forgotten is their willingness to labour for unity in the face of overwhelming odds. Late in 1560 Calvin called for 'a free and universal council to end the divisions . . . and reunite all Christianity.' When Archbishop Cranmer wrote to him proposing a consensus his warm reply was that he would 'cross ten seas' if he could be of service in consolidating the churches of the Reformation.

The unity of the visible church was a firmly held tenet of the Scottish church in the post-Reformation period. Men of such calibre as Melville, Brown, Rutherford, Gillespie, Durham and others, while unremitting in their protest against ceremonial impositions and doctrinal errors, reiterate and emphasize that the whole visible church is one. The Covenanters, so often maligned for intolerance, insisted on the oneness of all everywhere who love the Lord Jesus Christ in sincerity. National churches in Scotland, England or France were to our forefathers as provinces of a great empire, parts of an integral whole. Walker says: 'True churches of Christ, side by side with one another, forming separate organizations, with separate governments, seemed to them utterly inadmissible, unless it might be in a very limited way, and for some reason of temporary expediency' (*Scottish Theology and Theologians*, p. 97). In 'The Doctrine of the Church in Scottish Theology,' by John Macpherson, there is a most interesting chapter on 'Church Unity—The Sin of Schism,' where he tells of the anxious care the Fathers in Scotland had concerning the unity of the church. He quotes a passage from Durham which is well worth repeating: 'Never did men run to quench fire in a city, lest all should be destroyed, with more diligence than men ought to bestir themselves to quench this in the church; never did mariners use more speed to stop a leak in a ship, lest all should be drowned, than ministers especially, and all Christian men should haste to stop this beginning of the breaking in of these waters of strife, lest thereby the whole Church be overwhelmed.'

Such a high view of the real and essential unity of the church was strictly related to the true preaching of the Word and the right administration of the sacraments. There was a biblically-oriented ecumenism and across the Reformed church commitment to the gospel and a single system of doctrine found expression in a number of confessions. Christ's church in the world professed itself a community that had received grace by faith in Christ and knew Christ through the teaching of Holy Scripture. In the obedience of faith they listened together to His word and together learned the truth of 'one Lord, one faith, one baptism.' Norman Shepherd writes in *Scripture and Confession* (p. 23): 'The unity of the church visible does not achieve expression only after universal adoption of a single confession of faith, but is already present, for example, when one church denomination is able to recognize in the doctrinal standards of another denomination the same faith to which it is committed. On this basis an ecclesiastical assembly may welcome into its midst and participation in debate the fraternal delegate of another ecclesiastical body adhering to a different doctrinal formula. The church of Christ visible is always united under the uniquely authoritative standard of the written Word of God.'

Because we believe that the *sola scriptura* principle alone makes true unity possible we can see absolutely no hope for the church in the modern ecumenical movement where unreformed traditionalism and unrepentant liberalism dispense with even a formal acceptance of the Word of God and replace it with something directly contradictory to it. A vast, amorphous organization, full of unresolved contradictions and ambiguities, is far from 'the unity of the Spirit in the bond of peace.' To the Reformed, 'There is one body and one Spirit even as ye are called in one hope of your calling' (Eph. 4.4). Paul G. Schrotenboer in a penetrating study, 'Motives of Ecumenism,' pays attention to the ecumenical emphasis on communication and dialogue as means of establishing Christian truth and takes care to indicate clearly the essential qualitative difference between the truth of the Word of God in Christ Jesus and man's autonomous unliberated speculation. We should certainly seek the truth and that in fellowship with one another, but, 'In relation to the Truth of the Word of God, the "holy quest" should be transformed into a holy audience. In this holy audience in which men of communal faith seek for a deeper *understanding* of the unchanging truth of God, significant advances are made. Therefore there should be unity among Christians . . . for their richer understanding of and more fruitful obedience to God's Word' (p. 50).

The World Council of Churches is associated with a world-wide drive to unite churches in order to advance missions and point to our Lord's words in John 17. Christ did indeed pray that His disciples might all be one in order that the world might believe that God sent Him: 'Not for these only do I ask but also for those who believe in me through their word, that they all may be one, as thou, Father, art in me and I in thee, in order that they also may be in us, in order that the world may believe that thou has sent me. And the glory which thou hast given me I have given to them, in order that they may be one as we are one. I in them and thou in me, in order that they may be perfected in one, in order that the world may know that thou hast sent me and hast loved them as thou hast loved me.' The pattern after which this oneness is to be formed is the eternal and profound unity existing between the Father and the Son. It is a oneness of faith and hope and love and also of life itself. This was no haphazard assembly our Lord had in view but one that was defined in terms of His unity with the Father. Professor Murray writes: 'John 17.21 must not be divorced from John 17.20. To dissociate the unity for which Christ prayed from all that is involved in believing on him is to rend asunder what our Lord joined together. And this believing on him is not a faith that can be abstracted from the total witness of the New Testament to the identity of Jesus. Our Lord pointed to this when he said, 'those who believe on me through their word' (op. cit., p. 10).

Protestants agree that the church in heaven and on earth is one. There is one flock (not fold), one people of God, one body of Christ. Essentially the church has a given oneness which we cannot create or destroy. The plethora of divisions not merely between denominational groups but within them as well, makes us regard the church's unity, to say the least, as problematical. We recognize that Christians may 'bite and devour one another,' that members of the same family may disagree profoundly though they remain, nevertheless, members of the same family. Hodge speaks of these 'disturbing influences,' partly external (political and geographic) and partly internal, as distorting the unity of the church in her witness and life in the world. 'When men differ it is better to avow their diversity of opinion or faith, than to pretend to agree, or to force discordant elements into a formal uncongenial union' (op. cit., p. 95). This is in itself an acceptable conclusion. Men are not bound to unite when their differences would destroy harmony or involve them in unscriptural practices that would offend the individual conscience, but when 'the points in which they differ are either such as the Scriptures do not determine, or which are of minor importance, it is obviously wrong that all the evils arising from the multiplication of sects, should for the sake of these subordinate matters be continued' (op. cit., p. 96). While it is true that the essential unity is spiritual the body of Christ is not an invisible entity and the oneness for which He prayed was to be a demonstration to the world in a most tangible way. The lack of unity among churches that have a pure and identical confession of faith is a denial of the unity which the Lord's intercessory prayer obliges true believers to strive for. It has been observed frequently that the lack of unity among the strictly evangelical Reformed Churches calls for prayer that men would see this fragmentation and lack of co-ordination as an evil, destructive to the body, dishonouring to the Lord and maiming the active witness of the church. Divisions in the Christian church are a judgement or chastisement from God. 'It is plain enough that the anger of the Lord hath divided us, and rent us in twain, like the veil of the temple, from the top to the bottom. God is angry because we have sinned' (Ralph Erskine, *Diary and Life*, p. 152). The divisions of the church ought to exercise and humble us under the hand of God (Psalm 137.1–3).

Let us return to the statement at the beginning of this section: union with Christ forms the church in the vital fellowship of the Holy spirit. It has been said that the word 'fellowship' has 'come down in the world.' The Greek *koinonia* in its New Testament use would indicate participation, sharing, rather than association or, as in modern parlance, gregarious camaraderie. The core of *koinonia* is theological and constitutive rather than social: partaking of something of which others also partake. Clowney quotes J. Y. Campbell (op. cit., p. 51) as saying that the verb *koinonein* is often used as a synoym for *metechein*, to partake of, to share. In Heb. 2.11–12, 17 and 1 John 1.3–17 the direct concept of fellowship is emphasized, yet all fellowship rests on vital union with Christ. The fellowship of the Spirit (Phil. 2.1) must have reference to the way in which believers partake of the grace of Christ and share divine gifts the one with the other. In this rich and enriching relationship the Spirit works out His purpose for the church and directs her mission. He is at present Himself as Gift and Giver of a rich multiplicity of varied gifts for the service of the body: 'Now there are diversities of gifts, but the same Spirit. And there are diversities of ministrations, and the same Lord. And there are diversities of workings, but the same God who worketh all things in all. But to each one is given the manifestation of the Spirit to profit withal' (1 Cor. 12.4–7). Different gifts indicate different ministeries. God distinguishes ministeries in the fellowship for the good of the body. If the body were all an eye or an ear there would be distortion to the point of destruction. It is our Lord's requirement that we keep the unity of the Spirit in sharing the Spirit's gifts.

It is inside this fellowship that we consider dissensions (*kaire-*

seis). Paul says that they are necessary in order that the approved may become evident (1 Cor. 11.19), but they are regrettable (Gal. 5.20). They are the works of the flesh. Paul's two statements in regard to dissensions are very similar to what Christ said regarding 'offences,' *skandala*: 'Woe to the world because of offences. It is necessary indeed for offences to come but woe to the man through whom the offence comes' (Matt. 18.6–7; cf. Luke 17.1–3). In both contexts the word 'offence' means, *a cause of stumbling*, and the most severe condemnation is pronounced against those who injure the fellowship in this way. The fact that when the New Testament deals with obstacles to the developing life of the Body it points to people and not to churches is most important. Pride and party spirit, lack of love, lack of care, lack of forbearance, unwillingness to respect the other man's conscience in secondary matters break unity at the 'grass-roots' (Rom. 14; 1 Cor. 8).

Because the church is the church it has all that is essential to its basic unity in every age but the complete expression of this unity will appear only when she is presented to her Lord, 'a glorious church, not having spot or wrinkle or any such thing.'

How, we ask, are we to serve the expression of the church's unity in Scotland today? If our foregoing exposition has been right certain principles seem to arise as guides to duty.

First, we must insist that the only proper basis for closer church relations must be found in a clear and unwavering testimony to the absolute authority of the Holy Scriptures. We are charged and privileged to hold fast and to hold forth all the truth known to us.

Second, there is what Hodge puts first, mutual recognition of all Christians as members of the body of Christ. 'It is a great offence against Christian charity, and a direct violation of the command of Christ, to refuse to receive as our brethren those whom Christ receives as His disciples' (op. cit., p. 97).

Third, we should labour to create a worthy atmosphere for unity. We know that the build-up of good-will begins on the personal level, our individual words and actions must show that we are anxious to keep the unity of the Spirit. Living and working in mutual respect there should be persistent avoidance of divisive courses; a persistent friendliness even when misunderstood and repelled. No man 'is an island, intire of itselfe' in the church of Christ. This spirit must rule among our office-bearers so that one court will respect the decisions of another with meticulous care so that together they may build up and strengthen the body. The charge of isolationism should not lie at the door of an evangelical reformed church. Professor Collins in his valuable book, 'The Heritage of our Fathers,' gives a full discussion of the attitude of the Free Church to Presbyterian reunion. He writes (p. 157): 'The Free Church gave all serious attention to the questions relating to further Union, and made various pronouncements upon them, eventually, in a circular issued in 1929, clearly indicating her reasons for not participating in the Church Union that was soon to take place. 'It would be the occasion of much joy to us, as Free Churchmen'—so runs the pamphlet—to see the reunion of the sundered Presbyterians of Scotland on the ground held by our Reforming and Covenanting Fathers. It is a matter of sincere regret that we cannot regard the Union that is soon to be consummated as one that at all, worthily, answers such a description.' This is both clear and courteous.

Fourth, we should be ready to advance good works by co-operation in a non-sectarian spirit along with all our brethren. A sharpened christian conscience will itself urge toward a community of action. Federations, involving no sacrifice of principle or testimony, have been formed with this end in view and have been used of God for 'the increase of the body into the building up of itself in love' (Gal. 4.16).

Bibliography

D. D. Bannerman, *The Scripture Doctrine of the Church*, Clark, Edinburgh, 1887.

J. Bannerman, *The Church of Christ*, Clark, Edinburgh, 1868.

E. Best, *One Body in Christ*, London, SPCK, 1961.

Burn-Murdoch, *Church Continuity and Unity*, CUP, 1945.

C. B. E. Cranfield, *Commentary on Romans 12, 13*.

S.Hansen, *The Unity of the Church*, Upsala, 1946.

C. Hodge, *The Church and its Polity*, Nelson, 1879.

J. Macpherson, *The Doctrine of the Church in Scottish Theology*, Edinburgh, 1903.

J. Murray, *Nature etc. of the Church*.

E. Kasemann, *New Testament Questions for Today*, SCM, 1969.

H. Ridderbos, *Paul*, Erdmans, 1975.

Various pamphlets and articles by several writers inclusive of Schrotenboer, Paton, Clowney, Stibbs and Packer.

Infant Baptism

ALLAN M. HARMAN, B.A., B.D., M.LITT., TH.M., TH.D.
Visiting Professor of Hebrew and Old Testament Studies,
Hawthorn Theological Hall, Victoria, Australia.

1. The Sacraments

At the outset some remarks are apposite in regard to the term 'sacrament' which is used in all the Reformed confessions in reference to baptism and the Lord's Supper. The term is not a biblical one, but rather one of ecclesiastical origin. The Latin word *sacramentum* was the term for the military oath by which a soldier bound himself to obey the officer placed over him. Possibly the term was transferred to Christian use to signify the obligation of a Christian to serve Christ. Another explanation of its Christian use is that it refers to the mysteries of Christianity and to the fact that the sacraments, though outward signs, yet have an inward and spiritual meaning.

Our understanding of a sacrament does not depend, however, on the derivation of the term but rather on the teaching of Scripture in regard to it. The authority behind the sacraments is divine, not human, and in this respect they are similar to other ordinances which form a part of worship. In the preaching of the Word the truth is brought home to the heart and understanding, while in the sacraments the same truth is impressed by means of visible signs. They signify the benefits of the gospel as they serve as pictorial representations of covenant promises. Even the spectator at the administration of the sacrament may learn something of the gospel message, though the sacramental benefit is confined to worthy participants.

The sacraments must be understood in a federal or covenantal context. They are (as Paul says in Rom. 4.11 of one of the sacraments of the Old Testament church) seals of the covenant and of its blessings. This covenantal connection is stated explicitly of the Lord's Supper in the words of institution: 'This cup is the new covenant in my blood, which is shed for you' (Lk. 22.20). The connection of baptism with the covenant is seen primarily in the relation which baptism has to circumcision. The sacraments are sealing ordinances in that they confirm or seal God's promises and are perpetual witnesses to the fact that 'he is faithful who has promised'.

As sacraments, baptism and the Lord's Supper are means of grace. They serve to strengthen the faith of those who receive them, and are a means of upbuilding those who already possess God's grace. In applying the benefits of the gospel they do not work automatically, but serve as channels of God's grace in that they are among the appointed means for the advancement of spiritual life. There is no virtue in the sacraments in and of themselves, for they are entirely dependent on the operation of the Spirit of God and on the faith of the recipients. A merely physical participation in the sacraments conveys no blessing, but rather brings with it the condemnation of God.

Another fact which must be borne in mind is that the sacraments have significance as ordinances of the church. That is to say, they are not administered privately, nor do they have significance for an individual apart from his connection with the church of God. This fact explains why the administration of the sacraments falls to office-bearers of the church. In the Reformed churches the administration of the sacraments is the responsibility of the minister because of the intimate connection between the preaching of the Word and the administration of the sacraments. Those entitled to preach the Word dispense the sacraments, and in so doing act on behalf of the church. Likewise the sacraments are administered publicly in the presence of the congregation because they relate to congregational life, and to proceed to administer them in private is a denial of their corporate character.

2. The Unity of the Church in Old and New Testaments

Basic to a correct appreciation of the biblical doctrine of baptism is the doctrine of the church, and especially the essential unity of the church in both dispensations. The Old Testament speaks of an assembly of the covenant people gathered before the Lord as God's own possession (Ex. 19.5; 1 Ki. 8.14, 22, 55, 65; 2 Ch. 6.13). Such an assembly was a permanent feature of the believing community in the Old Testament period and not just a characteristic which belonged to a passing phase of Israel's history. The worship of the Old Testament centred on the tabernacle (see especially Ex. 29.42–46), and God promised to meet there with Israel, to dwell there and to be their God. That promise was central to the covenant theme of the Old Testament and was reiterated constantly, as well as finding its fulfilment in the New Testament.

This church of Old Testament days did not disappear with the change in dispensation at the commencement of the New Testament period. Stephen gave expression to the identification of the church in both eras when he said of Moses; 'This is he who was in the church in the wilderness with the angel that spake to him in the mount Sinai, and with our fathers' (Acts 7.28). Right throughout the New Testament there is the application to the New Testament church of terms and descriptions which were first applied to the Old Testament church (cf. 1 Pet. 2.9, 10). It is striking too how the redemptive events connected with the birth, ministry and death of Jesus are viewed as the fulfilment of the covenant made with Abraham (Lk. 1.54–55, 72–75; Gal. 3.6–29). This continuity of the church into the New Testament period is emphasized by the analogy of the olive tree which Paul uses in Romans 11.17–24. The whole point dominating Paul's argument is that there is only one olive tree, only one church, and that the apostolic ministry did not result in the formation of a new church. The effect of that ministry was to engraft the Gentiles into the already existing tree.

It is also helpful to bear in mind the fact that the terms for the Old Testament sacraments are applied to the New Testament sacraments, and vice versa. Thus in the New Testament 'circumcision' and 'the passover' can be applied to the rites of the New Testament church. Paul can say that seeing 'Christ our passover has been sacrificed for us, let us therefore celebrate the feast' (1 Cor. 5.7–8), while in Colossians 2.11 ff. circumcision and baptism are linked in such a way that the terms applicable to the rite of circumcision are predicated of baptism. The reverse procedure also takes place when Paul speaks of the children of Israel as having been 'baptized into Moses in the cloud and in the sea; and all ate the same spiritual food; and all drank the same spiritual drink' (1 Cor. 10.2–4).

3. The Old Testament Background

That baptism has as its Old Testament counterpart circumcision is not now such a matter of dispute even with Baptist writers, and there is no need to re-argue the matter here. Thus Paul Jewett can say: 'We do not deny the essential correctness of this approach (i.e. of covenant theology). Though most baptists do not believe it, it is indeed true that the NT fulfils the Old and that even the analogy between circumcision and baptism is beyond cavil' (*The Encyclopedia of Christianity* I, p. 524). David Kingdon similarly recognizes the connection between the two. He comments: 'It is my considered opinion that Baptists must recognize the analogy between circumcision and baptism. It seems to me pointless to deny the existence of this analogy, yet it is often done. One appreciates why there has been a marked reluctance to recognize its existence, namely, because of the fear that to recognize the analogy would mean the opening of the door to the practice of infant baptism, since as circumcision was applied to Abraham and his seed, baptism should be applied to believers and their seed' (*Children of Abraham*, p. 28). However, neither of these writers is prepared to accept identity of meaning between baptism and circumcision such as has often been set forth by those advocating infant baptism (for a typical example see James Bannerman, *The Church of Christ* II, pp. 84–86).

A re-assessment of the significance of the connection between circumcision and baptism is necessary though, both for Baptist and non-Baptist writers alike, because of the revision in our understanding of the nature of the Abrahamic covenant and the rite of circumcision. This revision has been the result of study setting the Abrahamic covenant over against its Near Eastern background. All of biblical revelation came in particular historical settings, and to neglect the historical and cultural background will only result in a distorted view of the particular revelatory data under consideration. In the case of the Abrahamic covenant it must be set over against the treaties or covenants which were well-known in the patriarchal period, and thus in the account in Genesis 17 all the regular features of these ancient vassal treaties appear (for a brief discussion on these treaties see *The Lion Handbook of the Bible*, pp. 198 f., and for the application of this background knowledge to the Abrahamic covenant consult *The New Bible Commentary Revised*, pp. 92–97).

The specific stipulation of the covenant in Genesis 17 is the practice of circumcision. Either circumcision was a practice already well-known, or else fuller instructions were given regarding performance of the rite, though this appears to be less likely than the former suggestion. The communal performance recorded in Genesis 17.23–27 served as the ratification of the covenant. Just as in the contemporary secular covenants, those who entered into the covenant with the Lord bound themselves by this oath to his service, and placed themselves under the curse expressed if they were unfaithful to their obligations. As was typical in covenants of that period, the knife ritual of circumcision vividly portrayed the judgment specified in the spoken oath (for secular examples see D. J. McCarthy, *Treaty and Covenant*, p. 195), and for the Old Testament covenants this oath was virtually synonymous with the covenant itself (cf. Deut. 29.12).

This background setting to the covenant detailed in Genesis 17 enables an emphasis to be placed on circumcision which has often been lacking. Rather than stressing qualification or purification (which is a secondary significance of circumcision) the emphasis must fall on circumcision as a sign of God's judgment if the stipulations of the covenant (including circumcision) were not kept. Rather than indicating primarily a new status, circumcision, when administered to a male Hebrew child, was to be a constant reminder to him of the obligations of God's covenant, and of the fact that if he proved unfaithful to those obligations, and therefore virtually denied the covenant, he would suffer under God's judgment. Thus in Genesis 17.4 there is a play on words in the Hebrew text, for the warning is given that breach of the covenant requirement would involve being cut off, which is an allusion to the rite of circumcision as a cutting ritual, as well as echoing the common Hebrew idiom for making a covenant (kārath berith, 'to cut a covenant').

When the institution of circumcision is seen in its historical setting in Genesis 17, then the emphasis can rightly fall on the significance of the covenant sign, rather than on questions relating to the status of the circumcised child. Too often the subsidiary question of status in reference to circumcision (and also in reference to baptism) has been allowed to overshadow the significance of the covenant sign and seal. It is clear from Paul's words in Romans 4.11–12 in reference to Abraham that his circumcision was subsequent to his possession of a righteous status with God, and that the circumcision he received was neither the cause of that righteous status nor did it enhance it. Circumcision, according to Paul's argument, does not exclude us from Abraham's descendants, nor does it contribute to our incorporation with them. It is also to be deduced from Paul's discussion that circumcision was a sign and seal for all who received it, and therefore in the case of infants it was not such a sign and seal subsequent to their faith but prior to it.

Another point which needs to be made in connection with the idea of status is that many discussions on circumcision centre too much on the question of circumcision as a sign of nationality. To do this is misleading, for during the first half-millenium that circumcision was administered under the Abrahamic covenant, those receiving the covenant sign were not members of an earthly kingdom. Hence to equate the right to circumcision with citizenship in the Old Testament theocracy is to ignore the setting of the institution in the patriarchal period and the long elapse of time until Israel became a nation.

Although the concept of circumcision as a mark of qualification was not taught contemporaneously with its institution, yet the idea is present from the Mosaic period onwards. Moses could say that he was 'a man of uncircumcised lips' (Ex. 6.12–13), by which he meant that they were unfit for service. The expression an 'uncircumcised heart' clearly meant a heart which was stubborn or rebellious, and the command to circumcise the foreskin of the heart (Deut. 10.16) meant that the state of heart had to be brought into conformity with the outward sign of the covenant borne in the flesh. Later in the Old Testament this distinction appears in a very graphic form when the Lord through Jeremiah declares that he will punish those who are circumcised yet uncircumcised (Jer. 9.25–26). This is the Old Testament teaching which is taken up by Paul, who taught that a true Jew was one who was circumcised inwardly, with the true circumcision being that of the heart, by the Spirit (Rom. 2.25–29; cf. Rom. 4.11–12; Phil. 3.3; Acts 7.51). Here is the constant teaching of Scripture that when the consecration symbolized in circumcision is truly fulfilled it is not just an outward matter but a thing of the heart. Any who were circumcised in the flesh but not in the heart were really in a state of uncircumcision.

Another aspect of the Old Testament background which requires comment is the matter of parental authority in relation to circumcision. To state the matter in another way, it is necessary to look and see what were the principles governing covenant administration, and these principles revolve around the choice of circumcision as the covenant sign. The account of the institution of circumcision given in Genesis 17 and the fact that it was performed on the male organ of procreation suggest that it had something to do with the descendants of the person receiving circumcision. At this point another look at the secular vassal treaties is helpful, because the vassal coming into the treaty arrangement did not enter as an individual but as a ruler of the people. All under his authority were brought within the power of the superior king, and his oath pledged his servants as well as himself. Moreover, his oath committed his descendants to obedience to the covenant requirements as well. For a biblical example Deuteronomy 29.9 ff. serves to show how those entering into the covenant (which was being renewed as the children of Israel were about to enter the land of promise) included the children and the aliens (vs. 11), and observance of the requirements of God's covenant extended to the generations to come.

In the vassal treaties there is reference to having one's descendants cut off. For example in a treaty which the Assyrian king Esarhaddon made with Ramataia it is said: 'May he [Ashur] never grant you fatherhood. May Sarpanitu who gives name and seed, destroy your name and seed from the land' (D. J. Wiseman, *The Vassal-Treaties of Esarhaddon*, pp. 60, 62). Biblical parallels to this occur in Deuteronomy, for among the pronounced blessings are those relating to the offspring of the body (Deut. 28.3–6), while among the curses are those which relate to the offspring (Deut. 28.16–19). The ultimate curse of having no descendants features in the biblical account, and reference can be made to the curse uttered against Jehoiachin, the last king of Judah (Jer. 22.24–30).

To return to Abraham and the covenant recorded in Genesis 17, the implication is that Abraham the patriarch was entering the covenant with all those who were under his authority. That such authority extended beyond his own children is made plain in Genesis 17 by reference to the fact that purchased slaves, those bought slaves who were then in the house, were to receive circumcision. Providing that Eliezer of Damascus, his adopted son, was still alive, then he too would have received the covenant sign. In himself being circumcised Abraham received the sign which spoke of God's curse against him if he was unfaithful, but also there was the reminder that God would cut off his descendants if he failed to keep the covenant obligations. All his descendants were being consecrated to God in his circumcision, but yet each of those descendants would require to receive the covenant sign for themselves.

The basic principle which becomes apparent from the administration of the Abrahamic covenant is that a loyal covenant servant had the responsibility to bring all those under his authority to the Lord and also to consecrate his descendants after him. If a man failed to fulfil this obligation then he became liable to the curse of being cut off from the people. From parallel passages in the Pentateuch it is clear that this expression 'to be cut off' did not just refer to social exclusion from the rest of the people but rather to the execution of the death penalty (cf. Lev. 18.8, 29 with Lev. 20.11 for an example of this usage).

There is one enigmatic passage in the Old Testament which is best seen as an illustration of the judgment curse being inflicted on an unfaithful covenant servant. This is the incident recorded in Exodus 4.24–26. Moses was returning to Egypt to assume the role to which he had been called of God, and at the lodging place the Lord met him and sought to put him to death. It was only after Zipporah performed the circumcision of her son that the Lord let Moses alone, and he was allowed to go on with his appointed mission. Seemingly Moses had failed to ensure that Gershom was circumcised, and therefore the ultimate curse of the covenant (indicated by circumcision itself) was to be executed against him. There are many features about the incident which are difficult, especially Zipporah's action and words after the circumcision. What does appear plain is that Moses was held responsible for the fact that Gershom was not circumcised, but that Zipporah's action resulted in the threat against his life being removed. This incident re-inforces the principle that a loyal covenant servant had the responsibility to see that his children bore the covenant sign, and thus it was not only an individual who made his confession of trust in the Lord but the head of a household brought that household into a relationship with the Lord as well.

4. The Institution of Christian Baptism
When we turn to the New Testament we find that in the period up to the death and resurrection of our Lord, there is the co-existence of circumcision and several forms of baptism. Thus John the Baptist was circumcised on the eighth day (Lk. 1.59) as was Jesus (Lk. 2.21), which was the current custom at that time (Jn. 7.22). But both John and Jesus' disciples practised baptism, and while these forms of baptism did not constitute Christian baptism yet there is a relationship to that baptism which was instituted by Jesus after his resurrection. John came with his message of repentance for the remission of sins, and the baptism which he administered was a special sign for that final generation living under the Old Covenant, and clearly it was intimately connected

with his message of judgment. There was greater significance in his baptism in relation to the impending judgment of God than to the thought of purification from sin.

The baptism practised by Jesus and his disciples has to be related to that of John. This becomes clear when it is realized that the cessation of the Judean baptismal ministry of Jesus (Jn. 3.22; 4.1 ff.) is linked with the imprisonment of John (Mt. 21.23 ff.; Mk. 11.22 ff.; Lk. 20.1 ff.). The final despising of that ultimatum, which John was issuing, ushers in the new era, and so when Jesus begins to minister in Galilee he can proclaim the arrival of the acceptable year of the Lord (Lk. 4.18–21). Presumably the significance of this earlier baptism of Jesus was similar to that of John's baptism.

When we come to the institution of the distinctly Christian baptism after the resurrection (Mt. 28.19) it is impossible to disjoin this absolutely from the earlier baptism of John. As Meredith Kline has stated it: 'Nevertheless, this new water baptism, appearing so soon after the other and still within the personal ministry of Jesus, would hardly bear a meaning altogether different from the earlier one. There would be a pronounced continuity between Christian baptism and the earlier, Johannine baptism' (*By Oath Consigned*, pp. 64 f.). One does not need to follow the position completely which Kline goes on to elaborate in order to observe the line of continuity which emerges in relation to the significance of circumcision, John's baptism, and Christian baptism. In each of them there is no thought of grace or blessing inherent in the sign itself. Rather in receiving the sign the recipient acknowledged the sovereign rule of the Lord over him, faithful submission to which would bring blessing, while rejection of it would incur God's ultimate judgment.

For our immediate purpose there are two aspects of our Lords' command to baptize which require emphasis. The first is the fact that baptism is subsequent to disciplining: 'Therefore in your going make disciples of all nations, baptizing them. . . .' The main verb is 'make disciples', and the method of carrying out this command is contained in the two co-ordinate participles which follow, 'baptizing' and 'teaching'. Discipleship involves not just acceptance of a body of knowledge, but submission to the Lord and obedience to his command. Only those who abide in the truth are truly Christ's disciples (Jn. 8.31). That acknowledgment an individual must make when he comes to seek baptism for himself and for his children, and whatever further instruction he must undergo that coming for baptism is in itself a confession of discipleship.

The second aspect, and one which re-inforces the point just made, is the significance of the clause 'into the name of the Father and of the Son and of the Holy Spirit'. By use of the singular 'name' emphasis is placed on the fact that it is baptism into the name of the triune God, while 'into the name of' has the connotation of union with someone, and also the acknowledgment of ownership. This appears so both from the analogous usage in the Old Testament (cf. Deut. 28.9; Is. 63.19) and also from our knowledge of Hellenistic Greek usage (cf. J. H. Moulton and George Milligan, *The Vocabulary of the Greek Testament Illustrated from the Papyri and Other Non-Literary Sources*, p. 451; W. F. Arndt and F. W. Gringrich, *A Greek–English Lexicon of the New Testament and Other Early Christian Literature*, p. 575). Hence those receiving the sign of baptism receive a mark which is indicative of union with the triune God and which is a recognition of their submission to his lordship.

5. The Administration of Infant Baptism

The remainder of our discussion must now concentrate on two specific aspects of baptism, namely, the administration of baptism to children and the significance which it has in their case. As we turn to look at the first of these matters we must note that it is not a matter which can be settled by appeal to specific texts of the New Testament which authorize the baptism of infants. There has to be the recognition that the argument for infant baptism is a cumulative one, and depends also on the position noted earlier in this discussion in relation to the unity of the church in Old and New Testament dispensations. The question of the unity of the church must be settled prior to approaching the question of baptism. The case for infant baptism is grounded in the recognition that God's covenant is basically one in both dispensations, and that as the gospel dispensation is the unfolding of the Abrahamic covenant it is to be expected that the relation of children to the sign and seal of the covenant would be the same in both dispensations. As Professor John Murray has expressed it, in the absence of any repeal of the practice of administering the covenant sign to children 'we conclude that the administering of the sign and seal of the covenant to the infant seed of believers is still in operation and has perpetual divine warrant. In other words, the command to administer the sign to infants has not been revoked: therefore it is still in force' (*Christian Baptism*, p. 53; see also pp. 48–53 for his main discussion on the inclusion of infants). By divine command the covenant sign of circumcision was adminstered to male children under the Abrahamic covenant, and without any intimation of the repeal of the incorporation of children we have to proceed on the basis that the new covenant sign of baptism is for children as well as adults.

While the New Testament contains no express command regarding the baptism of children (nor for that matter any command limiting it to adults), there is other evidence which does have a distinct bearing on the matter, and which lends support to the position already indicated.

(1) The New Testament teaches that the children of believers stand in a category different from that of unbelievers. Paul says: 'For the unbelieving husband is sanctified through his wife, and the unbelieving wife is sanctified through her believing husband; for otherwise your children are unclean, and now they are holy' (1 Cor. 7.14). Doubtless here 'holy' is not to be equated with 'regenerated', but appears to take its meaning from Old Testament contexts in which 'holiness' can be indicative of formal consecration to the Lord. Here then in the New Testament is the situation in which children are declared to be sanctified, not because of personal faith but because of a relationship which they bear to a believing parent. That this is Paul's meaning here finds confirmation in his reference to the status of the descendants of covenant members in Romans 11.16, 'And if the first piece of dough be holy, the lump is also; and if the root be holy, the branches are too'. In this passage 'holy' does not refer to what is morally 'pure' but to the consecration of the Israelites to God. Now while no argument for infant baptism rests on these passages, yet they are important in so far as they show that Old Testament ideas continue over into the New Testament and that parental authority was still viewed in the same way. The objections against this interpretation, especially with reference to the unbelieving partner also being sanctified, fail to recognize that the idea of sanctification does not necessarily have to be identical in the cases of the children and the unbelieving partner, for the implication may well be in the latter case that the marriage relationship is itself sanctified unto the service of God's covenant.

(2) While the account in the Gospels regarding the bringing of little babes to Jesus (Mt. 19.13–15; Mk. 10.13–16; Lk. 18.15–17) affords in itself no direct justification for infant baptism (Christian baptism not having yet been instituted and no mention being made at all of baptism in connection with this incident) yet it does afford evidence both of the fact that Jesus regarded little children as members of the kingdom of God, and of our Lord's approval of the parental authority which was exercised in bringing the children to him. That the membership of little children is in view is made plain by the context in which the words of our Lord come, and by the words themselves which must be construed to mean that Jesus was speaking expressly of little children being partakers in his kingdom. The emphasis on parental authority in the passage is important for it carries our Lord's commendation of those parents who brought their children to him and placed them under the authority of his ministry. It is also worth pointing out that the call of Jesus was to the babes (Lk. 18.16, *auta* referring back to *ta brephē*, the babes), and that this call was realized in the bringing of the children by their parents so that the idea of covenant headship was emphatically recognized.

(3) The accounts of household baptisms (Acts 16.15, 33, 34; 1 Cor. 1.16) comprise one-quarter of the accounts we have in the New Testament of the actual administration of baptism. In none of the accounts is express mention made of the presence of children, but as Meredith Kline comments 'households are mentioned along with the central authority figures in these instances, and these households had to consist of somebody in the category of household subordinates. Even with respect to the narrower question of whether parental authority is honored in the adminstration of the New Covenant, it would not matter whether conclusive evidence could be adduced proving that there were no children in any of these households; for if there were no children, then surely the household consisted of servants; and if it could be shown that servants were received into the church on the basis of the authority principle, it would follow *a fortiori* that the continuity with Old Testament practice included infants also' (*op. cit.*, p. 97). When viewed alongside announcements of salvation such as that in Acts 2.38, 39, the implication is that the confession of faith of the parent involved had as its consequence the incorporation of his household in the covenant community. In one of the instances of household baptism the faith of the father is singled out for specific mention.

Luke, in recording what transpired in the household of the Philippian gaoler, notes that while the rejoicing of the gaoler was accompanied by like rejoicing on the part of his family, yet in reference to faith it is the gaoler only who is singled out for mention. Many of the English translations fail to translate accurately at this point, but the RSV is to be commended for its faithful rendering: 'And he rejoiced with all his household that *he had believed* in God' (vs. 34). Though Kurt Aland and others have argued to the contrary, the Greek word for household used in these instances in Acts and 1 Corinthians (*oikos*) also points to a family group regarded as a unity. Thus Jeremias can say emphatically that 'nowhere in the whole of Hellenistic Greek literature nor in the Jewish literature' is the word *oikos* 'restricted to the adult members of the family' (*The Origins of Infant Baptism*, p. 14). It may also be true that this Greek word denotes the narrower family of parents and children as over against the word *oikia* which denotes household or establishment in the wider sense. This distinction was stressed by Douglas Bannerman in his book *The Scripture Doctrine of the Church*, pp. 76 f., 88–85, 320, 325, 504 ff., though more recently Jeremias has upheld the distinction between these two Greek words in that *oikos* denotes the members of the household while *oikia* is used when speaking of the social position of the family or of all the kin (*op. cit.*, p. 14 n. 2). It is interesting that in the two references to the family of Stephanus in the first in 1 Corinthians 1.16 *oikos* is used, but in 1 Corinthians 16.15 ('you know the household of Stephanus, that they were the first fruits of Achaia, and that they have devoted themselves for the ministry of the saints') the wider word *oikia* appears.

(4) The authority of parents over the children is stressed by Paul when addressing Christian parents. In letters to churches he also singles out children and gives to them, as to other groups such as husbands, wives, fathers, servants, and masters, definite instructions regarding their conduct (Col. 3.20, 21; Eph. 6.1–3). The children must be regarded as belonging to the saints to whom the epistles are addressed, and the obedience which is required of them is reckoned as being given to the Lord himself (Eph. 6.1, 'in the Lord'; 6.4, 'in the discipline and instruction of the Lord'). Parental authority is here regarded as the extension of the covenantal authority of the Lord himself. Another striking thing about the passage in Ephesians 6 is that the link with the Old Testament is made explicit by appeal to that stipulation of the covenant of Sinai

HOLD FAST YOUR CONFESSION

which dealt specifically with the relationship of children to parents, and Paul quotes it with the accompanying promise (Eph. 6.2, 3; cf. Exod. 20.12, Deut. 5.16). This conforms with the general impression which is gained of the New Testament teaching that the arrangements for covenantal teaching and authority seen in the Old Testament also carries over into the New Testament period.

Some comment is also required in relation to the profession necessary on the part of a parent when bringing a child for baptism. In the practice of Reformed churches since the Reformation there has been some difference in regard to the administration of infant baptism, and alongside a genuine profession of faith on the part of at least one parent, another lesser profession has come to stand as well. In the latter case no personal profession of faith on the part of the parent is required, and consequently no requirement of church membership (actual or prospective) is involved. Several points need to be made concerning this position, which cannot be defended on biblical grounds.

(1) The very nature of the covenantal authority of parents in the biblical sense presupposes a genuine profession on their part when bringing their children for baptism. Failure to make such a profession would in itself be tantamount to a rejection of the authority of the Lord and a spurning of the demands which he makes of his loyal subjects.

(2) The New Testament evidence shows that a profession of personal faith is a prerequisite for baptism either for oneself or for one's children. The New Testament knows only baptism for believers and their children, and there is no suggestion that a profession of nominal adherence to the Christian faith can serve as a substitute for a true and living faith in Jesus Christ as redeemer and lord. The principle of *nullum sacramentum sine fide* ('where there is no faith, there is no sacrament') applies very pointedly here.

(3) This position is confirmed by an appreciation of the fact that there is an identity of profession required for the sacraments of baptism and the Lord's Supper. As Professor John Murray puts it: 'It is a great fallacy and one fraught with grave consequence to suppose that there is such a thing in the New Testament as dual confession, one entitling to baptism and another, of a higher order, entitling to communicant membership' (*op. cit.*, p. 83; see also the discussion by William Cunningham, *The Reformers and the Theology of the Reformation*, pp. 268 ff.). Just as an adult

seeking baptism is required to make the same profession for it as for his admission to the Lord's Table, so no distinction can be made between the profession a parent makes in regard to his child's baptism and his own admission as a communicant member.

(4) Nor should it be forgotten that in bringing a child for baptism the parent/parents are required to vow to bring up their child in the discipline and admonition of the Lord. To come and take that vow while refusing to make a full profession of faith results in an incongruity which should be immediately apparent. Only those who have had a personal experience of God's saving grace can honestly vow to bring their child up in the discipline *of the Lord*. To come and take the vows while refusing (or unable) to make a profession of personal faith leads to a situation entirely out of accord with biblical standards both in regard to church membership and the nature of the sacrament.

6. The Significance of Infant Baptism

Whatever view we hold of baptism there has to be the recognition that the New Testament does not elucidate the doctrine of baptism with the same clarity it does the doctrine of the Lord's Supper. Hence in regard to the initiatory sacrament of the New Testament we are obliged to draw implications which necessarily depend both on a restricted number of New Testament passages and on the analogy of the initiatory rite of the Old Testament period. It is to the latter we have to turn for considerable assistance in setting forth our understanding of what is the precise significance of baptism when administered to children. Nor should we lapse into a position in which a sharp distinction is drawn between the significance of adult and infant baptism. In both it has to follow faith, in one case of the recipient himself, in the other of at least one parent. William Cunningham pointed out long ago that if we separate infant baptism from adult baptism we are led to form very defective views of the former. Cunningham also held that adult baptism is the proper fundamental type of the sacrament, but this is not a necessary consequence of asserting a close relationship between the two types of baptism (cf. *Historical Theology* II, pp. 145 f., *The Reformers and the Theology of the Reformation*, pp. 245–247; see also the comments by Murray, *op. cit.*, pp. 88–90).

It may also help to define the significance of baptism negatively first, especially in order to obviate some objections to infant baptism and also false understanding on the part of some who practise it. Firstly, it has to be stated emphatically that baptism does not regenerate. The New Testament makes this abundantly plain, for there is a case such as that of Simon Magnus, who though baptized, had the pronouncement made concerning him that his heart was not right in the sight of God and that he was still 'in the gall of bitterness and in the bondage of iniquity' (Acts 8.21, 23). Moreover, there are many cases recorded of regeneration and faith preceding baptism, as well as many expressions on the part of Paul and the other apostles that it was by the preaching of the Gospel, and not by baptism or any other sacramental means, that men would be saved. This acknowledgment of the fact that baptism does not regenerate also flows from the basic understanding of what a sacrament really is. The sacraments as signs point to realities beyond themselves, and to suggest that baptism causes regeneration is to confuse the sign and the thing signified.

Secondly, there is no presumption of regeneration either. Baptism is not adminstered on the grounds that we presume the child will be regenerated, though this view has been adopted in Reformed churches and goes back at least to the First Helvetic Confession (Art. XXII). In actual practice baptizing on the ground of presumptive regeneration has little to distinguish it from the view that baptism itself regenerates. The ground upon which we act in administering baptism to children must be that we believe that it is a divine institution to give the covenant sign to children of believers.

Looking at the matter now from the positive aspect, what significance does baptism have when adminstered to a child of believing parents?

(1) Infant baptism is a recognition that such a child is already a part of the covenant community. This participation in the covenant community does not depend upon such baptism, but upon the fact that a child was born into a family with at least one parent a true believer. Earlier we noted the import of Paul's teaching in I Corinthians 7 which shows that children of believers are by their relationship to a believing parent marked off from the unbelieving world. In this respect children of baptist parents are just as much part of the covenant community as children of parents who believe in and practise infant baptism, though in the former case the parents fail to mark their children with the covenant sign. Baptism is for the child the formal and outward acknowledgment of a relationship in existence by birth into a Christian family.

(2) The administration of baptism to a child (as of baptism to an adult) is a seal or assurance of God's promises. Added to God's verbal promises is a visible seal, which is a pledge that God's mercies are for ever sure to all who will put their trust in him. To both baptized adults and children this seal can only convey assurance of spiritual blessing providing that the recipient either now or eventually becomes a believer in the gospel. A mistaken notion sometimes arises from the brevity of definition found in the Shorter Catechism which speaks of baptism signifying and sealing spiritual blessings. However, baptism does not seal in the same sense that it signifies, for it is not a seal of regeneration to the individual but a seal of God's covenant, confirming the word he has spoken. The seal is that of a general assurance that God will unchangeably adhere to his covenant, and that he will bestow all promised blessings on all who by faith willingly receive them.

(3) The act of baptism does not convey grace to the child in and of itself, nor should it necessarily suggest the idea only that positive spiritual benefits are in store for those who believe the gospel. Earlier note was taken of the role of circumcision in denoting God's curse on an unfaithful servant. It is the teaching of the New Testament that the Lord's Supper signifies more than the spiritual benefits which believers receive through feeding on Christ, for the warning is expressly given that unworthy receiving of the sacrament, so far from conveying blessing, is but an eating and drinking of judgment (1 Cor. 11.29). Here there is continuity of thought with the Old Testament in regard to breach of the covenant oath, and unfaithfulness results in the fearful judgment of God. (cf. Heb. 10.26–31 for similarity of idea, though without mention of the Lord's Supper). It would hardly be surprising if the other New Testament sacrament also had an aspect which related to judgment or curse, especially as its Old Testament counterpart, circumcision, had such a significance. Moreover, the baptism of John was administered against the background of impending judgment (Mt. 3.7; Lk. 3.7). It served as a sign of God's curse, in the execution of which the axe was already laid to the roots of the unfruitful trees (Mt. 3.10, Lk. 3.9). There are passages in the New Testament which relate baptism to God's judgment in water ordeals (1 Cor. 10.1 ff., of the exodus from Egypt; 1 Pet. 3.19–21, of the flood), while baptism is also seen as union with Christ in the judgment he underwent in death, burial and resurrection (Rom. 6.3 ff.; Col. 2.11 ff.; cf. Lk. 12.50). In Colossians 2.11 ff. Paul understands the

circumcision of Christ, not as that administered to him as a child, but as a dying or death. Hence the sequence of ideas, circumcision: burial: resurrection, is parallel to baptized into his death: burial: resurrection, found in Romans 6.3 ff. Being baptized with Christ in his death, or circumcised with a circumcision made without hands, are both descriptions of union with Christ in the judgment of God he endured. The judgment theme inherent in baptism is highlighted by the way in which Paul links baptism with the Messiah's death, burial, and resurrection.

Those to whom baptism is administered need to be reminded of the fact that this water symbol not only depicts the positive benefits of union with Christ, but also reminds of the dreadful consequence of sin and unbelief. He who despises the gospel, though himself baptized as a child or adult, will in the end receive the due wages of sin and perish under God's judgment. What was said of the baptised Simon Magnus will be applicable to him: 'You have neither part or portion in this matter, for your heart is not right before God' (Acts 8.31). Those who despise the ordinances of God and continue in unbelief will in the end know that it is a terrifying thing to fall into the hands of the living God (Heb. 10.31).

(4) In administering infant baptism the church requires certain vows from the parents. This is important because it formally recognizes the covenant obligation which rests upon parents to bring up their children in the fear and admonition of the Lord, as well as in this way re-inforcing the truth that covenant privilege also involves covenant obligation. As Professor Murray puts it: 'What needs to be stressed in this connection is that we may never divorce the faith of God's covenant grace from the discharge of those obligations which inhere in the covenant relation. Covenant privilege always entails covenant responsibility. And this is just saying that the comfort and confidence of God's covenant mercy may never be severed from covenant keeping' (*op. cit.*, pp. 90 f.). To place confidence in the efficacy of baptism, and yet continue to show no fidelity in keeping the obligations which the Lord lays on us as individuals and as parents, is to be guilty of gross presumption.

This parental covenant obligation extends to the giving of precise instruction to children regarding why they were baptized and the need for them to be baptized in heart by the Holy Spirit. As with circumcision, the believing parent by baptism consecrates his child to the service of the Lord, but that consecration must in time become a personal matter for the child, or otherwise he must be regarded as having no part in God's kingdom. On the basis of the analogy of the initiatory ordinances of the Old and New Testaments we may apply Paul's words in Romans 2.28, 29, to baptism. He is not a Christian who is one outwardly; neither is that baptism which is outward in the flesh of any saving purpose; but the true baptism is that of the heart, and in the spirit, and not in the letter.

As an illustration of the type of parental instruction needed reference may be made to the way in which Philip Henry, father of Matthew Henry the commentator, taught his children the significance of their baptism. He drew up a short baptismal covenant for the use of his children as follows (text in *The Lives of Philip and Matthew Henry*, pp. 83 f.):

> I take God the Father to be my chiefest good, and highest end.
> I take God the Son to be my Prince and Saviour.
> I take God the Holy Ghost to be my Sanctifier, Teacher, Guide, and Comforter.
> I take the word of God to be my rule in all my actions.
> And the people of God to be my people in all conditions.
> I do likewise devote and dedicate unto the Lord, my whole self, all I am, all I have, and all I can do.
> And this I do deliberately, sincerely, freely, and for ever.

This he taught his children each Lord's Day evening, and endeavoured to lead them to a full understanding of its implications and to make their own dedication of themselves to the Lord.

(5) When a child is baptized there is the recognition that that child is part of a praying community. The Westminster Directory for Worship speaks of prayer at the time of baptism in words to this effect: 'That the Lord, who hath not left us as strangers without the covenant of promise, but called us to the privileges of His ordinances, would graciously vouchsafe to sanctify and bless His own ordinance of baptism at this time; that He would join the inward baptism of His Spirit with the outward baptism of water, and make this baptism to the infant a seal of adoption, remission of sin, regeneration, and eternal life, and all the other promises of the covenant of grace; that the child may be planted into the likeness of the death and resurrection of Jesus Christ; and that, the body of sin being destroyed in him, he may serve God in newness of life all his days'. Such prayer is not just to be prayed by the officiating minister, but the whole congregation must do so as well, for bap-

tism is an ordinance of the church. Furthermore, the church is the broader extension of the Christian family, and God deals with us not just as individuals in an atomistic way, but as members of organic and corporate relationships. God promises to be a God to the believer and his seed after him, and he works in fulfilment of his promise through the family and the church. God's method of working is in the lines of the generations, and he who executes judgment on the wicked to the third and fourth generation shows mercy to the thousandth generation of them that love him and keep his commandments (cf. Deut. 5.9–10 with Deut 7.9). Not only do the parents have responsibilities to the child, but the wider Christian family to which he belongs must also fulfil its responsibilities by praying for the child, setting examples of godly living, and supplementing the home instruction with further teaching and application of biblical truths.

(6) Baptism has a teaching ministry to fulfil as well, for every time one sees baptism administered this is a fresh reminder of the significance of it. In this way baptism (as also the Lord's Supper) appeals to our senses and functions as a pictorial representation of spiritual truth. For someone baptized in infancy this means the importance of baptism is brought home to him repeatedly as he sees it administered to others, and his own baptism takes on new significance as he is brought to profession of personal faith in Christ. By exercising such faith in Christ he shows himself to be a true heir of the promises, and the pledge of these promises given in his own baptism becomes a ground in itself for confidently relying on them. It is this benefit of baptism which the West-minister Confession has in mind when it affirms: 'The efficacy of baptism is not tied to that moment of time wherein it is administered; but that by the right use of this ordinance, the grace promised is not only offered, but really exhibited and conferred by the Holy Ghost, to such (whether of age or infants) as that grace belongeth unto, according to the counsel of God's own will in his appointed time' (XXVIII, 6).

It is also true that baptism and the Lord's Supper may both serve to portray vividly the gospel to those who are unbelievers. As the sacraments are dispensed in conjunction with the preaching of the Word, they witness to gospel truths and of the need to be made true partakers in Jesus Christ. The evangelistic note should always be present when the sacraments are administered.